JOHNNY CARSON

– – – –

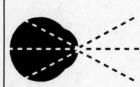

This Large Print Book carries the
Seal of Approval of N.A.V.H.

JOHNNY CARSON

HENRY BUSHKIN

THORNDIKE PRESS

A part of Gale, Cengage Learning

GALE
CENGAGE Learning·

Detroit • New York • San Francisco • New Haven, Conn • Waterville, Maine • London

GALE
CENGAGE Learning®

Thorndike Press® Large Print Biography.
The text of this Large Print edition is unabridged.
Other aspects of the book may vary from the original edition.
Set in 16 pt. Plantin.

LIBRARY OF CONGRESS CATALOGING-IN-PUBLICATION DATA

Bushkin, Henry.
    Johnny Carson / by Henry Bushkin. — Large print edition.
        pages ; cm. — (Thorndike Press large print biography)
    ISBN 978-1-4104-6523-8 (hardcover) — ISBN 1-4104-6523-3 (hardcover)
1. Carson, Johnny, 1925–2005. 2. Television personalities—United
States—Biography. 3. Tonight show (Television program) 4. Large type
books. I. Title.
PN1992.4.C28B88 2014
791.45092—dc23
    [B]   2013040079

Published in 2014 by arrangement with Houghton Mifflin Harcourt
Publishing Company

Printed in Mexico
3 4 5 6 7 18 17 16 15 14

CONTENTS

ONE:
1979: THE STAR AMONG STARS

You would think that by now the questions would have stopped. After all, he went off the air in 1992, and he died in 2005 — long enough ago for people to have lost their curiosity about Johnny Carson and to latch on to one of the many new stars, superstars, and pseudostars who have risen in the interim. But that really hasn't been the case. Indeed, in the years that he's been gone, Carson's status seems to have been reinforced. Talk-show stars have proliferated, but Johnny is now beyond a star: he is the Undisputed Champion, the Universal Standard. As talented and popular as all his putative successors might be, each of them is still doing a monologue about the day's events, still sitting at a desk making jokes with the band, still calling out tonight's first guest, still following in Carson's footsteps across a landscape that will be forever his.

People talk to me about Johnny because,

sooner or later, it comes out that I worked for him for nearly two decades. I was his attorney, although that term hardly expresses all I did; more properly, I was his lawyer, counselor, partner, employee, business advisor, earpiece, mouthpiece, enforcer, running buddy, tennis pal, drinking and dining companion, and foil. A good portion of my job entailed cleaning up his messes — business messes, personal messes, family messes. There are still a fair number of people around Los Angeles who had a business relationship with Carson that ended unhappily; they still love Johnny but hate that prick who was his attorney. Which was just the way Johnny wanted it. By any measure, this was the most complex and stimulating and challenging relationship of my life, the most rewarding and the most disappointing, the one that, a quarter century after its end, continues to provoke, irritate, delight, amuse, and sadden me. He and I were together longer than he was with three of his wives, and he and I were closer than he was with any of his friends, family, or professional colleagues. For all that, nothing shocked me more than the day, six years into our relationship, when I read a magazine article in which he said that I was his best friend. Friend? No, I don't think we were friends. The collar around my neck was usually quite loose and comfortable, but not always. There was never a question about who was in charge.

The question that people most frequently ask me is, What was Johnny really like? They are usually happy to hear the first part of my answer: he was endlessly witty and enormously fun to be around. Their interest flags when I add that he could also be the nastiest son of a bitch on earth. The truth is that he was an incredibly complex man: one moment gracious, funny, and generous; and curt, aloof, and hard-hearted in the next. Never have I met a man possessed of a greater abundance of social gifts — intelligence, looks, manners, style, humor — and never have I met a man with less aptitude for or interest in maintaining real relationships.

But to understand Johnny's complexity, one must first understand his artistry and the esteem in which he was held. This is not an easy thing to do. If we were to talk about a great movie actor, it would be simpler: his transformation into his character would be evident; the range of behavior he depicts would be obvious; the subtlety and nuance of the human experience that he illustrates would grab you by the throat. But what

Johnny seemed to do was more common-place. He came out and told a few jokes. He then kidded with Ed (McMahon) and Doc (Severinsen), played a game with the audience or performed in a ridiculous skit, and then made chitchat with celebrities. And it was the same thing every night. What was so damn special about that?

Perhaps I had begun to take him for granted, in the way New Yorkers can pass the Empire State Building every day without ever looking up. Then one night early in 1979, I recognized why Johnny was a star like no other. As it happened, I needed to be amidst a galaxy of stars in order to appreciate him.

By the start of 1979, I had been his lawyer for nearly one decade and had been watching him on television for almost two. I obviously knew he was a star — NBC paid him like a star, audiences applauded him like a star, and sponsors adored his stellar ratings — but I guess I had become used to him. It's true, I was more in awe of him when we first met in 1970, but that had a lot to do with the vast difference in our places in the world: I was a young attorney of no particular accomplishment, and he was the well-established host of the dominant program in the late-night time slot. But Johnny seldom played the star around me (whenever he called me, he'd begin every conversation by saying, "Hey, you got a minute?"), and we evolved a productive, low-key business relationship in which he always had the final say, but in which he almost always accepted my recommendations. We also had a personal relationship; we saw each other almost every day and commiserated about personal matters. I was privy to his finances, to the ups and downs of his marriages, to his concerns about his children, to all his interests and his moods, and I traveled with him every few weeks when he went on the road to play nightclubs. Maybe because I saw him at such close range, I lost sight of his immensity. But on that night in 1979 — a night that fell about halfway through our long association, and one that followed many high points in our relationship — I finally experienced a moment in which I recognized his true stature.

And what's funny is that for most of the evening I was in no mood to appreciate anything good about Johnny.

"Where is he, Henry?" Ginny Mancini demanded when she greeted me at her door. "You told me he would be here by now."

And indeed I had, here being the beautiful Holmby Hills house of Ginny and Henry Mancini. It was an hour after the start time that appeared on the invitation celebrating yet another of the seemingly endless honors and awards Mancini had received during his peerless career (the most prominent of which, his twenty Grammys and three — at that point — Oscars displayed on shelves around a large-screen TV built into a wall unit in the den). Several hours before, Johnny had phoned Ginny to confirm that he'd be attending and to ask that I be allowed to join him. It was a somewhat odd request, this being a strictly A-list event, but every Hollywood hostess has at one time or another had to accommodate a guest with special needs far odder and potentially more explosive than the presence of his business lawyer.

Frankly, I was surprised Johnny wasn't there already. He'd been famous for his punctuality since his early days in radio (and undoubtedly before — it's impossible to imagine Ruth Carson tolerating tardiness in her son). To say Johnny was late was almost like saying Old Faithful was late; somebody should alert the media.

But late he was, and the clock ticked on. The white-jacketed waiters from Chasen's had long ago rolled out the chili and the hobo steak, and soon Ginny would have to call for dessert. Like most of the wives in her set, Ginny treated hostessing as something between an art and a sacred mission, and she approached it with a seriousness of purpose that would have made General Patton look like "The Dude" from *The Big Lebowski*. Ginny, moreover, had been in show business, singing with the Glenn Miller Orchestra and with Mel Tormé's Mel-Tones, where she had no doubt witnessed enough celebrity misbehavior to leave her little tolerance for any more. "You know, when he says he is going to come," she huffed, "he can't send you in his place."

"I quite agree," I murmured. Of course I agreed. How could I have disagreed? I was standing in the home of the great Henry Mancini, who happened to be sitting on the couch in front of me talking shop with Lalo Schifrin, the composer, most famously, of the *Mission: Impossible* theme. (Throughout the evening, in what I assume to be Mancini's signature gag, whenever a new song would emanate from the speakers, he would lift his head and say, "What a great song! Did I write that one?") To their right was Jack Lemmon, straight off the set of *The China Syndrome,* sharing some story about Jane Fonda with his *Odd Couple* partner

Walter Matthau, who was still dissecting how the Steelers topped the Cowboys in the Super Bowl a few weeks before, apparently costing him a sizable wager. Nearby was Gene Kelly, still lithe enough to look like he could do his *Singin' in the Rain* routine on Ginny's new Provençal furniture, enthusing about *Xanadu,* the musical he would soon appear in that would turn into such a bomb that Carlos the Jackal should have claimed credit for it. There were two Bonds on hand — the smooth incumbent, Roger Moore, who was shooting *Moonraker,* discussing European tax havens, and his charismatic predecessor, Sean Connery, who interrupted his sotto voce discussion with Michael Caine to ask a waiter to bring him a fresh Scotch. One Hollywood icon, Jimmy Stewart, had driven with his wife across town to attend the party, and now he was talking with another, Cary Grant, who had flown from London with his wife to be there. There were so many other guests — Tony Curtis, the composer Sammy Cahn, the director Richard Brooks, the producer Ray Stark, André Previn, George Shearing, Michel Legrand — talking about so many other topics, like the overthrow of the shah of Iran, Caine's new brasserie in London, Moore's impending vacation in the South

14

of France, the flower arrangements that had been done by Fred Gibbons, whether *The Deer Hunter* was too intense to be nominated for an Oscar, and whether Kareem Abdul-Jabbar was ever going to take the Lakers to a championship.

My role — and it didn't have to be explained to me — was to stand back and smile and make small talk, although not much and only when spoken to. This was a Hollywood A-list party, and when Hollywood A-list celebrities go to a party, they expect to see the place full of other A-listers. If stars or studio heads or any other important show business personages find that they're sitting among a lot of nobodies, they get paranoid and begin to think that someone is trying to demote them. They don't mind a few unglamorous people like me because we usually listen well, but I didn't expect any of these people to chat me up (although Michael Caine, with whom Johnny and I had gone clubbing in London, genially tried to include me in conversations). But for at least some members of this group I was a functionary not much different from the waiters carrying trays around the living room — more useful if you needed a contract negotiated, less use-

15

ful if you wanted another bacon-wrapped scallop.

And thus I was surprised to realize that so many of these people made it a point, when getting a drink or another canapé, to detour to my side of the room and quietly ask a variation of the question that had been posed by Ginny Mancini the minute she opened her door. "So where's Johnny?"

It was the only question some of them would have bothered to put to me, but what was fascinating was the eagerness with which they asked. "Where the hell is he, Henry?" "Is he still coming?" "He's not standing us up, is he?" A few of them, like Caine, had been out on the town with Carson. Some had seen him at benefits and similar occasions, and nearly all had been on the show. But none of them knew Johnny well. It struck me that most of them genuinely wanted him to come, were genuinely interested in meeting him, curious to see him up close, and hoping to get to know him better. You could see how Johnny's general aloofness from the Hollywood scene actually drew people to him, how his relative unavailability on the social circuit restored the mystique that his nightly presence on the tube corroded.

Virtually everyone in that room grasped

the role scarcity played in maintaining celebrity; surely the performers did. They knew that they needed to keep hidden from public view until they were selling something. Then, when they had a new film or book or album to publicize, they would do the talk-show circuit, expose themselves to the crowd, and bare some part of their personality in the hope that this would help separate some portion of the audience from its money.

And that's when most of these people had met Carson, on the set of *The Tonight Show,* where they developed an incredible respect for what he did. Despite their enormous talents, none of these actors could do what Carson did. Lemmon could have played all of Matthau's characters and Matthau could have played Lemmon's, and Michael Caine could easily have been a Bond. That's what they did: they played characters, inhabited invented identities, brought to life a carefully constructed script. But Johnny took the stage just as himself, reliant mostly on his own native gifts. Night after night, he performed live to tape in a medium that permitted no rewrites if a line didn't work or no do-overs if someone messed up. As the great director Billy Wilder told *The New Yorker,* "Every night, in front of millions of people, he has to do the salto mortale," a circus term for a somersault performed on the high wire. "What's more, he does it without a net. No rewrites. No retakes. The jokes must work tonight." When guests like Stewart or Kelly or Lemmon came on *The Tonight Show,* they were naked — no lines, no characters, no costumes, no director — just themselves. Carson helped them by drawing out the qualities that made them seem interesting, glamorous, witty, and fun, frequently using self-deprecation to do this. He played the straight man to their jokester, the pupil to their master, the fan to their stardom. Only once or twice a year did they have to submit themselves to the talk-show grind, and even though most of them were veterans of multiple appearances, many still found it excruciating. (Some, like Rock Hudson, refused to appear on any talk shows at all, saying, "I can't order from a menu without two writers working up my lines.") But Johnny could just do it; and at that point in 1979, when he was hosting the program four nights a week for ninety minutes a night, he had been doing it for seventeen years, earning NBC $50 to $55 million per year. Perhaps only one other broadcaster in America could match that level of success, and just as Walter Cronkite set the gold standard for excellence and reliability in the news business, Carson's nightly exhibitions of wit, intelligence, grace, and sheer showmanship set that standard for entertainment. And on that night at the Mancinis, after hearing the eagerness and even tension in the voices of Hollywood's greatest luminaries as they asked for Carson, I saw the singular respect he'd earned among his peers. He was indeed a star among stars.

I told them all the truth: I didn't know why Johnny was late. But that didn't mean I didn't have a theory. Three weeks earlier, Johnny and his wife, Joanna, the beautiful, raven-haired, tempestuous third Mrs. Carson, had decided to split, and Johnny had packed his bags and moved out. This wasn't so unusual. He had walked out before, but what was different is that he usually checked into the Beverly Hills Hotel under my name or that of my loyal assistant, Carrie Becker. This time, however, he had me rent him a house, which Carsonologists like me took as a sign that the breach with Joanna was serious. You could tell the split was terribly distressing for Johnny; he was nastier and more abrupt than usual, and he had begun working jokes about marital strife and divorce into his monologues and comic bits.

Earlier that week, in fact, he was rehearsing a skit in which he played Adam to Betty White's Eve. The preposterous sight of a nearly naked Johnny in a fig leaf and a thickly matted wig was very funny, but the stinging punch lines about withholding intimacy and the expense of alimony and the heartlessness of lawyers showed that this was a rare occasion when Johnny was just as interested in sending a message as getting a laugh.

But what was the message? Johnny wasn't head over heels in love with Joanna anymore, if he ever was. He probably loved Joanna as much as he could love anyone, but women had always come and gone in his world; I don't think he would have been too torn up if she had merely gone. What he hated was to have emotional turbulence invade his world, and this storm was huge. It forced him to react to someone, which he only felt comfortable doing at times and in ways that he chose. But now Joanna had forced him to react to her. It was all that I or his team at *The Tonight Show* could do to keep him calm and focused enough each day to do his show.

Suddenly it was a moot issue. That morning, almost as abruptly as they'd split, he and Joanna had decided to reconcile. As a public declaration of peace, they had decided that he would come to the Mancinis' party, with Joanna joining him as a happy surprise. This was surely a good thing, but the timing made me worried — it might have been better to give the Krazy Glue a little more time to set. "You know, feelings are still a little fragile," I advised him. "The possibility that the two of you might start up again at the party can't be dismissed." Just that fast, I realized that I should have kept my mouth shut.

"Well, Henry Kissinger," Johnny sneered, "why don't you come to the party in case you have to mediate a new treaty?"

Great, I thought to myself. *He wants me there in case there's a mess that needs cleaning up.* Now I had to go to a party where I really didn't belong in case I had to play a role I thought I had outgrown: Henry Bushkin, the quicker picker-upper.

At long last, the Carsons arrived. They pulled up in the white Rolls-Royce Corniche that Johnny had given Joanna earlier that year, reparation for some earlier indiscretion. If nothing else, Joanna had helped Johnny redefine the Hollywood standard of an apology. He smiling, she hugging, they offered neither excuses nor explanations. It didn't matter; just as his absence had been feared, their arrival as a duo had not been anticipated, and the guests were happily surprised as they gathered around, the women cooing and fussing over Joanna, the men backpatting and handshaking with Carson. Michael Caine draped his arm around Johnny's shoulders, and Johnny responded with a wink. "You're looking good and fit," remarked Roger Moore, although Johnny, at six feet in height and in possession of a thirty-two-inch waist, had never looked otherwise.

"That jacket is amazing," admired Tony Curtis, fingering a lapel. Indeed, this gift from NBC, a navy blue cashmere blazer with fourteen-carat gold buttons, was pretty striking, but no more so than anything else in Johnny's bespoke wardrobe. Cary Grant and Jimmy Stewart clucked like uncles. When it was my turn, I leaned in and under my breath asked, "Is everything all right?"

"I'll tell you later," he said with a smile.

Johnny absorbed the welcome in stride. By this point, he took his status amid this entertainment aristocracy for granted and wore the admiration lightly. With his athletic build, he stood as ramrod straight as when he had been a junior officer in the navy at the end of World War II. The cropped hair was salt and pepper, his eyes clear, the irises a piercing blue; he was probably more handsome now than in 1951 when he first brought his mischievous charm into a television studio in Los Angeles. He carried himself with more elegance than his younger self could have summoned. He wore no wedding ring. If you didn't know how old he was (and he made no effort to disguise it), you probably would have guessed thirty-four or forty-four, but probably not fifty-four. In every aspect other than his age, this man looked like exactly what he was, king of the hill, top of the heap.

It was Johnny's usual practice at parties to greet the host or hostess and then commandeer a friendly face and retreat to a quiet corner. That evening, Johnny, friendly and on form, relaxed and said hello to everyone. In my peacekeeper capacity, I stayed alert for signs of strain; it generally took little to capsize Carson's mood, and who knew what state secret he was going to tell me later. But I sensed nothing untoward.

Soon enough, as happens at parties everywhere, the men gathered in one spot, and the women convened across the room. Johnny was at the center of the men, and Joanna of the women.

It was a very small and exclusive club to

which these women belonged. They shopped at the same chic boutiques, ate at the same upscale eateries, had their hair and nails done at the same salon, rose and fell on the fortunes of their husbands. In the men's group, the subject of the Carsons' marriage was being consciously avoided; chances were better that one of the men would confess to pedophilia before he'd ask how things were going between Johnny and Joanna. Among the women, however, it was Topic A. The ladies plunged into the deep end, demanding to know if Joanna was okay. That was their code for asking if Joanna needed their help. These ladies were a formidable force when protecting one of their own. They had all seen friends being dumped by their superstar spouses, and these women were there to ensure that if such a thing did take place, those husbands would pay a heavy price.

Among the connections that held these women together was their membership in SHARE — Share Happily and Reap Endlessly — a foundation launched in 1953 by Gloria Franks, Jeanne Martin, and other powerful wives that helps and supports emotionally disturbed children. Like at an army base, where a wife's status corresponds to her husband's rank, Joanna entered this

Old Hollywood community as a premier member of the club, and with her personality and intelligence, she was a particularly welcome one. A woman of the world, Joanna knew that it was risky for any wife to base her life entirely on her husband's continued affections, and she sought to enhance her own status by getting involved with SHARE's philanthropic efforts. She achieved this goal in no time, and before long, she'd become president of the organization. And that led directly to her split with Johnny.

SHARE's big fundraiser every year is its Boomtown party, a huge event that features top-of-the-line entertainment, auctions, and special stagecraft. Every year the event is a whopping success, and every year there is pressure to top the previous event. Joanna began her tenure by volunteering Johnny to emcee the next Boomtown affair. But for whatever reason, Joanna had failed to ask Johnny first.

Big mistake. Johnny Carson was one of the most generous people I've ever known, but he hated being obliged to do something, and he resented being needed, especially by people close to him. It almost automatically brought out a harshness in him, a nastiness. When Joanna told him of her grand gesture, he told her to forget it; he'd hosted the event before, it was a lot of work, and he didn't want to do it again. This led to words, which led to the separation, which resolved itself when Johnny capitulated. Why he yielded and how much he resented his surrender only he could say, and he never did. But as I learned the next day, the spectacular diamond bracelet Joanna had worn to the Mancinis was the price for the truce, and months later, the benefit would raise $500,000 for various worthy causes, with Johnny at the microphone. Still, he made it clear that he was still irked that Joanna had volunteered his services. "I was invited," said Johnny in his monologue, with transparently faux joviality, "in the same sense that Spiro Agnew was invited to return the money."

Once the backslapping had run its course, I could see Johnny growing restless. The eyes that could focus patient attention on Joan Embery's chimps, nonagenarian nut-carvers, and vacuous starlets began flitting anxiously toward the door. As much as he felt like he belonged in the company of Cary Grant and Jimmy Stewart and other show business giants, he didn't much care for their company. He often told me that all it took to turn the most electrifying film stars into dullards was to be around them for a while. But he felt that way around everybody. There were very few social scenes in which he was ever really comfortable, and dinner parties, unless the other guests were people he really liked, constituted real work for him; he was known to describe these events as torture.

Ed McMahon once said that Johnny "was comfortable in front of twenty million but just as uncomfortable in a gathering of twenty." Praise from strangers soured him: too much of it was insincere or clueless, and he found it tiring to pretend that it meant anything to him. The artificial intimacy also grated; the fact that he was constantly in people's homes made him a familiar figure in their lives, but they were never familiar to him.

Though attractive, popular, and charming, he was at heart a self-made Midwesterner — a habitual loner brought up to guard his emotional privacy. The year before, the playwright and critic Kenneth Tynan, a man Carson admired and might even have envied for his cool elegance and great anecdotes, mentioned in his *New Yorker* profile of Carson that someone had compared Johnny to the great Fitzgerald creation Jay Gatsby. Tynan dismissed the comparison, but I thought there was something there. Gatsby represented the American dream of self-made wealth and happiness, the spirit of youth and resourcefulness, and the ability to make something of one's self despite one's origins. He achieved more than his parents had and felt he was pursuing a perfect dream. Yet behind the façade, Gatsby was a lonely man. Drawn in broad strokes, that description also applied to the "King of Late-Night Television."

Johnny relaxed a bit once he spotted Jim Mahoney, who was a partner with Paul Flaherty, another Carson confidant, in operating one of LA's top PR agencies. Some PR people are famously abrasive, always ready to fight with the media and protect their clients. Jim was the opposite, always the easy-going diplomat. He was talking with his close friend, the hotel heir Barron Hilton. Carson had often bent elbows at the Bel-Air Country Club in their company, and he headed in their direction. I discreetly followed, as did the longtime *Tonight Show* producer Freddy de Cordova, who commandeered us a seating area in the Mancinis' den. Before long the jokes were flying. When a waiter came to get our drink requests, Johnny requested a glass of golden Montrachet, another sign of Joanna's effect. Once a notoriously hard drinker, Carson had, under her influence, developed into a true connoisseur. But even though he now knew what wine to have, he still didn't always know when he'd had enough. Drinking was always an adventure with Johnny; two drinks were enough to place Carson into a twilight zone from which could appear either a hostile, nasty, bad Johnny or a very funny good Johnny.

This night, thankfully, good Johnny emerged. "What movie star would you compare yourself to?" Hilton asked. "Lassie," Johnny immediately replied. "We're both lovable, and" — his eyebrows lifted, the corner of his lips turned down — "we both come when we're called." With this mock-affronted expression of disbelief, the impeccable delivery, and the punch line that pierced the nagging subtext of the evening, a deep, knowing, rueful laughter filled the room. Soon Johnny felt relaxed enough to take out some coins and perform several of the magic tricks he first perfected during the long Nebraska winters of his youth. A deck of cards providentially appeared, and Johnny stepped up his tricks. I was reminded of the scene in *Butch Cassidy and the Sundance Kid,* when we learn that Sundance couldn't hit anything when he stood still and shot, but when he ran, tumbled, and dodged, his aim was uncanny. "I have to move," Sundance explained. Carson standing in a living room making small talk was uneasy; Carson in performance, in front of a dozen pals or thirty million people watching the Oscars, was uncanny.

Jim Mahoney then asked Johnny if the oft-repeated story involving a guest appearance by Zsa Zsa Gabor carrying a white Persian cat was true. Gabor is said to have asked Johnny if he would like to "pet my pussy." Carson reportedly replied, "I'd love to, if you'd just remove that damned cat!" No, it never really happened, although Johnny did give a wink and a nod to the notion that at some point he did get to pet the real thing. Mahoney, the old pro at relaxing people, kept tossing slow softballs that Johnny cheerfully knocked out of the park.

After a while, Joanna Carson gracefully glided over and invited Johnny to join her at the dinner table. Just for a moment I thought I saw him bristle, and my antennae went up. But the mood swiftly passed, and Johnny left the men's club. But that was all right. The Mancinis had filled the room with friends of the Carsons', and they were soon joined by Suzanne Pleshette and her husband, Tommy Gallagher. Suzanne had long been one of Johnny's favorites, going back to one of her early appearances on the show, when the guest who had preceded her, the gossip columnist Hedda Hopper, kept patting Suzanne on the arm and trying to interrupt. "If you pat me on the arm again," the starlet said to the doyenne of gossip columnists during the commercial, "I'm going to knock you on your can." With her warm personality and bawdy sense of humor, she soon had Johnny laughing at stories about his good friend and her TV husband, Bob Newhart. When Suzanne asked Johnny and Joanna to join her and Tommy for dinner at Dominick's the next week, he promptly agreed. Clearly the king was feeling happy.

Only once more did his mood darken — when Johnny explained to a few of the guys the reason why he was late. The cause had nothing to do with Joanna, at least not directly. Johnny was delayed because he was engaged in a prolonged telephone discussion with Jerry Staub, one of my law partners, over the rental house that he had abruptly just vacated, almost as abruptly as he had taken occupation just three weeks before.

"Get me a goddamn place to live," an upset and angry Carson had demanded then. "I can't fucking stand her. Get me a place to stay, because I'm moving out."

"It's going to be expensive," I reminded him, perhaps needlessly, since he was presently holed up in his customary refuge, the Beverly Hills Hotel, which was hardly cheap. But no matter what it cost, the hotel wasn't going to prove satisfactory in the long run. Johnny had his own tennis court at home, and although he got to play with former Wimbledon great Alex Olmedo when he booked a court at the hotel, he felt too exposed on a public court. He wanted privacy. "I don't care what it costs," Carson said. "Pay whatever they ask but get it quick."

With price presenting no object, Marty Trugman — a well-regarded realtor who happens to be my cousin and a good friend of Johnny's — cut a deal in no time. Fred Roven owned a gated property on Loma Vista in Beverly Hills that was very private and had the required tennis court. Marty got Fred to agree to vacate his home on a day's notice. In turn, Johnny agreed to rent the place for three months at $25,000 a month and to pay the entire $75,000 bill up front for the place. Under ordinary circumstances, the cost would have been significantly lower, and Roven snapped up the cash.

But now that the crisis with Joanna had

ended and Johnny had moved back home, he wanted his money back — a third of it, anyway. "I only stayed there for less than a third of the time," he argued. "All I want back is a third of the money. That's fair, isn't it?"

"Sort of," I tried to explain, "but not really. You can't walk into a restaurant, eat a third of a steak, say you're full, and ask for a third of the cost back. Besides, you signed a contract."

Johnny waved me off; such legalities just didn't square with his basic Midwestern sense of fairness. "Look, just be my lawyer and get the money back." He insisted that I take up the issue with Fred.

"Carson can go fuck himself," Roven replied, and there the matter ended.

After the party, standing outside the Mancinis' home waiting for the valet to retrieve our cars, I bid Johnny and Joanna a good night.

"You're coming over tomorrow at eleven?" he asked, referring to our standing tennis game. "Can you hang around a bit afterward? There's something we need to talk about."

"Sure. Care to give me a preview?"

"You're going to New York next week to see Mike Weinblatt?" he asked, referring to the president of NBC Entertainment.

"Yeah, it's time to get contract extension talks rolling."

Johnny shook his head. "You need to tell him that I won't be renewing. In fact, you need to tell him that once we do this year's anniversary show, I'm going to quit *The Tonight Show.* I'm out."

"What?" I was shocked. From time to time, Johnny spoke vaguely about what he might do when he was finished hosting *The Tonight Show.* Never had he made it seem like that moment might be imminent.

"Tell the boys that I've had enough. Their schedule is a wasteland, I have to maintain ratings without having a single worthwhile lead-in, and I have no confidence that the genius Fred Silverman will be able to yank his nuts out of the fire. Plus the grind is killing me."

"They'll fight like hell," I said. "They'll have just six months to find a new host."

"That's plenty of time," he said adamantly. At that, the Corniche appeared. Johnny tossed the valet a twenty, and the newly reconciled Carsons motored happily into the night.

TWO:
1970: BREAKING IN

Johnny Carson, his famously puckish face obscured by sunglasses and disguised by distress, led a squad of men with down-turned mouths and upturned collars through a rain-swept Manhattan evening. Carson strode purposefully, and his four followers hurried behind, dodging taxis and avoiding umbrellas and jumping puddles to keep pace. Their destination: a modest high-rise in the East Forties near First Avenue. Their mission: a dubious if not downright illegal cloak-and-dagger caper to enter an apartment to which they had no title, let alone keys. Their identities: Joe Mullen, a licensed New York private eye, straight out of Mickey Spillane, serious and capable; Mario Irizarry, his tall, gaunt aide-de-camp, adept at lock picking and as conversational as a clam; and Arthur Kassel, my best friend. A security expert/crime photographer/police groupie with slightly grandiose ambitions, Arthur had made it his business over the years to befriend important people; and about a year earlier, at a police benefit, Arthur made friends with the event's emcee, the host of *The Tonight Show,* Johnny Carson.

And then there was me, the last in line, the one hustling hardest to keep up, the one beset by worries — worried that I'd fall behind, worried that I'd collapse, worried that five hustling men in Manhattan who didn't resemble the Knicks would draw the attention of the police. But everybody on the sidewalks had their heads down, and we didn't stand out more than the average bustling New Yorker.

Sucking wind, I was glad when we finally reached our destination, although as we stood in the lobby, shaking the rain off our London Fogs, I began to feel a sense of panic taking hold. What was I doing here? I was a graduate of Vanderbilt University Law School! I had sworn an oath to uphold the law, not violate it, and breaking and entering in the state of New York is a felony. As if sensing my panic, Johnny looked over at me. "Don't worry, kid," he said reassuringly. "Nothing's going to happen to you. Trust me."

And trust him I might have — after all, he

was famous; he must know more than I —
but then he turned to my friend.

"Arthur," he asked, "are you packing today?"

Arthur nodded and patted his hip.
"There's nothing wrong with a little shooting," he said, "as long as the right person
gets shot."

Breaking and entering while in possession
of a deadly weapon: that's a whole other
class of felony in New York State.

In 1970 I was twenty-seven years old,
born and raised in the Bronx, the child of a
thoroughly middle-class couple, my mom
the secretary to a union leader, my dad a
salesman in the garment district. I attended
Lehigh University, where I played on the
varsity tennis team, and then went on to
law school at Vanderbilt. There I acquired a
law degree and a wife, a pretty blonde
Nashville girl named Judy. Now we were
back in New York, in a very nice apartment
in Forest Hills, with a newborn son whom
we loved dearly. I got a job as an associate
at a small but competitive entertainment
law firm, Beldock and Kushnick, with offices at 720 Fifth Avenue in Manhattan,
right near Central Park, and I was a happy
man. I was no highflyer, but I felt good
about where I was and where I was going.

Entertainment law was constantly interesting, and I felt fortunate to be able to study by the side of Jerrold Kushnick, who was highly regarded in music industry circles. Among the firm's clients were The Who, Led Zeppelin, and Frank Sinatra's colorful longtime manager, Jerry Weintraub (who would later produce *Ocean's Eleven* and its sequels). Brought in to replace an attorney who had left the firm to represent the affairs of Bette Midler, the firm wasted little time tossing me into the fray. My first case involved copyright infringement, and I won, which gave me the confidence any freshman lawyer needs as he begins his career, especially in New York City. Now the firm had entrusted me with executing all the contracts that were required by the producers of a big rock festival in Atlanta that was going to feature one of our up-and-coming acts, Grand Funk Railroad. I was a little fish in a relatively small current in the middle of an entertainment ocean, but I was excited. I had a wife I loved, a kid I adored, a job I found interesting — things were good. Then Arthur Kassel called.

I had met Arthur through Dan Paulson, a childhood friend. Dan had partnered with Arthur to make police training films, and they came to me for legal advice. I was amused by this guy Arthur, a born raconteur who lived and breathed NYPD. He wore Nino Cerruti suits and monogrammed shirts garnished with solid-gold revolver-shaped cuff links, and raced around the city in a long black Cadillac that sported four antennae, just like official cop cars. In normal conversation he would describe people as mutts and mopes and perps and skells, and he once said a police officer subdued a suspect by giving him a wood shampoo. I thought he was a riot, and we hit it off from the start.

Arthur still lived with his parents in Brooklyn, and our apartment quickly became his second home. Judy didn't seem to mind. She was a flower of the South, and I think she was beguiled by this authentically Runyonesque character in her kitchen. A genuine man about town, Arthur knew everybody who might be anybody, or at least said he did. (Later, after he moved to Los Angeles, he would marry Tichi Wilkerson, who owned the *Hollywood Reporter,* which gave him great clout in the film industry, and he partnered with Sylvester Stallone in opening the Beverly Hills Gun Club.) No doubt Arthur parlayed his connection to Carson and the other celebrities he glommed on to to gain entrée to the politicos and city officials who would buy his products and services. That was his method; although he was a very good friend to me and many others, Arthur primarily looked out for number one, which is why I was slightly skeptical when he called me one afternoon with an offer that seemed a little too good to be true.

"How would you like to meet Carson?"

"Carson who?"

"Johnny, you jerk."

"Like on *The Tonight Show*?"

"The same."

"Look, Arthur, I'm up to my neck in contracts. I'm not much interested in padding the audience at some taping."

"No, my friend, nothing like that. How would you like to go up to his offices at NBC and talk to the guy?"

Actually I thought maybe Arthur was playing some kind of joke, but that really wasn't his style. "Why would anyone like Johnny Carson want to meet me?"

"You're a lawyer, aren't you?" Arthur then explained that Mr. Carson and his wife were going through a rough patch in their marriage. "I told Johnny that you were just the man who could help."

"That's ridiculous," I said. "Carson could have every high-priced matrimonial attorney in Manhattan standing in his office at the snap of a finger. He'll take one look at me and throw us both out."

"You'd be surprised," Arthur said. "Carson doesn't trust lawyers — not any he's met, anyway. I convinced him that you're a straight shooter and the two of you should talk."

Skeptical but excited, I agreed to a meeting with Arthur and Johnny the next day. I couldn't wait to tell my bosses.

It was almost comic to see the surprise on their faces. "Why you?" Kushnick asked, stating the obvious question. But my bosses had both been in entertainment long enough to know what a funny business it was. Every year people emerged from nowhere to become major stars, and they brought all sorts of peculiar ideas with them. "Enjoy yourself," Howard Beldock advised in his gravelly voice. "Just don't be too disappointed if nothing happens."

Sleep did not come easy that night. Try as I might, I could not imagine how I was supposed to fit into the star-studded world of Johnny Carson. This was a man I had been watching since high school, when I'd come home and flip on his ABC game show *Who Do You Trust?*, the show that first brought him national prominence. And I was a regular viewer of *The Tonight Show,* which Carson had been hosting now for the past seven years, during which he had surpassed the popularity of his illustrious predecessors Steve Allen and Jack Paar. Most everyone I knew tuned in nearly every night. We could all imitate Ed McMahon saying "Heeeeeeeeere's Johnnnnnyyy" and "Hey-yo!" and we could all perform our own a cappella versions of the Paul Anka–composed *Tonight Show* theme. Everyone could quote lines from Carson's monologue and from Carnac the Magnificent and his other bits, and you'd hear them snapped out at water coolers, cocktail parties, and barbershops for weeks after Johnny first uttered them. Carson was the guy so many of us wanted to be: confident, suave, full of fun, and fast with a quip. Plus, he was cool. He looked cool; he dressed cool; he was likely the first handsome comedian of the television age. The medium's pioneers, performers like Milton Berle and Sid Caesar and the other comedians our parents liked, traced their roots to vaudeville, where they had to mug and vamp to get the attention of the patrons in the back row. They carried that style into their TV work. Carson was part of the next generation; he grasped that he owned the camera the way Bing Crosby and Frank Sinatra had grasped that they owned the microphone. That understanding made him more natural, more relaxed, cooler. He didn't have to fight for attention because the camera found him. He didn't have to bug out his eyes and gape to get a laugh; all he had to do was arch an eyebrow. At forty-five, he was reaching the pinnacle of his craft, and under his administration, *The Tonight Show* had ceased being an interesting lagniappe tossed in at the end of the broadcast day. It had become an essential part of the culture.

Between the moment I hung up the phone with Arthur and the time I walked into Johnny's offices at NBC, I spent as much time as I could researching the man and his career. He was born in Iowa in 1925 but raised in Nebraska by his mother, Ruth, and father, Homer (called Kit), a power-company manager. He served in the navy, went to the University of Nebraska, broke first into radio and then into television in Omaha, and then went to LA, where, in a typical up-and-down television career, he apparently took a shot at every opportunity that came down the pike. He wasn't NBC's first choice to succeed Jack Paar, but after rejections from Bob Newhart, Jackie Gleason, and Joey Bishop, Carson got the gig and debuted on *The Tonight Show* in October 1962, with guests Groucho Marx, Tony Bennett, Rudy Vallee, Mel Brooks, and Joan Crawford.

He caught a break and made the most of it. Television was a more earnest medium then; Carson set himself apart with his easy command. He just never seemed ruffled, and, in fact, he would invite the worst of circumstances, leaving a few stinkers in his Carnac routines so that he could glower at a groaning audience and say, "May a love-starved fruit fly molest your sister's nectarines." One writer had once noted that Johnny could spot a flaw in his delivery before uttering the first syllable; another said that he possessed the fastest, most exquisite audience reaction meter of any comedian alive.

The next evening, after the late-afternoon taping of *The Tonight Show,* Arthur and I entered the art deco lobby of NBC headquarters at 30 Rockefeller Plaza. I was nervous and excited. Would I make the right impression? Would he see me as just another stumbling boob with a briefcase? What awed me as much as anything was going into the building. Headquarters of the Rockefeller family, home to NBC News, source of significant cultural and public affairs programs, the splendid art deco skyscraper was a symbol of power, wealth, and pride. All my life I'd passed by it without ever going inside, even though my office was less than ten blocks away. Like a Londoner passing Buckingham Palace or a Roman walking by the Vatican, I felt Rockefeller Center was something that would always be within my sight but never within my grasp — until today.

Carson's secretary, a cute redhead in a short black dress, escorted us into Johnny's private office. It was impressive. Wide windows presented a panoramic view of the Midtown skyline; with dusk falling, the lights in the office buildings twinkled against the pink and orange smears of the sky. I couldn't tell you how the room was decorated, other than to say it was sleek and modern and looked like it might have served as a set for photographs in *Esquire* or *New York* magazine. The men I worked for had nice offices, but theirs were places where money was earned; here it was taken for granted. Before I sat down, I noticed a needlepoint pillow on the sofa, something that seemed stylistically out of place. Then I read its embroidered message: ASSUMPTION IS THE MOTHER OF ALL FUCKUPS. Funny — but was I in on the joke or the butt of it?

45

Carson came in and immediately got down to business. There wasn't even any small talk with Arthur. A man who I thought embodied the genial, witty host acted like the guy at the B. Altman's department store where I interviewed for a summer job in high school, indifferent to me and impatient to be done. It seemed like something was distracting him, maybe even making him tense. When he asked questions, he did little more than read my résumé back to me. "You went to Vanderbilt Law School? You're a member of the New York Bar?" It was as if I were the last guest on the program as time was running out and he was throwing me questions until the music came up. I was becoming seriously confused and not a little impatient at what was shaping up to be a big letdown. "Just don't be too disappointed if nothing happens," I could hear Howard Beldock saying. Finally he asked a question that surprised me completely. "You play tennis, right?"

"Yes. I played on my team in college. Why?"

"I play tennis. It's my sport." He added that he'd recently joined the Vanderbilt Tennis Club, whose members played on two courts directly above Grand Central Terminal. It was a very expensive club, named for the old tycoon who founded the railroad and endowed my school. "If you work for me, I'll expect you to join me occasionally."

"I'd look forward to it."

That was it. Interview over.

Outside in the hallway, I commented to Arthur, "Strange interview. I probably blew it."

"No, no, my friend. He liked you."

"How do you figure that? He barely showed a flicker of interest."

"Trust me," Arthur said. "He's going to call you again. And soon. Maybe tomorrow."

Although the interview didn't seem to amount to anything, just the fact that I had actually met Carson earned me some instant celebrity with my family and friends, and I went through rounds of phone calls with my uncles and cousins and in-laws in Tennessee. What was he like? What did he say? Did he have a fancy office? Was he funny? I evaded most of their questions or embroidered answers. I had barely met the man. With my wife, though, I was candid. When she asked how it went, I said, "It was stupid. He didn't seem very interested in me." Still, I couldn't let go of the idea that Arthur seemed so sure that Johnny would call.

■ ■ ■ ■

The next day was probably one of the least productive of my life. I spent the entire time at my desk, acting like a thirteen-year-old girl. I told myself he would never call and then tried to will the phone to ring. I chased my thoughts in circles, at first convincing myself that he hadn't liked me and that there was no chance that he would call, and then persuading myself that Arthur thought he liked me and that maybe he would. When five o'clock rolled around, I gave up and snapped shut my briefcase. I would do my worrying at home.

And just like that he called. Him personally — no secretary. "Can you meet me this evening?" he asked. He gave me an address on East Forty-ninth Street, which I recognized as the United Nations Plaza, the premier cooperative apartment complex in Manhattan. Senator Robert Kennedy had lived there, as well as various CEOs and the celebrated author Truman Capote. First I had gone to Rockefeller Center, now UN Plaza. This just kept getting better.

When I arrived at Carson's apartment, I was met at the door by his next-door neighbor, who just happened to be Sonny Werblin. Now, had I not just met Johnny Carson, meeting Sonny Werblin would easily have been the biggest event of my week, month, year, whatever. Sonny Werblin alone would have got the uncles and cousins calling (though probably not the in-laws in Nashville). Sonny was one of the leading sports impresarios of his era, the former president of the New York Jets who just a couple of years before had daringly signed the brash superstar quarterback and league-of-his-own sex symbol Joe Willie Namath and brought home a Super Bowl trophy in a game that was a historic upset. Bald and pudgy, wearing glasses with clear plastic frames, Werblin had once been one of Lew Wasserman's top agents at MCA, and he still favored the MCA agent's uniform of a black suit and starched white shirt; I felt my self-image rise just by shaking his hand. Werblin, as I would shortly learn, was Johnny's manager.

Carson lived in lavish style. His apartment, a two-story duplex on the thirty-fifth and thirty-sixth floors, took up five thousand square feet of extremely scarce and expensive floor space. The living room was beautifully decorated in dark wood paneling accented with shades of deep brown; it was a little overwhelming for my taste, but I couldn't help but be impressed with the wealth on display. Scattered throughout the apartment were heavy cut-glass ashtrays from Steuben and Cartier, along with sterling-silver boxes full of Pall Mall cigarettes, which accounted for the heavy cloud of blue tobacco smoke floating over the room. Johnny and Sonny and I made some small talk about Sonny's horses — this made me think that maybe we were waiting for someone else to arrive — while Johnny's houseman, George Smith, a cordial African American, busied himself serving drinks and emptying ashtrays.

Suddenly Sonny got down to business. After stressing the confidentiality of our get-together, he offered what he obviously considered a telling observation: "Jack Benny was the unhappiest man I have ever known. And Benny is Carson's idol." Of course I knew who Jack Benny was but knew nothing about his private life, so I kept my mouth shut and summoned all the sang-froid I could muster.

Sonny continued with astonishing bluntness. "Johnny is the second-unhappiest person I've ever known. I'm telling you this for a reason. Right here in front of Mr. Carson. Watch your step. Johnny's mood can go from up to down in milliseconds. The situation about to be discussed would be dangerous if word gets out. Keep a tight lip." This pronouncement did not appear to embarrass the star, but it sure had me flushing red. I waited for an opening to respond.

Johnny, meanwhile, seemed impatient, as if he had somewhere else to be. He lit one cigarette after another, exhaling smoke that drifted up to merge with the floating haze. He looked at me as though he found my presence a distraction, and I became increasingly uncomfortable. Both men were drinking. Sonny nursed a Scotch while Johnny sipped red wine. I neither drank nor smoked, which added to my growing discomfort. Finally, out of desperation to fit in, I asked Johnny for a cigarette. He smiled, and I felt an immediate vibe, a relaxation. Just like that, I had passed some invisible test and was now more accepted. "I started smoking in 1939," Johnny said without emotion, the first remark he'd made since I'd arrived that was directed at me.

"Yes?" I didn't mean for it to sound like a question, but it did.

"I have no plans to quit smoking. I can't quit. What's more, I don't want to quit, and I don't want people around me telling me I should quit." I hadn't had the slightest inclination to say anything to him about

51

smoking, but I wasn't about to argue. Then, happy to have made that point, he changed the subject. "Henry," he said, finally arriving at the purpose of our meeting, "I have reason to believe my wife is cheating on me. I also have an idea who the son of a bitch is that she's shacking up with." No wonder he had been restless — he'd been sitting on a bombshell!

Joanne — née Joanne Copeland — was Johnny's second wife. His first wife, Jody, was his college sweetheart. It was, as I was to learn, a fairly typical first marriage between young people. It produced three sons — Chris, Ricky, and Cory — but it did not withstand the demands or the sexual temptations of Johnny's increasingly successful career. During his years hosting the quiz show *Who Do You Trust?*, the Carsons had a beautiful home in leafy Harrison, New York, but Johnny was seldom there, spending long hours at work before moving the party to Danny's Hideaway or some other club until closing time, when, more often than not, he and a young lady adjourned to somewhere more intimate. Their divorce became final in 1963, and within months he married Joanne, a cute, vivacious former stewardess who had briefly worked as the hostess on a TV game show called

Video Village. Now, seven years later, Johnny had substantial evidence that Joanne had secretly leased an apartment within blocks of their UN Plaza home, which she used for clandestine rendezvous with her lover.

"Well, I'll be happy to file for divorce, if you want . . ."

"No, I don't want you to file for divorce," he interrupted. "I want you to go with Arthur and me and some other guys when we break into the apartment to find evidence to prove the bitch is cheating on me."

My first reaction was to be appalled. *No way,* I thought. Members of the bar do not break and enter apartments. I am an officer of the court. I am the heir to a great legal tradition. I thought of Clarence Darrow. I thought of Learned Hand.

And yet . . . this was an immense opportunity at the beginning of my professional life to land a very major client and launch my career into the stratosphere. I hesitated.

Carson continued. "I need a lawyer to accompany the team tomorrow night in case shit happens. I have very experienced people who have assured me that there won't be any problems, and Kassel has already cleared things with the cops. But somebody needs to be there in case something goes wrong . . ."

"You'll prevent that," said Werblin. "Like a rubber."

"Like in case some cop who didn't get the message shows up," said Carson. "Now, I know Joanne is out of town, probably with Prince Charming, and she won't be around." He then sat back. Getting to the core of our encounter had removed some of his tension, and he was visibly more relaxed. Still, his eyes never left my face.

The act he proposed clearly bordered on ethical misconduct or possibly criminal behavior. Not even as a teenager had I ever knowingly broken any laws. But I wanted to become his lawyer, not his conscience. And maybe the whole thing wasn't so illegal.

"Let me ask you," I said, "does Mrs. Carson have any money of her own?"

"No, not really," Johnny replied.

"Then let me suggest that you have been the person who has been paying for this apartment. So arguably it's your apartment."

Johnny slapped his hands together and Werblin chuckled. "There we go!" Johnny laughed. "Arthur said you were smart." Frankly, I had no idea if this argument had any legitimacy, but it was a reasonable line and might well provide enough cover for a fast-talking lawyer to get his coconspirators out of trouble if some nosy cop started being fastidious about the law. "Good," said Johnny. "You're part of the team."

I spent the next twenty-four hours alternately thrilled and petrified. All of a sudden, it seemed everyone around me had turned into Perry Mason–level interrogators. At home, Judy pressed me for details. "Please, Judy! We had a conversation about some personal matters that I can't talk about," I said, tersely cutting her off. The next day I was even more abrupt with my bosses. "It's between me and the client," I said, and shut the door of my office, where I quietly freaked out.

I was better in the evening, back at Carson's apartment, when I finally met the rest of the crew, and I was able to step into my role. Joe Mullen was the indisputable leader of this little group, but I showed no hesitancy in taking charge of the legal aspect of things. "You're now working for me," I told the private eye. "All your future bills must be sent to my office." That meant that everything Joe did was protected as attorney work product, and that would begin to insulate Carson from any legal ramifications of what went on. Mullen quickly agreed.

Suddenly, without any preliminaries or pep talks, we were off — into the night, into the rain, through the traffic, entering the door of the suspected love nest. In the bright light of the lobby, the sunglasses Johnny had been counting on to cover his identity proved useless. "Hey, Johnny Carson!" the burly doorman bellowed. "Hey-ohhh!" But his delight at the sudden apparition of a celebrity in his lobby did not translate into a willingness to admit strangers into a resident's apartment. Joanne must have used her husband's money to tip generously. "Oh no, can't do that," the doorman shook his head. "You wait here. I have to go get the building manager."

Fortunately the building manager turned out to be less committed to the sanctity of his tenant's domain. When I gave him my spiel about Mrs. Carson being the tenant but Mr. Carson actually paying the bills, the manager made like Earl Warren and actually appeared to be pondering the merits of my argument, which he did right up to the moment the thick-necked Mullen grabbed his hand and slipped several hundred dollars in cash into his palm. "Yeah, okay," the manager nodded. "Come on up, I'll let you in."

With Irizarry left to stand guard in the

hallway, the four of us entered Joanne's snuggery. Almost instantly, Carson discovered evidence of his cuckoldry: the whole living room — in fact, almost the entire pad — was furnished with discards from the couple's UN Plaza apartment. There were even some pieces that Johnny hadn't realized were gone.

"Look, it's him," said Arthur. He was pointing to a table in front of the window, on which sat about six or seven framed photographs of Joanne's playmate. For the first time I realized her noontime buddy was Frank Gifford, the former New York Giants football great who had made the Pro Bowl at three different positions — flanker, halfback, and defensive back — and who had, since his retirement, showed promise as a sportscaster for CBS. One of the pictures showed Frank and Joanne at a restaurant table against some tropical resort-like background.

"Bingo," said Arthur, just as Joe Mullen emerged from the bedroom. "I got men's and women's clothing hanging together." Then he held up a robe of sorts, although it seemed awfully sheer to be the kind of thing a girl would wear to sit around and watch *Bonanza* in while she put curlers in her hair. "Recognize it?"

Johnny nodded. Crushed by the overwhelming amount of evidence, Carson leaned against the living room wall and began to weep. It was a painfully uncomfortable moment. Arthur busied himself taking photos of the premises, while the rest of us tried to look away and give Johnny his privacy. It was, however, a small space, and I couldn't always keep my eyes away.

During one of those glances, I could see that Carson's raincoat had fallen open. I was shocked to see that Johnny was carrying a .38 revolver in a holster on his hip. Mullen, seeing what I saw, shot me a look that warned, *Don't say a fucking word,* and then he quietly flipped the framed pictures of Gifford on the windowsill so that their backs faced the room. Across the room, the silent Joe Mullen deftly swept some lingerie under the sofa with the toe of his shoe. He wanted to spare Johnny the sight. There was little else that could be done.

I was beginning to feel exceedingly uneasy. Armed men, an emotionally ugly scene, a man in turmoil — I wasn't very experienced, but as any reader of the *Daily News* could tell you, many an inferno has erupted with less kindling. Just as soon as Carson regained control of his emotions, I shot Mullen a look. "Let's go," the PI barked. I asked Kassel if he had all the photos he needed, and as he shot me a thumbs-up, Mario stuffed some of Joanne's personal items into a monogrammed pillowcase. Items of this nature could be useful if presented in court, but the truth is that they are more useful in keeping you from having to go to court.

Very little was said on the walk back to Johnny's apartment. The rain had subsided, but no one felt like recapping the raid. When we reached Johnny's apartment, he thanked us and said he was tired and wanted to be alone. He asked his houseman to give me a ride back home. As the car headed over the Queensboro Bridge, I realized that I was probably one of the very few people who had ever seen Johnny Carson cry.

Frankly, with the job done, I had no idea whether I would ever hear from Carson again, but the next afternoon he called and asked me to meet him at his apartment the following morning. I was thrilled — the game was still on. My parents were joining my wife and me for dinner over the week-end, and I bought a bottle of expensive wine to celebrate. I could tell by their voices how proud they were of me. I doubt they would have been very impressed if they'd suspected what I'd been part of the night before.

That evening, exhausted by the events of the past forty-eight hours, I hit the sack shortly after nine p.m. and soon fell deeply asleep. But at two a.m. the phone rang. It was Carson, and he was obviously tanked.

"I'm sitting here with Ed at Jilly's," he slurred. "Can you please come down here right away." I considered putting him off until our scheduled meeting the next morning, but knowing how shitty he must have been feeling, and realizing that he might still have a gun, I told him I'd be there shortly. I dragged myself out of bed, put on a suit, and grabbed my briefcase. I managed to hail a cab (no easy feat at that hour in Queens) and arrived at Jilly's around three a.m.

There have always been a lot of good nightclubs and bars in Manhattan, but there are always two or three in any given era where there's a real scene, a Toots Shor's or Elaine's or Nell's, where people come as much to look, or to be looked at, as they do to eat or drink. Jilly's Saloon, on West Fifty-second Street at Eighth Avenue, was a lounge that in the late sixties and early seventies had a reputation for catering to celebrities. People were forever reading in the gossip columns that Judy Garland or

Dean Martin or Peggy Lee or Elizabeth Taylor had been to the place. Jilly's was owned by a big slab of humanity named Jilly Rizzo, whose best customer happened to be his boyhood pal and frequent drinking companion, Frank Sinatra. When Frank was in town, he could be typically found sitting in a chair in the back room, and when Frank wasn't in town, the chair was empty and leaning against the back wall awaiting him. Over time, the chair became a tourist attraction in its own right.

A dark-leathered tomb of a place, Jilly's was frequented not only by celebrities but also by a criminal element that gave the setting a dangerous allure. It was said that when he walked in one night, Sinatra had quipped, "Jesus, there must be forty-two indictments sitting at the bar." He loved the place so much that he set a scene from *The Manchurian Candidate* there.

At the wee small hour I arrived, the club was dark, lit only by lamps above the smoked-glass mirrors that cast a light so frail that it quit before it reached the banquettes. The back room where Sinatra held court was dark except for a red neon exit sign, and everything was so quiet that the only sounds you could hear were sounds you never otherwise heard, like the hum of the cooling units under the bar. All the regulars were long gone; even the hatcheck girl had checked out. Behind the bar was a barkeep in a bow tie, and at the bar was one patron, Johnny Carson, his head in a cumulous cloud of cigarette smoke, nursing a drink; all that was missing was Ol' Blue Eyes singing "One for My Baby and One More for the Road."

It was suddenly clear that Werblin had not been exaggerating. Johnny looked like the loneliest man I had ever seen, and the sight intimidated me. "Henry, get the hell out of here; you're out of your league," a small voice inside me said, and I nearly turned and walked out. Of course I didn't listen. I rejected the voice of reason and instead succumbed to the lure of ambition. Or maybe it was compassion. Perhaps I just felt drawn to the guy. Maybe it was just that the last two days of my life had been so incredibly different from the first twenty-seven years that I figured I owed it to myself to see what happened next.

I approached him, and when I was about five feet away, Ed McMahon wobbled out of the men's room, steadying himself on bar stools as he moved. He still had a few feet to negotiate, but then Johnny straightened up and said, "Ed? We're done here, right?"

"Yes, sir," Ed replied, and with a slight recalculation of his course and direction, Johnny's sidekick was gone in thirty seconds.

I took the empty stool to form a new trio: me, Carson, and the bartender, who brought me a Heineken and then slipped discreetly away. The silence was oppressive, and the pressure to make small talk was overwhelming. I was about to start chatting about the last time I had been to Jilly's, back before the baby, when Judy and I had set up another couple on a blind date, but I was spared that embarrassment when Johnny, sighing heavily, finally spoke. "I'm not surprised that Joanne did this to me," he said, "but it hurts. Hurts like hell."

That he was devastated was obvious. "Maybe I drove her to it. I wasn't the best husband in the world." He stared at the ceiling as though reflecting on the accuracy of this statement and then pounded the bar for emphasis when he apparently reached a judgment. "I shoulda been home more," he said with a drunk's certainty. "Not out running around."

I didn't try to respond. There was nothing to say. Johnny was lost in regret and self-loathing. "I'm a shit. I have three kids with my first wife and I don't see any of them."

The more Johnny talked, the weirder this moment seemed. People I'd known all my life, my best friends, none of them would ever unburden themselves to me. But here's a man I'd known for two days baring his soul, and I had nothing to say? Maybe that's why I was here.

Abruptly he changed topics. "Ever been to Nebraska, Henry?" he asked. Nebraska, of course, is where Carson was raised. "No, of course you haven't; why would you have? Let me tell you, Henry — it's terrible. The roads, the wind, the snow, the mud, the freezing weather. But the people . . . they couldn't be nicer or friendlier." He stopped abruptly. "Nature calls, I'll be right back." He headed woozily to the men's room.

I sat there dumbfounded, like an actor in a play that had no script. Nothing in my relatively young life had prepared me for this situation. There must be some way men in my circumstances are supposed to behave, but I hadn't read the handbook. I had no choice but to be me. Then Johnny returned.

"Where was I?"

"You were telling me about weather in Nebraska," I reminded him.

"Oh yeah. Bad weather. But Cornhuskers? Cornhuskers never complain. I love 'em all. Tough as nails, the people from Nebraska. Whiners wouldn't last a year there. They can put up with all the shit nature throws at them." He shifted on his stool. Anger rose in his voice. "Especially my mother. She's the toughest son of a bitch of them all. There is no goddamn way to please that woman. She's Lady Macbeth! My marriages failed because she fucked me up!"

Up to this point, he'd been speaking into some middle distance situated between him and the rows of liquor bottles standing in front of the mirror. But now he spoke specifically to me.

"You're married, aren't you, Henry? I bet you love her. I bet she's a wonderful girl. But let me tell you, be careful because women will take anything they can. Money, jewelry, clothing, shelter, even children. And they can have it all! I don't give a shit, I really don't. But it's never enough, is it?"

He really wasn't interested in an answer. He wanted a sounding board. Carson was sharing with me thoughts he probably never unloaded on anyone else in his life. But why me? Maybe he unloads like this all the time, and all he needs is to spot a fresh set of ears and off he goes.

"Joanne has broken my heart . . . to the extent I even have one."

Now this was getting to be too much. It was one thing to let a guy get something off his chest, but I didn't want to stand around while he wallowed in self-pity — at least not until he was officially a client. "Johnny, would you like me to take you home?" I asked.

"Fuck no, George is outside with my car. Have a drink, Henry. I'm not finished yet." Like magic, the bartender appeared with another Heineken, and Johnny continued. "If a doctor opened up my chest right now, he couldn't find a heart, or any goddamn thing. Just a lot of misery. My mother made sure of that. She deprived us all of any real goddamn warmth. My dad, Homer, should get the fucking Medal of Honor for endurance. The fucking Medal of Honor! I love them both — but from a distance." He stared into his drink and brooded. I wished I could say something to comfort him, or at least help him wrap up the evening. If nothing else, I hoped just listening would help.

Carson lit another cigarette then looked me straight in the eye. "I can't quit smoking and I get drunk every night and I chase all the pussy I can get. I'm shitty in the marriage department. Make sure you understand this."

Understand what? What was he saying?

And why was he saying all this to me? Maybe because nobody else would listen to him. The wife didn't. Werblin certainly didn't; Werblin talked about him in the third person while he was sitting right there! Ed McMahon was a guy you sent home. I don't know what he saw in me in our initial meetings; I don't know what I had done, but I suddenly realized that he was going to let me stick around. He was telling me all these things so I would realize what he expected of me.

Carson's mood then turned on a dime. He shot me a smile and said, "Henry, did you know that it's a proven fact that married men live longer than single guys? It's also a proven fact that married men are far more willing to die." I burst into laughter, and he did too. And suddenly the dark cloud lifted.

"Why Frank Gifford?" he asked. "What's that asshole got that I don't have?" I wasn't sure where he was going with this but maybe nowhere good. The mood appeared to be swinging back.

"That guy plays three positions on the field," he said. "I could never get Joanne to go for more than two." His deadpan timing was perfect. I nearly fell off my stool laughing. He was smiling appreciatively. "I think

I'll use that line in tomorrow's monologue."

From the front of the bar, the creak of the door opening and the thrum of a passing car broke the silence of the room. We turned to see a woman enter. As she drew closer in the dim light, one could gradually see that she was a young woman — tall — with long brunette hair — and even longer legs, in a short skirt and thigh-high boots — and as nearly famous as Johnny was.

Next to me, Johnny rose from his stool. "Henry, we're done here, right?"

I knew my line. "Yes, sir," I said, and the handsome couple left. All the trauma and misery from Joanne's betrayal vanished the minute he had another woman on his arm. Whatever cares he had were melting faster than the ice cubes in his Tanqueray and tonic.

Later that same morning, not long before noon, he called. "Hey, what did we talk about last night?" he asked. "What the hell did I say?"

"Nothing much," I replied. "Nothing important."

He paused for several seconds. I think that he was impressed that my discretion extended even to him. "You must never, ever repeat a word from last night," he finally said. "You understand that?"

"I do."

"So what did I talk about?"

"You talked about everything last night — everything. Your mother, your family, your heartbreak over Joanne, a lot of stuff. But if you're worried, just realize that I'm your lawyer; everything that is said between us is confidential and covered by attorney-client privilege. I would lose my license if during your lifetime I repeated it to a soul."

I heard him laugh. "Well, Henry, I guess you're my lawyer now. Can you come over this afternoon? I want you to file for divorce as soon as possible."

THREE:
1970: CALAMITY JOHN

I was now officially Johnny Carson's lawyer, an amazing turn of events, as astonishing as if I had won a lottery. But I didn't have much time to savor my good fortune.

People have often asked me how the hell a young, wet-behind-the-ears lawyer got himself hired to represent one of the biggest names in entertainment. Well, I've described the how, but I don't know if anyone can fully explain the why. All I know is that one of Carson's favorite sayings was "It's all in the timing," and timing had a lot to do with what happened. I met Johnny at just about the moment he had begun to suspect that the icons who had been representing him hadn't really done a very good job protecting his welfare. After that, all I can say is that I was then able to offer the qualities needed at the moment — earnestness, interest, willingness, and sufficient intellect.

And a certain tenacity. My first employers

and mentors, Jerry Kushnick and Howard Beldock, taught me to be alert and always on the lookout for new clients.

In the New York of that era, lawyers tenaciously vied for clients, entertainment lawyers especially. From the moment I signed on as a young associate, my bosses drilled me in the techniques of client protocols. Never decline a case until I had spoken to them and never admit to a potential client a lack of expertise in any legal discipline. If Johnny Carson needed a divorce lawyer, my complete lack of expertise in matrimonial law was immaterial; I would just work like hell to turn myself into the best divorce lawyer in New York. My job was to go the extra mile to prepare myself and rely on the senior partners if I found myself in over my head. But pass up a client? Never!

You won't be surprised to learn that things grew complicated fast.

As soon as we filed papers for divorce, Joanne hired Raoul Felder. To this day, Felder is feared and revered as one of Manhattan's premier divorce lawyers, having represented Mayor Rudy Giuliani, Robin Givens, Richard Harris, Carol Channing, David Merrick, Riddick Bowe, and the less famous (and now former) spouses of such notables as Elizabeth Taylor, Liza

71

Minnelli, Carl Sagan, Tom Clancy, Patrick Ewing, and Martin Scorsese. Just thirty-one years old in 1970, Felder was himself relatively new to matrimonial law practice, not quite yet the Duke of Divorce of tabloid fame. But he had spent nearly a decade in the trenches, first prosecuting cases as an assistant U.S. attorney, and then arguing appeals in federal court as a special assistant U.S. attorney; both posts usually draw lawyers who are aggressive, relentless, and whip smart.

Carson and I were perhaps fortunate that we encountered Felder when he knew only most of the tricks in the book, not every single one of them.

Felder promptly went on the offensive. He filed a brief that sought an alimony payment of $35,000 a month, an amount that was, as all the newspapers loudly reminded me the next day, the largest such payment ever sought in the state of New York. All at once it was clear that in the very first matter I was handling for my precious new client, I had hit the trifecta: I would be facing a matrimonial-law gladiator in a case that would get played out in national headlines and that would involve unprecedented stakes, affecting my client's wealth and reputation. Welcome to the major leagues.

The first step in the normal process of negotiating a divorce settlement is straightforward, or at least it is if people don't lie. It involves taking an inventory of the couple's property and then evaluating its worth. Once that's settled, the parties figure out how to split things up. As we worked through that exercise, facts revealed themselves, little by little, like the layers of an onion. Curious facts. Disturbing facts. Like the fact that Johnny Carson wasn't wealthy. Indeed, he had very little money.

He had little money because the people around him, whom he trusted, were serving him poorly.

He was being taken advantage of.

He was, by and large, alone.

And his life was a wreck.

The mess in his personal life was obvious. Carson was forty-five years old, had been through two marriages that had ended painfully, was the father of three sons whom he seldom saw, and he drank to excess nearly every night.

Plus, *The Tonight Show,* the cornerstone of his life, was not quite as solid as it appeared. The ratings were good and Johnny was popular, but behind the scenes there was turmoil. Carson had already fired two veteran producers, Art Stark and Stan Irwin. The current producer, Rudy Tellez, was on shaky ground, not only because of the quality of his work, but also because Rudy's wife, Jeannie, who had long been a friend of Johnny's, had accompanied Joanne when she went apartment hunting in search of a love nest and then leased the apartment for her in the Tellez name. Johnny didn't feel entirely justified in taking out Jeannie's betrayal on Rudy. On the other hand, did he really want to come to work every day and work with a man who would serve as a constant reminder of his wife's faithlessness? Rudy may not have known he was on his way out, but the only thing that would have made it more obvious would have been somebody pinning a target on his chest.

But beyond the show, Johnny was underserved. In addition to having an executive producer, a star of Carson's stature would often have a retinue of advisors. Among them would be an agent, whose job is to find the artist work and negotiate the terms of employment; and a manager, who would help plan the course of the performer's career and who often finds opportunities for endorsements, investments, and other business opportunities to augment the performer's income. Often the manager is a lawyer, but many performers have a separate attorney to provide advice and counsel. Many celebrities also solicit guidance from their publicists. The point is, the bigger the stars, the more people they have to advise them and look out for their interests.

Johnny Carson was badly underserved.

You've already met me, the lawyer. You know how unimpressive a résumé I had, but at least I was present.

Johnny also had an agent, at least nominally, at the William Morris Agency, then, as now, one of the major Hollywood talent agencies. But as I discovered when I began examining Johnny's files, the agency had temporarily suspended working on Johnny's behalf and had filed a claim against him for a commission on earnings that not only he had yet to receive but that also exceeded the amount he actually did bring home. This seemed insane to me. I couldn't understand why Carson's manager, Sonny Werblin, hadn't cleared this up. The more I got into every aspect of Johnny's financial life, the more mystified I became about what Werblin was doing.

From what I could tell, Johnny had poor luck with managers. His first managers were Al Bruno and Tom Shields, a Runyonesque pair, always chasing the broads and closing more bars than the Temperance League. They worked hard for Johnny and believed strongly in his talent and his future; when Jack Paar quit *The Tonight Show,* they campaigned hard for Carson to get the job. Their persistence paid off, first when NBC decided to offer Johnny the job, and yet again, even more crucially, when ABC refused to let Carson out of his contract to host *Who Do You Trust?* The managers had to persuade NBC to use a parade of temporary hosts while they waited six months for Johnny's liberation. But after all their effort, they made a big mistake: they allowed a sliver of daylight to come between their interests and Johnny's. They let Johnny suspect that they were not completely committed to him when they signed Mike Douglas.

Mike Douglas may not be well remembered today, but he was a singer with a popular and successful ninety-minute talk show that was syndicated by Westinghouse Broadcasting. In most markets it was an afternoon or dinner-hour show that did not compete directly against *The Tonight Show.* Still, it had the same format, and being based in nearby Philadelphia, it drew guests from the same New York talent pool, so it always had the potential to book an act that *The Tonight Show* wanted or do a bit that was too similar to something *The Tonight Show* had been contemplating. Douglas was nothing like Carson; he was a crooner from the Big Band era, a thoroughgoing square, a blandly good-looking diversion for women forced by the constraints of motherhood or wifedom to stay at home. Neither witty nor handsome nor cool, he represented no threat to Carson, except that he existed. Because if he existed, there could always be some strange, perverse, bizarre, macabre, self-destructive way that NBC could imagine Douglas replacing Johnny.

Carson felt that Bruno and Shields were wrong to represent Douglas. It was like representing Bing Crosby and then signing Frank Sinatra; sure, they came from different generations and had distinct styles and personae, but you couldn't say that there would never be a conflict. Indeed, there could be a lot of conflicts, and Johnny didn't like it. As I would come to see again and again, Carson not only valued loyalty, he demanded it. And yet he was generally a fair man. Although he was angry that these agents had created the potential for a conflict, he didn't think he had actually been neglected yet, and until that happened,

Carson wouldn't pull the trigger.

Of course, it didn't take long. They booked Carson a gig performing at the Fontaine-bleau Hotel in Miami Beach — two shows on Friday night, two shows on Saturday, and nothing but sky, beach, and luxury in between. The agents flew down with Johnny for the date, but then they disappeared. During rehearsal and sound check, it became evident that the sound system was on life support. This disturbed Johnny, as it would most performers who cared very much that they sound their best and that people who were paying to see them get their money's worth. The hotel tried to reassure Johnny that the sound could be fixed, but time passed and no repairs were made. Johnny wanted Bruno and Shields to step in and perform the role that managers are paid to play, that of the heavy; the enforcer; the bad cop; the insane guy who yells, threatens, and implies dark consequences for his adversaries and all their future generations. But Johnny's managers were not available to him in his hour of need. They had driven up to Fort Lauderdale with some newfound female friends.

At least they weren't with Mike Douglas.

The first show got under way, and the sound proved no better than at rehearsal.

Carson, furious, immediately packed his bags and left for New York. "Good luck finding those assholes!" Johnny said as he exited. Don Rickles, fortunately for him, was in the hotel playing the lounge, and the hotel immediately slotted him into the big room. He did not seem to have an issue with the sound.

As soon as Johnny returned to New York, he fired Bruno and Shields, and he never spoke to either of them again. He did, however, tell the story of that evening many times over the years, mostly because he loved the punch line. "The sound was so bad that the audience was getting restless," he'd say. "There were twelve hundred angry Jews in that room. They got Jesus but they were not going to get me. I got the hell out of town as quickly as I could."

Bruno and Shields were replaced by Werblin, now in his third year with Carson. David "Sonny" Werblin was a major executive, a certified "big macher." Originally a high-status show business agent — he had served as the president of the TV division of the powerful MCA (Music Corporation of America) agency — he had gone on to become a major sports impresario. For part of the time that he represented Johnny, he was the minority owner and president of the New York Jets, and also owned Elberon Farms, a large stable where he bred and raced thoroughbred horses. Later he became chairman of Madison Square Garden. These are outstanding credentials, but it wasn't as if Johnny had convened a search committee to find the best possible candidate to manage his affairs. Neither had the mighty Werblin surveyed the landscape and selected Johnny as a singular talent worthy of his ministrations. He was simply Johnny's neighbor. One day Sonny ran into Joanne at the elevator, and when she came back, she suggested his name to Carson. As we shall see, Johnny might have been better off had he limited his interactions with his neighbor to borrowing sugar.

As I mentioned before, the first thing I discovered when we began our inventory of the Carson holdings was that Johnny had very little money, nothing like the sums a star of his stature would be assumed to have. He had no investments, owned no real estate, had no real savings — and this was a man who for more than a decade had been generously paid like the popular network television star that he was. What's more, he had a second highly lucrative career doing his comedy act at nightclubs and concert halls. Obviously he lived lavishly and had a big overhead paying alimony and child support, but his lack of funds was shocking.

Carson had only one real asset: deferred compensation owed him by NBC. In 1967 his lawyer, Arnold Grant, a man described by a mutual friend as a "razor-sharp tax attorney" (and the husband of the former Miss America, television personality, and New York City Consumer Affairs Commissioner Bess Myerson), negotiated a contract that was nominally paying Carson $100,000 a week to host *The Tonight Show*. That's $5,200,000 a year, but Carson didn't have access to even a tenth of that income. Instead, he was receiving $3,000 a week — that's just $156,000 a year — with the rest being deferred. Grant, the brilliant tax attorney, negotiated this deal in 1967 when the income tax rate on big earners was 70 percent. The deal prevented the government from devouring Johnny's income, but it left Carson with just enough to cover his admittedly extravagant expenses and nothing for savings or investment. NBC was delighted to oblige Carson's wishes. The company wouldn't have to pay the balance for decades, and then it would be in dollars that had been devalued by inflation. And if in some weird, unforeseen way the deal somehow turned out to be against NBC's interests, the executives who negotiated the deal were going to be long gone when the bill came due.

The loser in the deal was Johnny. He was pocketing $3,000 for hosting five ninety-minute shows a week — or in other words, just $600 a program, which wasn't much more than the $450 his celebrity guests were paid for their fifteen-minute guest spots. It's true that the deal did shelter Johnny's income from taxes, although there would have been other ways to do that: through investments that would have been more profitable, more productive, and less restrictive. It's also true that the real value of the deal was as a hedge, a bet against Carson's talent. Had he flamed out after a few years and become a pop-culture footnote like Jack Paar, then the deal would have been an insurance policy that would have protected his money and preserved his capital for the years after his popularity had evaporated. It was a very conservative strategy, a case of being prudent to a fault.

When I explained to him that there were other ways to handle his money that would have left him with more to spend, Johnny sadly shook his head.

"Arnold Grant told me that this would be

the best thing to do, and I took his advice."

Not until the bill arrived was Carson's skepticism fully engaged. The lawyer charged Carson $250,000, which, thanks to the contract Grant had just negotiated, Carson did not have enough money to pay. The solicitous Grant then helped Carson acquire a bank loan to cover the fee. Carson took out the loan and then fired Grant. As with Bruno and Shields, he never spoke to Grant again.

To make matters worse, the William Morris Agency then chimed in and billed Carson for their 10 percent commission on the weekly $100,000 salary. Carson tried to explain to them that his real earnings were $3,000 a week, and that the rest of the dough was just a number on a promissory note that would sit in some safe until Johnny retired, at which time Johnny would be happy to pay the commission. Surely they completely understood that this was a tax ploy; surely they could wait to get their cut.

By 1970 things had changed. The top marginal tax rates on high earners had been reduced, and Johnny, a much bigger star than in 1967, was a beneficiary. The new contract that Werblin negotiated ended the deferred compensation scheme and upped Johnny's take-home pay to $30,000 a week, or $6,000 per show. Still, after paying the bills for his lavish lifestyle, Johnny had little money left for growth.

Little by little, however, it became clear that in hiring Werblin, Carson had repeated the mistake he had made with Grant: he found someone with a big reputation and invested his faith, and his earnings, in that reputation. But Sonny did not have the patience or time to devote to his famous client. He had other fish to fry. Plus, it was a drag to live cheek-by-jowl with a client and his needy wife, each of whom could be relied upon to end one of their frequent arguments by stomping down the hallway and banging on Werblin's door.

Sonny didn't have the time. Sonny didn't have the interest. Sonny didn't have the patience.

Sonny should have quit.

But here's the thing: Sonny was milking Johnny for too much cash.

Johnny Carson, famously dapper, wore a new outfit on his show each night. Like any good manager, Werblin recognized an endorsement opportunity. He negotiated a deal with Hart Schaffner & Marx to launch a new label, Johnny Carson Apparel. This was a very shrewd idea. Johnny wore new duds every night, and it wasn't wasted on the men in the audience — or on the women who picked out the men's clothing — that Carson always looked stylish and sophisticated.

But as I studied Johnny's contracts, I was shocked to realize that he owned no equity interest in the new company. Instead, half was owned by the manufacturer and half by Sonny Werblin. Carson, in effect, was paid a salary to wear clothes from the company that bore his name, while the man he had entrusted with his affairs lined his own pockets. And the company was doing well; Johnny should have been building equity in the product plus pulling down a substantial income.

In another questionable deal, Werblin had set up a company called Raritan Enterprises to produce *The Tonight Show.* The main reason Werblin did this was to allow himself to serve as executive producer of the program and pay himself $6,000 a week for the very little work that he performed. This was a classic show business tactic that management types still use in Hollywood to get slices of various pies. Had he actually contributed anything to *The Tonight Show,* or had he used Raritan to produce other programs that would have put money in Johnny's pocket, then no one would have begrudged Sonny his take. But this was a no-show, do-nothing position that would have delighted a mafioso, and Sonny's cut amounted to a 20 percent commission on Carson's then weekly salary of $30,000. Raritan also paid the rent on a suite of very posh offices that Werblin had rented at 641 Lexington Avenue, at Fifty-fourth Street. Shutting down that company would mean Johnny would be paying that rent since he guaranteed the lease. So far as I could see, enriching Werblin was Raritan's sole function.

One evening Judy and I were invited to dinner with Sonny and his wife, Leah. As Leah Ray, she had been a well-known vocalist in the Big Band era, performing with the Tommy Dorsey and Phil Harris orchestras and acting in a dozen films opposite Maurice Chevalier, Bob Hope, and other notables. They took us to Lüchow's, the famous German restaurant on Fourteenth Street in Manhattan. Its old-world style and décor — one wall was lined with beer steins, another with animal heads — could only be described as early oompah. I was looking forward to hearing some inside sports gossip and some bawdy show biz tales, but that was not to be, because in no time, both Werblins were plastered. One was accustomed in those days to seeing drunk patrons in bars and tipsy diners in restaurants, far more so than today, but it was still shocking to see an older couple like the Werblins get absolutely blotto in the middle of a prestigious eatery. Judy was just speechless at the sight. On the plus side, the sauerbraten and dumplings were excellent.

Crossing the Queensboro Bridge on the way home, Judy and I discussed Johnny's predicament. "Look what's going on," I said. "His wife is cheating on him. His manager is screwing him, his agents are exploiting him, and his producer's wife has been conspiring with Joanne to cuckold him. What a goddamn mess."

"He's going to have to fire Rudy," Judy said. "The divorce proceedings are going to get ugly and you might have to call Jeannie as a witness. Johnny can't have Rudy being the producer under those circumstances."

"No, of course not."

"And he's going to have to get rid of Sonny." I guess I must have registered some shock at Judy's cold-bloodedness, but she went on. "You don't think so? You saw him tonight. Sonny can't manage his own affairs. How's he going to manage Calamity John's?"

"Calamity John. That's pretty funny. But

what am I going to say to him? I hardly know the man."

"Just be honest with him, Henry. It probably doesn't matter — he runs through managers, agents, wives, and producers like tissues. You'll probably be gone in a month yourself."

Judy knew me well enough to know that I was already thinking that the best thing — indeed, the only thing — for me to do was just lay out the situation in all of its unappealing detail. When I did, one day at his new apartment on East End Avenue after tennis, Johnny took it surprisingly well; maybe so many people had been blowing smoke up his ass for so long that the facts were a refreshing change.

"That cocksucker!" said Carson. "How dare he! I signed whatever Sonny put in front of me. I guess I wasn't paying attention, but he's an asshole for doing that to me. But I was the schmuck. This should be a lesson to you, Henry. Don't ever let me sign something like that again."

Sonny didn't seem to mind getting the heave-ho. I worked out the details with his lawyer, Bob Shulman, who at least had the decency to act a bit embarrassed by his client's avarice. Of course, it was easy for Werblin to go. We weren't looking for blood or compensation, we just wanted to see him gone. Very well fixed, he hardly needed the income. And he might well have been relieved. At least there would be no more evenings disturbed by one angry Carson or the other banging on his door.

Once Werblin was out, one of my first priorities was to undo the ties between him and Johnny. The clothing deal was rewritten. First I flew to Chicago and met with the CEO of Hart Schaffner & Marx. I told them that Werblin was out and that unless Johnny replaced Werblin in the deal, Carson would no longer wear their clothes on television. I'm not sure exactly how things were handled, but Werblin's stock was transferred to Johnny, who would also be paid a $400,000 annual modeling fee for posing in the suits for advertisements. Raritan was shut down, and with Sonny's departure, there was an immediate and substantial increase in the funds flowing straight to Johnny's wallet. Carson was still stuck with the lease on the office space, but I found myself in a position to help Johnny with that in a more direct way.

I had resolved to make a bold move and start my own firm. Beldock and Kushnick had been very good to me. As soon as Carson became my client, they made me a partner and raised my salary to $35,000 a year, a princely sum back then. But I thought I could do better. I knew that Johnny would pay me $6,000 a month and that I could attract other clients. Moreover, I had met two smart, energetic young attorneys who had invited me to open a firm with them. Jimmy Walsh represented Joe Namath and several other football players (the famous Noxzema shaving-cream ad with Namath was entirely Jimmy's doing). Arnold Kopelson had considerable expertise in the financing of motion pictures by virtue of representing Chemical Bank. He went on to become the producer of such enormously successful films as *The Fugitive, Twisted,* and the Oscar-winning *Platoon.* Not only did I respect them as attorneys, but we were good friends and I felt more simpatico with them than I did with Howard and Jerry. I brought my secretary, Melissa Webster, from the old law firm, who was someone Carson liked very much. He never minded speaking with her, and she often assisted him in making arrangements that he didn't want to discuss with his own secretary. For obvious reasons.

Of course we needed offices, and the availability of the Raritan space was a godsend. Johnny was on the hook for six grand a month. Jimmy and Arnold and I agreed that we would each pay $1,000 a month to Raritan, saving Carson a bundle, and getting a pretty sweet deal ourselves. The beautiful offices were perfectly located and fully furnished. Judy loved the move, her parents loved it, and nobody loved it more than my mom and dad, who were very proud of their son, Johnny Carson's lawyer. Johnny always kidded me about my parents, Mary and Al. When I took my dad to *The Tonight Show* studio, you'd think by the way he acted that he ran the network. Perhaps he was slightly uncomfortable with all the trappings of his son's success, and at times he behaved insufferably. Yet Johnny always treated my parents warmly.

Now that I was up to my ass in alligators, I needed some help. So as a parting gift to my friends at the firm of Beldock and Kushnick, I asked them to handle Johnny's issue with the William Morris Agency. We all recognized that they were entitled to 10 percent of what Johnny was actually making on the contract that had been negotiated by Arnold Grant, and every week they got $300. Their position, that they were entitled to 10 percent of the deferred compensation, was just crazy. Their weekly bill for $9,700 that they insisted on sending was something Carson found galling and insulting, since they knew that they were asking for more than triple what Johnny was actually earning. Naturally this infuriated him.

"William Morris can go fuck themselves. How dare they charge me for money I don't have?"

With my time absorbed by the divorce, I turned the matter over to Jerry Kushnick. Jerry solved the problem with one phone call. He got on the line with his good pal Norman Brokaw, an important figure at the William Morris office.

"Here's our offer," he told Brokaw. "Drop the claim or no William Morris clients will ever be booked on *The Tonight Show* again."

It's hard to say if Carson was prepared to carry out the threat. Pretty far, I would say, although there comes a point when you are just spiting yourself. There certainly would have been times, for example, when NBC would have wanted stars of their shows who were Morris clients to be booked, and it would have been hard to explain a refusal to play ball. It didn't matter; William Morris yielded easily, and in gratitude, Johnny gave Jerry and me his tickets to the Muhammad Ali–Joe Fraser fight in Madison Square Garden, the hottest tickets in town. But Johnny never forgave William Morris. In 1979, when Johnny was hosting the

Oscars for the first time, one of the big films that year was a sci-fi release from Disney called *The Black Hole*. During the show, Johnny did his Carnac the Magnificent routine (wearing the cheesy nylon cape over his smart Certo tux). Holding an envelope to his forehead, he intoned, "And the answer is *The Black Hole*." He then opened the envelope and read the question: "Where does your career go when you sign with William Morris?" The most prestigious audience in all of show business hooted its appreciation.

In the weeks to come, my involvement in Johnny's affairs kept growing. As I worked on the divorce, I fully expected to hear that he was looking for a new manager, or an agent, or even that he was considering a new lawyer. Instead, bit by bit, the items that had been in Werblin's portfolio were handed off to me. Before too much time passed, I was acting as his attorney, agent, personal manager, business manager, public relations agent, messenger, enforcer, tennis partner, and drinking and dining companion. If Johnny needed something done, I was the one who did it. And instead of paying three advisors, he paid one.

Then came the day when I was sitting in

Johnny's apartment and he asked me to join him while he interviewed a candidate for the job of executive producer of *The Tonight Show* (yes, Rudy had been fired). "Sure, I'd be happy to," I said, but I was surprised. "But what do you expect me to add to the discussion? I don't know anything about the production of *The Tonight Show,* or any other show for that matter. And this guy knows a ton."

"Henry, it's time you got to know some of these things," Carson said. "Look, I've been screwed so many times by other people, you're the only one around I trust right now. Whatever you do, don't bullshit me. Just lay it on the line. Okay? Just say what you think. Is he full of crap or can he really pump new energy into my show? I'd like your opinion."

"Okay," I replied. "What should I be looking for?"

"Most people in this business will do or say most anything to get a job," Carson said. "Tell me if you think he'll be able to challenge me.

"Your role as my lawyer is going to involve a lot of different things. But the one thing I don't need is any advice on how to run my show. Stay away from that. From time to time, I'll need you to cover my ass when I do or say something stupid. Mostly make sure I don't get fucked over again."

With his affairs in an obviously shambolic state, was he grasping at straws by having me sit in on such an important meeting?

After the interview, he asked for my opinion. "Well," I said, "since you want my honest opinion, here it is: I have no clue if he's capable or not, except that he has an excellent background. He's charming and as smooth as a baby's ass. But he lived with his mother until he was fifty-three years old, and that seems a little fucked up to me."

Carson grinned. "I'd like to see him live with my mother for a week! If you think he's fucked up now, wait till he's spent time with her." Even genial George Smith laughed at that.

"But he sure seems to know every big name in the business," I added, "unless he's full of shit. But personally, I liked him a lot."

"Yeah, me too," said Johnny. And with that, Johnny decided to hire Fred de Cordova, the man who would produce *The Tonight Show* for the next twenty-two years.

During this period, somebody — Judy, probably — showed me a copy of an issue of *Life* magazine that was published just a few months before Johnny and I met. If I'd read it when it came out, it didn't stick with me. Reading it after having met him, it struck me like a thunderbolt. In the piece, journalist Joan Barthel describes Johnny as a man "burdened by layers of shyness . . . of insecurity and suspicion built up over years of feeling deserted by agents, let down by associates, taken for granted by NBC, surrounded by yes men, and misled by bad advice. When a friend said to him recently 'Sometimes you've got to trust people,' Carson replied bleakly, 'But who?' "

It was shocking to realize that he'd been searching for an answer to that question for months and that the answer he found was me.

FOUR:
1972: JOANNE AND JOANNA

Very soon, I came to a significant and life-changing epiphany: representing Johnny Carson wouldn't be like any of the typical strictly business attorney-client relationships I had seen during my early years of practice. When I worked for Beldock and Kushnick, I had seen many clients. Some of them needed more attention than others, and some were closer friends than others, but none of them absorbed the kind of time I was devoting to Carson. I was his lawyer, agent, manager, janitor, and more. Like the proverbial slowly boiled frog, a story often used as a metaphor for people who are unable to react to gradual changes, I suddenly found myself up to my neck in Carson's professional and personal drama.

From the start, I saw him nearly every day. Several times a week we played tennis at the Vanderbilt Club, usually between ten-thirty a.m. and noon. Located in the Grand

Central Terminal Annex in what had once been CBS studios, the club had just undergone a posh makeover and was the popular new place where luminaries like Mayor Lindsay and Baseball Hall of Famer Hank Greenberg came to play. Hank and I became good pals, and later he sponsored me for membership in the posh Beverly Hills Tennis Club.

It is no exaggeration to say that I acted on the assumption that playing tennis with Johnny was part of my job description. Had I stopped, he might have found a different partner, but I didn't feel secure enough to risk it.

These would be the first of hundreds of tennis matches that the two of us played, and anyone who has ever played a game against a boss will understand what I mean when I say we practiced more diplomacy in those games than Henry Kissinger did during his entire career. Johnny was not a particularly gifted player, but he was devoted to the sport, and he thought he was better than he was. I did my utmost to make any match closer than it really was, usually by calling many out balls in. It was an informal handicap system. The worse he played, the bigger the handicap, and therefore the more often I had to shout "Great shot!" in order to make him feel better on the court. Some days his game was too wild and there was nothing I could do, and on those days I knew I would be getting a call from Freddy de Cordova. "How bad did you beat him today, Henry?" the producer would gripe. "I hope you enjoyed it, because he's taking it out on the rest of us. For Christ's sake, Henry, would it kill you to let him win once in a while?" I sympathized with Fred and, in fact, I frequently threw games. But I would never, ever acknowledge to Freddy that this was anything I could control because he'd call me every day and campaign to have me throw every set. "Are you sure he wasn't talking to his mother?" I would invariably respond. Even more than losing at tennis, a call from Ruth Carson could drive Johnny nuts.

After we finished playing, I showered and went to my office, just fourteen short blocks away in Midtown, while Johnny went back to his place to shower and change for work. New York was perfectly set up for Johnny. He loved everything about the city, and his driver was always standing by. "New York is an exciting town where something is happening all the time, most of it unsolved" was one of his most favorite lines.

Three or four times a week, we got together again in the evening. We hit all the favored hangouts of the rich and celebrated: Patsy's, Toots Shor's (before it closed down), the 21 Club, and the Playboy Club. For a while we were joined by Arthur Kassel, who felt that his role in brokering this union entitled him to inclusion. But for Johnny, a little of Arthur went a long way, and I regularly had to explain to Arthur that Johnny and I would be discussing matters covered by attorney-client privilege, and therefore he couldn't join us. "Say no more," Arthur would discreetly reply.

Arthur would eventually get himself exiled permanently from Johnny's circle through a singularly stupid act. One day Johnny was flying from New York to Los Angeles with his son Rick. Arthur wanted to sit with Johnny, but the flight was fully booked, so Arthur used his law enforcement juice to have Rick bumped to a later flight, and Arthur took his seat. Once Carson got wind of the lie, he cut Arthur out of his life. But Kassel and I maintained our friendship.

Along with Arthur, others would often join us — Ed McMahon, Sonny Werblin for a while, Joe Mullen, and Johnny's accountant, Warren Shine, were regulars, and we constantly ran into people from the network or other comedians who joined us.

I particularly remember one amazing night when Johnny and I went to Le Club in the East Fifties, one of the first cosmopolitan dinner clubs in New York. We ran into George Plimpton — prolific journalist, editor of the *Paris Review,* elegant man about town. He and Carson settled into a dazzlingly witty repartee, which eventually led to Carson doing magic tricks, which Plimpton hilariously and unsuccessfully attempted to imitate. We then ended the evening at P. J. Clarke's with Carson issuing a blanket invitation to Plimpton to appear on his program. Plimpton, in return, invited Johnny to one of his upcoming parties. Plimpton frequently accepted; I'm sure Johnny never did.

Johnny's favorite places to eat were the restaurants of Steak Row, the steakhouse-rich group of blocks between Lexington and Second Avenue in the East Forties. Carson loved them all — Christ Cella, Colombo's, the Palm, Joe & Rose's, Pietro's, Scribe's, the Pen & Pencil. But his very favorite had to be Danny's Hideaway, which the inimitable Dante Charles Stradella — a dynamic personality packed in a five-foot-two, 130-pound body — had started in the fifties as a six-seat, one-room eatery with his Mamma Rosa cooking and him waiting tables and tending bar. A decade later the restaurant's eleven dining rooms, the walls of which were covered with photos of celebrities, most of them posing with Danny, filled a four-story building and seated three hundred. Outside there was a sixty-foot awning that read Danny's Hideaway and His Inferno; His Music Room; His Menu Room; His Key Room; His Nook.

In those days, Carson always picked up the check when we went out (later in our relationship, we alternated paying the tab, with total disregard for whether the previous check had been for two burgers or dinner for eight). This was true everywhere but Danny's, where we ate at least once a week, and where Danny always picked up the tab, something he did for his favorite customers. Of course, Johnny would in turn always leave a few hundred dollars on the table as a "tip." It was a game they both enjoyed. The first time I accompanied Johnny to the restaurant, Danny told me, "As long as Johnny comes to my joint, he will always be my guest. He did me a real good turn two years ago and now the same goes for you." I was stunned and Johnny said, "Don't look a gift horse in the mouth." The next time I went to Danny's, I was with Judy for our anniversary. I was quite prepared to pay the check when, true to his word, Danny picked up my tab. I often wondered how many of the celebrities in the photos on his walls were in his free-meal program.

Some years later, after we had moved to California, I had heard that Danny was having some tax or financial problems. I mentioned this to Johnny, who then instructed his accountant to send Danny a check for $100,000. "Just tell Danny that it's a small repayment for all the meals that he bought for me over the years."

That gesture showed Johnny in all his complexity: he was often generous, frequently on a grand scale, but he often had trouble responding when the people around him needed him for something, particularly emotional support. And in the same way that he often had trouble accepting compliments and praise from people, he sometimes had trouble expressing himself, and he would delegate even his great acts of kindness to intermediaries. In this case, Danny got to thank Johnny personally, and he broke down in tears as he did so.

And in between tennis and dinner? Yes, almost all of that time was absorbed with Johnny's many issues as well. His divorce, his business dealings, and many matters associated with his *Tonight Show* contract took up most of my office hours. Along with the apparel deal, Werblin had placed Carson in a number of other arrangements that were far more rewarding to Werblin than to Carson, and they had to be undone. There was Raritan to button up, and contracts to execute that covered the many personal appearances Johnny made for badly needed cash. My practice and my life were subsumed by all things Johnny. We talked about everything — women, children, wives, parents. After *The Godfather* debuted in 1972, Johnny would refer to me with that great new old word we learned from that movie — *consigliere.* It wasn't a perfect term for me: the disparity in our ages and stature in the world made me chary of fully asserting a lawyer's customary authority and bluntness. And yet we both realized that in order to meet my responsibility, I would have to advise him candidly. We agreed that we should always speak as equals on all matters of lawyer and client. This wasn't easy for me at first, but I got better at it.

And so we embarked on a complicated relationship. We were friends, but it wasn't a friendship of equals. We were business associates, and although we were very friendly ones, in any business arrangement the question "What have you done for me lately?" is never long out of the room. But we were close, and what bonded us was trust. Carson had been looking for, and had really needed to find, someone he could trust — trust to be competent, trust to protect his interests, trust to be on his side. And the more he trusted me, the more trustworthy he found me to be.

One day early on, I learned that Rick Carson, the second of the three sons Johnny had with his first wife, Jody, had been locked up in the military psychiatric ward of New York City's Bellevue Hospital. Rick had joined the navy in hopes of impressing his father, who had served in that branch, but whatever payoff he earned was soon overwhelmed by reality. Stationed in a desolate Alaskan outpost, the twenty-year-old soon became bored, lonely, and isolated. He began drinking heavily and exhibiting suicidal tendencies. The navy shipped him to New York to determine if he was fit to serve. He was at risk of being dishonorably discharged. Or killing himself.

Johnny was, of course, very concerned about Rick, but he didn't want to go see him. "Think of the media attention!" he said. "It would be a circus, and it would just piss the navy off. And it would mortify

Rick. I can't see how this wouldn't end up doing him more harm than good." This seemed like a colossal rationalization to me, but whatever the real reason was, I could see that Johnny didn't want to see his son in Bellevue Hospital, and so when Johnny asked me to handle the matter, I agreed. But this is not the sort of thing they teach you how to handle in law school.

Every day for most of the next two weeks, I passed through the wrought-iron gates and the ominous brown brick walls of Bellevue to visit Rick. On the first few occasions, he was confined to his bed, restrained and sedated. It wasn't until the third or fourth visit that I could speak to Rick without him being medicated. Schizophrenia and bipolar disorder were the conditions afflicting the young Carson, along with an awful case of the hiccups, and Thorazine was the treatment of choice. The young man (although he was not much younger than I) was scared and overwhelmed by his surroundings. Bellevue was actually part of the New York University Medical School, but every New Yorker knew it as an intake facility for the mentally disturbed. Rick was being held in a lockdown facility, and a more depressing place one could not imagine. Each day I would bring magazines and food, and gradually he began to trust me. He admitted that he had failed to follow orders and had then begun to drink heavily. Unfortunately, both of his parents were drinkers. He denied the navy's contention that he had attempted suicide, maintaining that he had only faked the attempts. He had no explanation for the bandages on his left wrist.

"Can I see my dad?" he asked.

"Your dad thinks if he came, there would be a million cameras, and it would turn into a big publicity spectacle that would just impede your recovery." I was speaking the truth — that is what Johnny thought — but I don't know if I was mustering much conviction.

Rick nodded and said he understood, but I could see by the way his shoulders slumped that he was terribly disappointed. He wasn't getting any other visitors, even though his mother lived in Westchester, only an hour away. I don't know if she knew he was there or if she didn't care to visit. I was willing to call her, but Johnny declined to give me her phone number. "Rick and his mom are not getting along," he told me. I argued that under the circumstances she should be advised and should visit, but I was too new on the job to press the point. This part of the problem was being delegated to me.

After a couple of weeks, I did manage to get through to the navy commander in charge of Rick's fate. We reached an acceptable solution. Rick would be given a general discharge and would enter a rehab program, and the navy commander would receive four tickets to *The Tonight Show* for himself and his boss and their wives. I went to the show that the officers attended. I thanked them effusively and then brought everyone backstage to meet Johnny. He also thanked the officers and posed for pictures.

Whether or not Johnny was right to avoid seeing Rick under such circumstances, it's true that by any standard Johnny was not a very good father. He was concerned about his sons — we had innumerable discussions in which he expressed real worry about their well-being — but he was not a significant presence in their lives, and he knew it. Johnny was very much a member of a generation of men that saw their principal paternal obligation as providing for their family's material well-being. That notion was used not only to excuse long hours and demanding schedules but, let's face it, also to excuse a lot of selfish behavior. Once his first marriage started to fall apart, there were a lot of nights when Johnny used work as an excuse to get away while Jody lived in Harrison and raised the boys alone. But that pattern dated almost from the day they were married in 1949; by 1959 they had separated, and in 1963 she had obtained a Mexican divorce, under the terms of which Carson agreed to pay $15,000 a year in alimony and $7,500 in child support. It was a reasonable settlement at the time but not very much in light of the huge income he would eventually earn. Jody never succumbed to the temptation to air her grievances in public; asked by one interviewer to describe what went wrong, she said, "We had three children right away and there was no money. It happens all the time to a lot of people." For his part, Johnny spoke of that marriage more than once as his "greatest personal failure."

To Johnny's credit, he sent Jody money many times over the years when she had a particular need. It would be wrong to say that he possessed a lingering affection for his college sweetheart, but he didn't want to see the mother of his children in want. Eventually, Jody had me on her speed dial to call me for some sort of help, either financial or legal. I always refused the legal assistance, but Johnny rarely refused her money.

Obviously, not all men availed themselves of the "work comes first" excuse, but it was perfect for Carson. Johnny had many virtues: he was generous and charming, and he could be warm, but he didn't like to be needed. He liked his relationships to be on his terms, and over the years, wives, children, friends, and associates found that Johnny was prepared to give a great deal to those he was close to, but that if you needed something more or something different than he was offering, you were almost always denied, and you risked being rather harshly rebuffed.

The hostility between Joanne and Johnny intensified. The longer their divorce dragged on, the more I learned the Carson's marriage had long been a troubled union filled with booze, fireworks, and sexual infidelity. I suppose these were the ordinary problems of many couples, happy and unhappy, but few had the wherewithal to underwrite their indulgences that Mr. and Mrs. Carson did.

Johnny wasn't any good at marriage. He made that very clear to me at the beginning of our relationship, when the second of his marriages was disintegrating, and his aptitude didn't improve very much with subsequent unions. Nonetheless, he firmly believed he should be married. That was just something you did when you became a man: you got married, had a wife, raised a family. Look at Homer and Ruth: they had been married more than sixty years. Being married was what a man did, and Johnny always married. There were things he liked about it. He liked having a home, and a home wasn't a home without a wife. He liked the stability. When he had a wife, he never had to bother to find a date for the many events that he attended each year, and in what struck me as a weird piece of celebrity logic but which Johnny truly believed, having a wife meant being less bothered by the media. As he put it to me one day, "If I'm single and I show up at a restaurant or some obligatory red-carpet or black-tie event, anybody I take with me will be fodder for tabloid speculation for months. It's really a big pain in the ass for both of us. If you show up with your wife, there's nothing to write about." Oddly, this rationale is similar to the one he gave for not visiting Rick in Bellevue.

But having a wife did not limit his behavior. There may have been times during his marriages when he was faithful, but fidelity was not the defining characteristic of husband Carson.

Certainly this caused him trouble. Years after Johnny left New York, Jilly Rizzo told my girlfriend at the time, the actress Joyce DeWitt, that there were many nights in the late 1960s when he had to put Johnny in a cab to get him back to his apartment. One night before Jilly got his chance to play dispatcher, an attractive brunette at the bar caught Carson's eye, and soon Johnny was doing his considerable best to convince her to leave with him. Unfortunately, the lady was not unattached, and when her boyfriend — a major figure in the underworld — arrived, he was not grateful to Johnny for entertaining his "goomar" during his absence. He and several large associates lifted Johnny off his bar stool and threw him down a flight of stairs, an apparent overture to a rather more serious beating. Only Jilly's intercession prevented the kind of punishment that would have kept Carson off the air for weeks, but as Jilly told the story, he had won only a temporary reprieve: the mobster took out a contract on Carson.

What prevented Johnny from a gruesome exit? As it happened, an infamous rally was about to take place, and that saved his life. Taking the threat seriously, Carson holed up in his UN Plaza palace for three days, missing three shows. Not good for the network. Soon David Tebet, an indispensable NBC executive, went to speak with George Wood, an important agent at the William Morris Agency. Wood was well known for having the "right" mob connections, and Tebet wanted to know if something could be done to patch things up. Just possibly, said Wood. He had heard that Joseph Colombo, widely reputed to be the head of one of the Five Families of New York and New Jersey, had formed the Italian-American Civil Rights League and was planning to hold a big Italian-American unity rally on Columbus Day in 1970. He was deeply, deeply disappointed that so far all of the networks had refused to cover the rally.

"Oh, I don't think NBC has completely made up its mind yet," said Tebet.

Soon an accommodation was reached. NBC News covered the event, and Johnny could leave his apartment.

The second Italian-American unity rally was held the following year. Colombo was shot three times at the rally and left in a coma from which he never recovered. That was the last of the rallies.

This, by the way, was not the only occasion when Carson's antics earned him a beating. For some reason, Johnny had started making jokes about Keefe Brasselle, an actor of modest talent and a would-be producer of several failed television shows. Around this time, before *The Tonight Show* moved to Hollywood, the show would travel to Los Angeles two or three times a year. During these sojourns, Johnny had taken a liking to a restaurant on Sunset Boulevard called Sneaky Pete's, where he often sat in with the jazz trio after hours, playing the drums and sometimes singing. One night a rather burly man named Walter Stevens came in. He found Johnny and Ed McMahon having a late dinner in a banquette. Stevens politely asked to have a moment alone with Johnny, and after Ed removed himself to the bar, Stevens told Johnny that he had been hired by some friends of Keefe Brasselle's to tell Johnny to lay off the Keefe Brasselle jokes. Apparently Johnny was unconvincing in his reassurances because Stevens then launched a flurry of punches to Johnny's stomach and liver. He was still pounding away when he was hauled off. "What the fuck, I'll drop it," said Johnny later. "No one gives a shit about Keefe Brasselle."

Johnny was always a player, but now that he was separated from Joanne, he did not have even the notion of a wife to limit his escapades. With Joe Mullen's arrangements freeing him from the scrutiny of Joanne's divorce investigators, Johnny was free to enjoy — discreetly — his de facto bachelorhood.

Discreetly, however, wasn't a word that described Johnny's adventures during this separation period (nor any other period, I suppose). Early in 1972 there was a Friars Club roast of Buddy Hackett. Johnny was the emcee at this stag affair that featured George Burns, Jack Benny, Sammy Davis Jr., Dean Martin, Red Buttons, George Raft, Flip Wilson, Jonathan Winters, and seemingly half of Hollywood was on the dais (it had three tiers). He started the evening off in great form with one of the few jokes from the event that I can repeat. "Most of you know I'm an astronomy buff. In fact, I had an observation deck and telescope installed at my home. I use it almost every night, sometimes even to look at the stars. We're very fortunate to live so close to the Palomar Observatory. They have an amazing telescope there. The glass that formed the lens took seven years to cure, and then the Steuben Company spent another three years polishing it. But it was worth it. You can look through that thing and see back billions of years into space. And I actually visited the Palomar Observatory to look through that famous telescope. And as I looked back into billions of years of history from that device, I could not find a single reason why this goddamn club is giving a dinner for a son of a bitch like Buddy Hackett."

It was surely one of the funniest nights of my life. The next comedian was more hilarious than the last. The incident that topped everything, though, came during a momentary lull in the proceedings, when Flip Wilson (seated behind Johnny on the third tier of the dais) suddenly burst out laughing in his inimitable high-pitched cackle. It seemed that Johnny, who was quite drunk (and in the middle of the second tier with ten guys on either side), had taken a wine bucket and was peeing into it. Of course the audience couldn't see this; they could only hear the growing mirth. But when Jonathan Winters joined Carson, the whole room collapsed with laughter.

The next day Johnny was to have a life-insurance physical for a ten-million-dollar policy. A doctor from New York had flown out to conduct the exam. One problem: Johnny was nowhere to be found. He never made it home that night. We were concerned enough to call the police. After a few hours, his car was spotted outside a massage parlor on Sunset Boulevard. It turns out that he had been there all night. I drove over and got him.

"You have a physical!" I reminded him.

"Oh, call the fucking thing off. If they examine me today, the only thing the tests will show is that I died last night."

So we postponed the physical, but I drove him to Burbank, and he taped that evening's show.

Despite striking out in two marriages, Johnny was still prime husband material, and with his divorce inevitable, his marriageable status was high. Handsome, debonair, intelligent, witty, and famous, he was rich and fast becoming richer, thanks to a new deal with NBC (which I negotiated) that was paying him $5 million a year, terms that made him one of the highest-paid entertainers in the world. And unlike so many other stars at the pinnacle whose insecurities were painfully transparent, Johnny Carson lived comfortably in his own skin. He may have been troubled in certain areas, but he was never tormented by insecurity.

During this time, he was linked with many

attractive women, including Eartha Kitt, Peggy Lee, and singer Joanie Sommers. Another was Angel Tompkins, a slinky blonde for whom the word *nubile* was invented and for whom clothing wasn't. A fixture in *Playboy,* she had featured roles in films with Gene Hackman, Lee Marvin, Elliott Gould, and other stars. I crossed paths with her as she was leaving Carson's apartment one morning, and while I was sure she was slipped in undetected by Joe Mullen the night before, she took no precautions in leaving; after all, if I could see her, so could detectives hired by Joanne's attorney, Raoul Felder. "You're nuts to be doing this and to be so careless," I said. "If Felder finds out, you could be screwed."

"Fuck him," said Johnny. "A stiff prick has no conscience." And he would not discuss it further.

Several weeks later, I asked what was going on with Ms. Tompkins. I told him it was relevant to the case, but really I was just being nosy. I was surprised to hear that he had dumped her. "She's done," he said. "She's in some sitcom, and she said in an interview that we were dating. Well, we're not." Just to reiterate, I started to review the relevant passage in New York matrimonial law for him, but he waved me off. "I know the ground rules," he said. "In fact, I told her my lawyers made me give her the ax because of her big mouth." In reality, discretion was always his rule, and he enforced it ruthlessly. "Don't worry," he told me. "I won't screw up again. The furthest thing from my mind at this moment is getting involved with another woman."

That lasted until the moment he met Joanna Holland.

Tall, with jade-colored eyes and long, lustrous dark hair, Joanna was a thirty-one-year-old model. Raised in New York in an Italian family, her first husband was the handsome, raffish Tim Holland, who had fashioned a career gambling, playing golf in stakes matches, and winning backgammon tournaments (between 1968 and 1973 he was the world's reigning backgammon champion). Though happy at first — Joanna was certainly impressed with the glamorous lifestyle she and Tim enjoyed in Biarritz, Monte Carlo, and St. Moritz — they divorced in 1966.

"It wasn't her fault," Holland later told *People* magazine. "Our lives didn't mesh. She wanted someone who went to business and worked. I played golf." After the split, Joanna began supporting herself and her son, Tim, in their small but elegant Park Avenue apartment by modeling for such celebrated designers as Donald Brooks, Geoffrey Beene, and Mollie Parnis, who takes credit for introducing the couple one evening at the 21 Club, where Johnny was dining with Parnis, Freddy de Cordova, and Jack and Mary Benny. "I was flirting like a sophomore," Johnny later said. In the opinion of Parnis, "Joanna was much more sophisticated than Johnny."

Sophisticated indeed, the decidedly up-market Joanna was no trifle. "Dark haired, of medium height and voluptuous build," an obviously smitten Kenneth Tynan would later write, "the third Mrs. Carson is the kind of woman, bright and molto simpatico, whom you expect to meet, not in Bel Air, but at a cultural soiree in Rome." (Something about her brought out the continental in writers: in the *Hollywood Reporter,* George Christy said she had "the sexiest strut this side of Montmartre.")

The men she dated were substantial figures. Prior to meeting Johnny, Joanna had been involved romantically with the chairman of the Hertz Corporation and other highly successful men who could and did spend extravagantly in their pursuit of a woman with her class and beauty. One former boyfriend, having loved and lost, forgot that he was supposed to behave like a gentleman. He sued Joanna, claiming the large sum of money he had provided to furnish her apartment was a loan. Joanna's position was that the money was unambiguously a gift. (Later it fell to me to defend Joanna and then settle the case. Johnny parted with some cash to make the man go away.)

Some people have muttered that Joanna was a gold digger, but that was not a shrewd or subtle or insightful assessment. Joanna realized she had been dealt a hand full of high cards and that for the benefit of herself and her son, she was determined to play the hand brilliantly. And she did.

Joanna had style, she had class, and I thought she'd be terrific for Johnny. Certainly in the beginning of their marriage she very much was. And, not long after they started dating, I could see that Joanna had fallen in love with him. She was not naive. She was a smart and sophisticated woman who understood from the start what she was getting into, in no small measure from the tutelage she received during her first marriage. Johnny's lifestyle — the boozing, his infinite attraction to women and their overwhelming interest in him — was well known. In the singles game, Johnny was the ultimate "get," and he enjoyed his status. No matter to whom he was married, no matter how happily, when an alluring woman came within range, the instinct for new adventure was an impulse he saw little need to restrain. In the realm of women, it was Johnny's world. He had the pick of almost anyone.

So with all of this as a backdrop, I was more than a little astonished when over dinner Johnny said to me, "I think Joanna is the one." It took me several beats to absorb this news until I finally pointed out, perhaps a little stupidly, "You're still married to Joanne. And the way the divorce is going, it will be at least a year before you're not married to her." I had no interest in standing in the way of Joanna per se, but I knew that if the relationship became public, it was going to cost Johnny a vastly larger sum to free himself from Joanne. But, as I was to discover so many times, the realities I feared mattered nothing to Johnny Carson when there was something he wanted. "Please just get it done. No more meetings on the subject. Give Joanne what she wants and end it."

From my point of view, the proceedings should have ended long ago. Joanne had been caught in an adulterous relationship. That was grounds for divorce. There were no custody issues. There was property to divide, alimony to negotiate, but she was a young woman who had a somewhat successful television career and had previously been an airline stewardess; it should have been an easy settlement. But it wasn't. Raoul Felder, defining his style as a matrimonial litigator, was intransigent, and Joanne, unfortunately, was hysterical. She phoned Johnny and harangued him, and then phoned me and harangued me. She showed up at NBC in an inebriated condition to annoy and provoke him. It got to the point where we had to move for restraining orders.

Sometimes her behavior made me feel that I was in over my head. Once I sought the advice of the great lawyer Louis Nizer, who had briefly represented Carson, as well as Charlie Chaplin, Salvador Dali, and many other famous clients. I was happy I did; he was the Yoda I had been hoping for.

"Nothing is more bitter than litigation between husbands and wives," he told me. "The nastiness and anger exceed that of any other relationship. Don't get caught up in it. Leave all the emotions to the psychiatrists. Focus on creating an equitable settlement." It was very sound advice; even more flattering, Nizer called me a few weeks later to see if I would be interested in joining his firm. I wasn't.

The turning point came when Joanne, for whatever reason, replaced the militant Felder with the even-keeled, highly professional Morton Bass. Once he got involved, the case resolved itself. We agreed that Joanne would receive the sum of $6,000 per month until she remarried or until Johnny's death (which she did, until Johnny died in 2005), as well as a pretty nice little art collection. It was a fair settlement, but given the millions Johnny was earning at the time, I think I did a damn good job for him.

The case did not end without a further outburst. On the very day in June 1972 when the divorce settlement was to be put on the record at the Bronx Supreme Court, Joanne fired Bass and introduced her new attorney. The judge would have none of it and made it clear that if she did not approve the settlement, there would be severe repercussions. Joanne came to her senses long enough to recant, and the settlement was approved. As part of the deal, Carson had agreed to pay Bass $35,000 for his fees. I gave him the check at the courthouse once the settlement was approved.

Now that the path was clear for Carson to

marry Joanna, the question became whether he should. The two of us sat down and had a talk. "Are you sure?" I asked him. "Do you know what you're really getting into?" I felt ridiculous, playing the cliché role of Pa Walton. Who was I to advise Johnny to be cautious? I was not yet out of my twenties, in practice for only four years, and married myself a mere four years (less than a quarter of the time Johnny had spent as a husband). Both Johnny and Joanna had been around the block and knew perfectly well what they were doing. Who was I to intervene?

Happily, Johnny took it well. He wasn't much interested in my advice to wait a bit until the fallout from his divorce had settled, but he did indulge my request to call Joe Mullen and have him do a thorough background check on Joanna and her family.

Joe's dossier was quite thorough. The details of Joanna's marriage to Tim Holland and their subsequent divorce were covered. Her later relationships with rather affluent men were scrutinized. She lived with her son in a well-furnished Park Avenue apartment. Her mother, Linda, and brother, Peter, were very much part of her life. Nothing in the report caused Johnny any concern.

Which was good. I certainly wasn't rooting against her. I liked her, I got a kick out of her mother, and I thought her brother was a good guy. And so it was on with the show. With two wives behind him, Johnny quietly proposed to Joanna and was delighted when she said yes.

Just two things remained. Determined to avoid the predictable media insanity, Johnny made it very clear that he wanted the marriage to Joanna to happen in complete secrecy — CIA dark ops! No leaks! And it had to happen soon. In one month, NBC was throwing a party for Johnny at the Beverly Hills Hotel honoring his tenth anniversary as host of *The Tonight Show,* and Johnny wanted to surprise everyone by announcing that he and Joanna were married — not just engaged, but actually married — at that event.

The most obvious clue that a couple intends to marry is to be found on display at city hall, where the couple has to take out a marriage license, and where loose-lipped clerks on columnists' payrolls are happy to leak the news. Therefore, the first key to having a secret nuptial is to engage the cooperation of a romantic judge who will keep the paperwork out of the usual traffic. As it happened, my cousin, Richard

Trugman, was a lawyer in Los Angeles, and he arranged a lunch for me at the Friars Club in Beverly Hills with Judge Mario Clinco, a superior court judge at the Santa Monica courthouse. Fortunately, Judge Clinco was not only romantic but also a bit starstruck, and he was only too happy to help America's biggest TV star prevent his special day from being ruined by a media melee. "Tell you what," he said. "I'll keep the license application and the marriage certificate in my chambers until after the event has been announced. The press will be none the wiser until Johnny breaks the news." Carson was so pleased that he graciously invited Judge Clinco and his wife to the upcoming party, where he made sure the three posed for numerous photographs together. It had all been something of an organizational nightmare but we achieved success.

But with the wedding day at hand, a lone detail remained unaddressed: the prenuptial agreement. Nobody was more aware than I was that Johnny's important affairs had been badly handled in the past, and I was determined to make sure this matter was correctly concluded. The new marriage was governed under California law and California is a community property state, which meant that in the event of divorce, in the absence of some other arrangement, the couple would split their estate in half.

I really wanted Johnny to make some other arrangement. Joanna was a fine woman, but there was no reason on earth that she should get half his dough. Prior to the wedding ceremony, I tried repeatedly to get Johnny to focus on this issue, and I knew he understood its import completely. He was the highest-paid performer in television. He was bringing a fortune to the union; her assets were negligible. A proper agreement was essential to protect everything he had earned over all his previous years of hard work. It was also designed to protect the bulk of what he would go on to earn.

I prepared the agreement for Joanna to sign. She was waiting for it; her counsel was standing by ready to review the papers, and she had expressed no resentment about making such an arrangement. And why would she? The amount we had proposed to settle upon her in the event of divorce was extremely generous, and Joanna, a sophisticated woman, knew it. Whatever destiny had in store for them, she and her son would be very secure.

It was Johnny who balked. Trugman and I had gone over the prenuptial details with

Carson repeatedly, and he had yet to sign. Finally, with time running out and guests on the verge of arriving, Johnny shook his head. "This is no way to start a marriage," he said. "Tear the goddamn thing up."

I was stunned. I had been Johnny's lawyer for slightly more than two years, which was not yet enough time to say, as I later certainly would have, "What the fuck are you doing?" Instead, I argued as best I could. "A prenuptial agreement is just common sense. A man like you needs one. Joanna understands. She has no problem with it. She expects it! Honestly, this could really come back to bite you in years to come."

"I hear you, Henry," he said. "It just doesn't seem like the right thing to do."

In desperation I played my hole card. "Remember that first night we talked in Jilly's? Remember how terrible you are at marriage?"

"I remember," he said. "But I don't care."

I did the only thing I could. I wrote him a letter that required his acknowledgment, which stated that against all advice to the contrary, he was going forward with the marriage without the prenuptial. He countersigned the letter. I next called his accountant in New York, Warren Shine. I insisted that Shine make notes of the conversation so that I had some further protection for this massive mistake.

"You know, Johnny, Henry's right," Shine said. "Why, the tax implications . . ."

"Piss off, Warren," Johnny said, and hung up the phone. Then he turned to me.

"Why the hell did you tell Shine about the marriage?" he yelled. "This could ruin the surprise at the party. You better make sure he keeps his fucking mouth shut." With that, the matter ended. Johnny had no regard for the potential cost of this failure; the only thing on his mind was the surprise.

At least for the moment, he had his bride, he had his marriage, and he had his surprise. The next evening, as Lucille Ball, Bob Hope, Jack Benny, Burt Reynolds, Rowan and Martin, and hundreds of other guests looked on, Johnny Carson cut a twelve-foot-high cake in celebration of his anniversary and then made an astonishing announcement.

"A lot of columnists have been asking why me and my gal haven't set a date for the wedding, so I think I will tell you that we were married at one-thirty this afternoon." Johnny then leaned down and kissed Joanna. Flip Wilson, wearing his Geraldine drag, kissed Johnny. Noting that all three of Johnny's wives had names that started with the same letter, Bob Newhart concluded, "Obviously Johnny didn't want to have to change the monograms on the towels after every marriage."

The secret had been kept, romance had triumphed, the laughs were plentiful, and the party rocked. No marriage ever had a more promising beginning.

In time, when the marriage ended and the divorce was settled, this romantic gesture would cost Johnny $35 million.

FIVE:
1972–1978: STAIRWAY
TO PARADISE

In a long-anticipated move, *The Tonight Show* left New York in 1972 for Los Angeles. Although the television industry had been cradled in Manhattan, building on the infrastructure of the creative and technical talent and investment that had produced radio, significant segments of the industry had by 1970 located in LA, especially the big sound stages where most of the TV series were filmed. Nearly everything having to do with entertainment, including most of the game shows, was now being produced in the studios in Burbank in the San Fernando Valley, leaving the news broadcasts and the talk shows in New York. Three of those programs — *The Tonight Show* on NBC, *The Dick Cavett Show* on ABC, and *The Merv Griffin Show* on Westinghouse — were produced within blocks of one another, and the battle for guest stars was intense. The bookers could hardly avoid duplicating

132

one another; in the meantime, on the opposite coast, a mother lode of talent was idling by the pool.

There was another factor: New York was becoming an increasingly stressful place to live, with crime, strikes, disruption, and deteriorating conditions leaving people feeling beleaguered and depressed. Johnny, who liked the time he spent in Los Angeles early in his career, was perfectly happy to kiss the Big Apple good-bye. As he told an interviewer, "At this point in my life, I enjoy playing tennis, enjoy going to the beach. I lived in New York seventeen years; I like the idea, as corny as it sounds, of a yard and a house. Maybe that's the old Midwestern values, but I like being able to walk outside in the morning and sit around; you can't do that in New York."

But my question was: What about me?

Even after Johnny had moved across the country, he still counted on me to handle all his issues, including that period when divorce proceedings with Joanne were being conducted in New York and his wedding plans with Joanna were being made in LA. In the year following his relocation, I made sixteen round trips to Los Angeles. It wasn't that much of a hardship. Flying in those days was easier and more pleasurable — so loose was security that a passenger could not only take a gun on an airplane but little bottles of shampoo as well — and it was always a pleasure to leave whatever was going on in New York and get out into the Southern California sun. My cousins, Richard and Marty Trugman, gave me a warm welcome whenever I showed up, as did the staff of the luxurious Beverly Hills Hotel, whose costs I passed on to Carson. No matter what else was going on, we met every day and played tennis at the hotel or the Bel-Air Country Club. More and more with each trip, I could see myself living in that environment.

The secret, subtle hand that facilitated the move belonged to Joanna. She saw the need for Carson to be surrounded by friends and allies. She not only encouraged me to make the move, she also quietly persuaded Johnny that he needed me to make the move. Once, when we were all sitting together, she subtly led the conversation to the subject of Sonny Werblin. "How did it happen that he owned half the business, and you were just a paid employee?" Her tone was full of sympathy and dismay, with not a hint of reproach.

She had caught him in a reflective mood. "I was a dumb fuck back then," Johnny said.

"He used you," I said.

"Well, it won't happen again."

"No," I assured him. "I'll make sure of that."

It was then that he suggested that I move to Los Angeles. He offered to help underwrite the move; what was even more surprising, he said that he would help me attract new clients. "I don't expect to be somebody's only client," he said, "but I need to know that I'm number one. When Bruno and Shields signed Mike Douglas, I didn't feel like I had their complete focus anymore. But I have confidence that I'll have your personal attention, even if you have to have other clients."

"You will," I assured him.

The concern now was Judy Bushkin. It was not that she was against the move per se. It was just another leap into another great unknown. She had already made the adjustment from Nashville to Manhattan and was happy about how things were going. We no longer lived in an apartment in Forest Hills; we were now the Bushkins of Park Avenue, living in a beautiful apartment at Eighty-fourth and Park, a short stroll from Central Park and the Metropolitan Museum of Art. Judy liked New York from the beginning, but lately she had begun to think of it as home. She was even planning to resume her studies at NYU once our son, Scott, was in preschool.

The one thing that bothered her was the amount of time I was spending with Carson. When he first became my client, she was very understanding of the hours I devoted to him. Maybe she was as excited as I to have this rare and exciting creature in our lives and was willing to do her share of the sacrificing. Or maybe she felt some sympathy for this lonely, troubled man who had been magically entrusted to my care. But as time wore on, and my relationship with Carson apparently solidified, she begrudged my absences, particularly my many visits to California, and especially when she became pregnant with our second child, our daughter, Dana.

One weekend we went to Connecticut, supposedly for a little peace and quiet together. It didn't turn out to be a very happy few days, with Judy spending much of it in tears. "Why do you have to spend so much time with Johnny and that Arthur Kassel?" she demanded. "I spend half my time alone."

I didn't have any answers. I saw her point entirely. By that time, even men had heard enough about Betty Friedan and the women's movement to know that no matter how much we scoffed and sneered, there were certain inequalities men profited from that were hard to justify. But Johnny was a big client, and he was my ticket. I didn't know how many times I could tell him I wasn't available to have dinner with him at Danny's Hideaway, but I was reluctant to find out. I was a young man, and I didn't have the confidence to find out whether Johnny would keep me around just on the basis of my fine legal skills, or whether I had to be his Swiss Army knife of a companion, attorney, manager, agent, henchman, crony, tennis pal, and corkscrew all in one.

During that bicoastal year, Joanna kept encouraging me to make a deal with Johnny that would justify a permanent move. "Just talk to him, Henry," she told me. "He likes you. He thinks you do good work. Just make your case." Eventually she persuaded me, and on the fateful day when I arrived at their home to discuss my terms for relocating, I was more nervous than I had ever been in my life. "Relax," she told me as she led me to Johnny's den. "It's in the bag."

She was more correct than I would ever have believed. The two-page, handwritten document stated that he would no longer pay me by the hour but would pay me a monthly retainer of $10,000, which was sufficient to cover my personal and office nut. He also agreed to pay my moving expenses and to loan me the down payment I would need to purchase a home. He spent less time reading the terms than you just did.

"Okay," he said, "you have yourself a deal. Let's go hit some balls."

With that deal done, my cousin Marty began looking for a place where Judy and I could live. He found us a Spanish-style house to lease on the 700 block of Linden Drive in Beverly Hills. "This place is just terrific!" Marty exulted over the phone to us back in New York. As he described its features, I grew more and more excited, even as I could feel Judy grow cooler. No reflection on Marty, but she was reluctant to move into a place she hadn't seen. When I mentioned her feelings to Johnny, he drove over and checked the house out for me — he lived just five minutes away. "It's perfect!" he shouted over the phone, in a reprise of Marty's call. "You'd be crazy not to take it."

"We'd be crazy to pay $2,000 a month on a place sight unseen," Judy said, but she was beginning to feel ground down. "I suppose if Johnny says do it, you'll do it," she said. "Nipper hears his master's voice."

Once again, it was Joanna who stepped

into the breach. She was so welcoming to Judy, so gracious and inviting, that whatever reluctance Judy may have had about Los Angeles was replaced by an eagerness to keep building a friendship with Joanna. Several years older and worldlier, Joanna schooled Judy, treated her like a sister, introduced her around, and made her see what possibilities were in store. I know that as much as she genuinely liked Judy, and she did, Joanna was making this effort for Johnny. If Judy was happy, then I would be happy, and then I could focus on making Johnny happy.

Judy finally decided she could cope with all this change under one condition: that we bring our nanny with us. That was fine with me. The Linden Drive house was owned by Aaron Ruben, the producer of such TV hits as *The Andy Griffith Show* and *Gomer Pyle, U.S.M.C.* Compared to my New York apartment, this was a palace. It was a Spanish-style hacienda with four bedrooms, a pool, and guesthouse. Al and Mary Bushkin loved it, as did Judy's parents, Max and Ruth Beck, and, of course, we did too. Life was good there. Our daughter, Dana, was born while we were living in that home. Johnny and Joanna sent mounds of flowers and baby gifts galore. We considered asking

Johnny to be the godfather, but as Judy correctly pointed out, he had no ability to relate to kids, not even his own, so we asked Arthur Kassel instead.

We lived there a year until the lease was up. We loved the house and offered Ruben $200,000 to buy it, but he declined. Judy began looking, and after a long search, settled on a Paul Williams colonial on Whittier Drive, north of Sunset. It had been the home of Paul Newman and Joanne Woodward, which in and of itself gave it a special cachet but it was pretty wonderful in its own right. It sat on a double lot with a separate guesthouse and pool house. I blanched at the $270,000 price tag, but Judy loved it, and Johnny and Joanna fed her enthusiasm. "Go for it!" Johnny said. "I'll cover the down payment, you go get the mortgage, but don't miss out on this one. It's beautiful."

Between the purchase price and a few repairs and alterations, the house cost us literally every penny we had. There was no money left for furnishings. For a while, three adults, a five-year-old, and a newborn lived among the pieces that had previously filled an apartment. We added a couple of lawn chairs, but when we dreamed of having a spacious house, we didn't think in terms of being able to play handball in it.

Fortunately, the composers and music publishers Buzz Cason and Bobby Russell came along. In six years they had built a catalogue that included such hits as "Honey," "Little Green Apples," and "The Joker Went Wild," and now they wanted to cash in. They hired me to negotiate a sale to the Lawrence Welk Publishing Group. When the deal went through, I received a $75,000 fee, much of which Judy used to create the home of her dreams. Marty Trugman's wife, Ellin, was the decorator and did a tremendous job. My parents were thrilled when they saw it. "Can you believe it?" my father kept asking. "Paul Newman's house!"

Some months after the sale — and, thankfully, after the redecoration had been completed — I looked out my front window and saw, sitting in the driver's seat of a Porsche parked at the end of my sidewalk, the home's former owner, Paul Newman. I went out and said hello. It turns out he and his wife were each running errands and decided to reconnoiter at their old home when they were finished. "Well, come on in and have a beer," I said, and he accepted. He was delighted to see what we had done to the house. When I went upstairs to tell Judy that Paul Newman was in the living room, she was in shock. "Come down and say hello," I encouraged, but she was too nervous, and as a result missed not only Newman but also Joanne Woodward when she later showed up.

Meanwhile the Carsons now owned a splendid mid-century modern on two acres on St. Cloud Road in the tony part of lower Bel Air. Mervyn LeRoy, the producer of *The Wizard of Oz* and other great films, had owned it and as much as Johnny wanted it, he was reluctant to take out a mortgage. "See if you can figure out how I can pay for it in cash," he told me. It turned out to be pretty easy. NBC owed him millions from his 1967 deferred compensation agreement. With several calls, they agreed to provide the funds for the house, and Johnny and Joanna moved in. Sonny and Cher were on one side of them, and Jerry Lewis on the other. Ron and Nancy Reagan were on the next block.

Joanna Carson was a woman with great taste and style, and for perhaps the first time in her life, she had enough money to get the best of everything. She redecorated the house to reflect not just her persona but also the stature of her husband, and the results were stunning. Joanna made sure to include features specific to Johnny's wants and needs. The grand living room was equipped with 35mm projectors (thanks to Mr. LeRoy), and ten or twelve guests could come over to have dinner and enjoy the latest movie in grand style. The first film I remember seeing there was a Jack Lemmon film, *Save the Tiger,* which Johnny insisted I see over my pleas that I needed to study for the California Bar exam that I was taking the next morning. (I guess he had confidence that I would pass; as usual, he was right.) As would befit one of the best-dressed men in Hollywood, Joanna provided Johnny with a dressing room that was as big as the master bedroom, where he could house the vast wardrobe that had been crafted by tailors in Chicago who were flown in three times a year for fittings. Carson's favorite tailor in town was Barry "Dino" Certo, who probably made fifty outfits a year for Johnny at his shop on Brighton Way in Beverly Hills. Joanna took as much pride in Johnny's appearance as he did.

Joanna also tried to make their home a place where Johnny's family would feel welcome. They were important to him, and so they were important to her, and her Italian sensibility told her that if you make the proper formal gestures of respect and affection, then not only will they be returned, but eventually they will also become heartfelt. In the house, there was a sumptuous set of rooms called the Princess Grace Suite because Mervyn LeRoy had built the suite as a separate addition exclusively for Princess Grace to use when she visited. Joanna thoughtfully decided that the suite should be redone and reserved for Johnny's parents to use on their visits. They would refer to it as the Ruth and Homer Suite. Other than his folks, no one would be invited to stay in that posh set of rooms.

On Ruth and Homer's earlier visits to Los Angeles, Johnny had always put them up at the Bel Air Hotel or the Beverly Hills Hotel. Now, with a new home, and with a new wife who was really working to establish a bond with Ruth and Homer, a hotel was out of the question.

As the day of their first visit to the new home approached, Johnny grew increasingly tense. I had yet to meet his folks, but Johnny warned me how difficult his mother could be, how begrudging of compliments and how withholding of affection she was. "Everybody likes Dad," he said, "but he lets her walk all over him. Every once in a while he lets out a peep, and it's like the Soviet

Union and Czechoslovakia — she just rolls in the tanks." I was going to get my first taste of her the next day at lunch.

The next morning Carson called to cancel the engagement. "Joanna was bending over backward to make Mom feel welcome," Johnny reported. "She took her on a tour of the house, explaining all the features. Mom said nothing. Silent. Like a fish. And I could see this was making Joanna anxious. Finally I said, 'Well, Mom, how do you like the job Joanna did? It's beautiful, isn't it?' And Mom said, 'Well, John, the wall covering reminds me of your aunt Maude's dining room in Norfolk.' And that was it!"

I burst out laughing, and in a second, he did too.

On all their subsequent visits, infrequent as they were, his parents stayed at a hotel.

This was hardly a unique incident. As far as I could tell, Ruth Carson was a person who was impossible to impress and impossible to please. She seemed to take no pride or pleasure in her son's accomplishments. The next day, Johnny took his parents to a party thrown by Kirk Douglas and his wife, Anne, where all the Hollywood elite were present. I had seen how hard it was for Johnny to socialize in crowds; it must have exhausted him to suffer all that backslapping and small talk while entertaining his parents. When they got back home, Carson asked, "Well, Mom, how did you like the party?"

"Well, son," she said, "I guess parties are the same all over the country."

When Johnny repeated her line to me the next day, he started to laugh again. "Yeah, all parties are the same. I've been to the volunteer fire department's potluck supper in Norfolk, Nebraska. Fucking Kirk Douglas has got nothing on that. Chasen's would kill to know the secret of June Olafsen's macaroni and cheese casserole. Can you imagine? Joanna was crying after Mother's remarks."

"How long are they staying?" I asked.

"I just chartered a plane for them. I'm sending them up to my sister's place. Catherine's much better at dealing with them."

Once I saw how hard it was for Ruth to give a compliment, I wondered if this was connected to how hard it was for Johnny to accept one.

A few years later, Johnny sent his parents around the world on a cruise to mark one of their wedding anniversaries. It was a forty-seven-day trip, with all accommodations entirely first class. Johnny even gave them an American Express card to cover anything they wanted to buy. "Dad," he said, "use the card for everything you buy on the trip. It's all on me." A lot of us fantasize about being able to give our parents a gift as wonderful as that.

Johnny never heard from them during the trip. Every few days he would bring up the fact that they had not called. "Can you believe it? Not a goddamn word. I send them on a fucking trip of a lifetime and they don't call." This continued on for the month and a half that they were gone.

Johnny knew exactly when they would be arriving back in Scottsdale. Days passed, and he still hadn't heard from them. Furious at their lack of fundamental courtesy, he finally called them. His dad answered. "How was the trip?" Johnny asked.

"Hold on, son," his father responded blandly. "I'll get your mother on the line."

"All she said when she picked up the phone," Johnny reported later, "was 'Well, son, we are so happy to be home.' That was it! No talk about the sights they saw, no comments on the food or rooms, no comments even about the weather! And certainly no thanks!" As before, Johnny laughed at his mother's rudeness, but he didn't really find it funny.

Another time, Johnny sent his mother a

mink coat for her birthday. This time Mom called to say she was sending it back. "It's too fancy for Nebraska," she explained, adding that better than a fur coat would be spending the winter in a warmer climate. That led to Johnny buying his folks a home in Scottsdale, Arizona. It would be nice to say that this made Ruth happy, but nothing did. The best that can be said is that she and Homer moved there, and that she didn't complain.

Once Judy and I settled in, I began focusing on work. I eventually closed my practice in New York, but Arnold Kopelson joined me in Los Angeles, and we partnered with my cousin Richard Trugman in forming a firm. Arnold and I had grown very close; he was more than my partner, he was now my best friend. I did nothing of significance without seeking his advice. Judy and I were also fond of his wife, Joy, who not long after moving to Los Angeles was diagnosed with an incurable form of cancer.

One terrible night shortly after the Kopelsons moved into a home near us on Whittier Drive, Joy was rushed to the hospital. Judy and I hurried to the Kopelsons' house to care for their children, and there we learned that Joy had passed away. She was a lovely woman who died far too young, and her family and friends were devastated.

Fortunately, Anne, Arnold's assistant of many years, was able to step into the void and give ongoing comfort to the children. In time, Arnold and Anne fell in love and married. Eventually they became partners in the film business as well.

A big part of every day continued to be devoted to my number one client. His show taped at five-thirty in the afternoon and he didn't go to the office until around two p.m. He had lots of time to kill, and I made sure to swing by and spend at least an hour with him every day. Sometimes that meant sunning ourselves by his kidney-shaped pool, but more often it meant hitting the courts at the Bel-Air Country Club, at least until his home court was built. Later I often met Johnny at the studio after the program. He and his producers critiqued every show immediately after completion. There were days when everything was perfect, and there were days that nothing worked. The skit sucked, the comedian flopped, and the sound went bad for ZZ Top. Fred de Cordova was the master of blowing smoke up Carson's ass. Bobby Quinn and Peter Lassally were far more accurate in their observations. But Johnny always knew if the show worked. He always knew.

I never said anything, and that's why people tolerated my presence. I never tried to use my relationship with Johnny to undermine anyone at the program or force a role for myself in a place I didn't belong. People knew that I had only one interest and that was Johnny's well-being, and for that reason, I was treated warmly, like a friend of the family.

One of the first deals I did for Carson in Los Angeles was actually in Las Vegas. During the seventies, the same well-funded legitimate interests, personified by Howard Hughes, that were cleaning up at the hotels and casinos were putting money into other enterprises. Having known serious development for only about twenty-five years, Las Vegas was suddenly a booming metropolis that offered major business opportunities to anybody who had cash available. With my advice, Carson headed a group of investors who bought the local television station KVVU. The ownership name was changed to Carson Broadcasting.

This marked an important milestone in our relationship. It was the first major investment that Johnny made where I was the chief architect of the deal; there would be many more, to our mutual enrichment.

Our group bought the station for $1 million. Not too many years later, we sold it for $25 million, landing a far larger jackpot than any high roller in a casino ever did. For me, there was also the satisfaction that I was serving my client well. It was a deal that stood in sharp contrast to the Johnny Carson Apparel arrangement designed by Sonny Werblin.

With Carson as the cornerstone and unrivaled number one client, the law firm prospered, and in 1976 we opened impressive new offices at 2025 Century Park East in Century City. Johnny came by for a visit. Inspecting my office, Johnny said, "You know what you need here, Henry? A red phone."

"A red phone?"

"A red phone. Like the one used to communicate between the White House and the Kremlin. A dedicated line that only I know the number to and that only you can answer. Or Carrie, if you're out. A phone where I can always reach you."

I had the line installed the next day.

Before long, Johnny and Joanna and Judy and I were all great friends. Not surprisingly, Judy was at first shy when she was with Johnny, but after moving across the country so her husband could work for the man, she agreed that it would make sense to get to know him better. Johnny made it easy by inviting us over for drinks and hors d'oeuvres. Reserved and very attractive at five feet seven inches, with brown hair and a very good figure, Judy was the prettiest girl in the world in my opinion. She certainly made a great impression on Carson.

Rick Carson was present when Judy first met Johnny. He was recently released from Bellevue and the navy, and Judy was able to draw him into the conversation in a way that impressed Johnny. Indeed, in the years to come, Judy would develop a rapport with Rick that Johnny really appreciated. Judy was also able to go toe-to-toe with Johnny in the smoking arena (butt-to-butt doesn't sound right). Over time, he grew quite fond of Judy, and little by little began including her in his jokes. It would take a full two years before I knew that he really accepted her, which he signaled by pretending to make a pass at her one night after a few drinks at the Hôtel du Cap in Antibes on the French Riviera. (At least I think he was pretending.) Indeed, there was a period when Johnny was quite fond of a lot of people in the Bushkin circle. He liked playing tennis with Marty Trugman. He enjoyed the company of Judy's dad, Max Beck, a great deal. On one amazing day, at Johnny's instigation, he drove Max, me, and Scotty in the Rolls down to Long Beach to see Howard Hughes's fabled wooden airplane, the *Spruce Goose.* The tour was conducted by none other than Hughes's right-hand man, Robert Maheu, at a time when the plane was not open to the public. Very cool.

But at the heart of this little social set were two couples, the Carsons and the Bushkins. The two men took care of business together, and the two women worked on charity projects together. The two men played tennis together, and the two women shopped together. The two couples dined together, weekended together, traveled together. Some of those trips rank among the most memorable moments of my life.

The summer of 1976 was the hottest summer London had experienced in at least 350 years, with fifteen days in a row exceeding 90 degrees. It just so happened that Judy and I were coming to London to meet Johnny and Joanna during those fifteen days. The plan was to spend a week in London at the Wimbledon Championships, and then go on to the South of France. Originally we were all going to stay at the elegant Inn on the Park Hotel in the May-fair section of London, but Johnny wanted no part of it. Too many NBC execs would be at that hotel. NBC was broadcasting the tournament, and the Inn on the Park had become a virtual satellite of 30 Rockefeller Plaza. Leaving us at the Inn on the Park, he booked rooms at the Dorchester.

When Judy and I arrived in London from New York (where we had deposited Scotty at sleepaway camp), we went directly to the Inn on the Park and unpacked and changed our clothes. We had a posh room that was well air-conditioned.

Johnny and Joanna had flown in from Los Angeles and had arrived earlier than we did. As soon as we settled in, Judy and I crossed Hyde Park to join Johnny and Joanna for a late supper. The stifling heat made the short walk seem endless, and we were sticky and thirsty by the time we got there. A great landmark hotel, the Dorchester had a magnificent, brightly lit marquee outside and marble columns and enormous chandeliers in an awe-inspiring lobby inside. What it didn't have was air-conditioning. The minute I entered, I knew Johnny was going to be unhappy. The lobby was an inferno. When I asked for Johnny's room, the sweaty receptionist told us to go right up. "He said to go right in — he's left the door unlatched."

We walked into the magnificent drawing room of his six-room suite and found it to be strangely empty. "Johnny?" we called.

"I'm in here," we heard him reply. We followed the voice into a bathroom, where we found the King of Late Night sitting naked in a tub filled with ice and water. "I don't care what you have to do," he said, "but get us the hell out of here tomorrow. Charter a 747 if you must, but get us out of Dodge." It was a very funny scene. Fortunately David Tebet, NBC's vice president for talent, arranged for room air conditioners to be installed the next day. The Carson six-room suite was then made livable, and everyone got to enjoy seeing Chris Evert defeat Evonne Goolagong in a three-set thriller, and Björn Borg top Ilie Năstase in straight sets.

Dave Tebet, by the way, was one of the best executives who ever worked with Carson, and his capabilities were widely recognized. Freddy de Cordova said that Tebet's title should be "vice president in charge of caring."

The president of CBS, Robert D. Wood, called Tebet "the ambassador of all NBC's goodwill, which he sprinkles around like ruby dust." An executive with the network since 1959, Tebet recruited such talents to the network as Michael Landon, James Garner, Dean Martin, and Carson himself; Tebet led the campaign within NBC to hire Johnny for *The Tonight Show.* A solver of problems, a stroker of egos, a fountain of compliments, Dave was the guy who calmed stars down when they were throwing tantrums, the guy who paid people off after stars misbehaved, the guy who gently broke the news to stars that their series had been canceled. Rumor had it he was authorized to bestow an endless array of gifts whenever he thought it appropriate, and Tebet was famously generous to people who helped him. Using NBC's connection to RCA — the network was owned by the electronics and appliance company — Tebet was said to give away color TV sets "like Rockefeller tossed around dimes."

"Mark my words," said Johnny, "when I die, the graveside services are going to be interrupted when a truck pulls up and delivers a color television from Dave Tebet."

As much as I was looking forward to the vacation and the tennis and all the rest, coming to London meant rewarding myself with a special treat: a brand-new Aston Martin. At the time, I was a shareholder in the Panther Car Company, which imported sports cars from Great Britain into the United States, and Bruce Kallenberg, the head of the company, helped me negotiate the endless red tape regarding modifications related to fuel and emissions and so on that were involved in acquiring the Aston. I paid roughly 13,000 British pounds for it, at a time when the pound was worth about $2.50. I was over the moon when I arrived at the Aston Martin Sloane Street show-room and found a pale silver Volante coupe waiting, a smashing two-seater with a V-8 engine. Every day, Judy and I were the embodiment of arrogant Americans as we rolled up to the tournament in our fantastic, brand-new, air-conditioned British sports car. And we loved it.

Johnny had been provided a suitable car by NBC, a Daimler limousine. It was air-conditioned, too, but only if you rolled down the windows.

We decided to take a break from tennis one day and arrangements were made to have lunch at the Angler's, a charming inn situated on the Thames River about an hour outside of London. It was still brutally hot, but the hope was that the drive would help cool us down. Judy and I drove out in the Aston, and we arrived cool and fresh about twenty minutes ahead of Johnny and Joanna, who arrived wet and cranky. Lunch was a disaster. Angler's was charming, but it had no air-conditioning, and we couldn't get out of there soon enough.

Judy and I took our time on the way back, stopping in small towns to do some leisurely antiquing before deciding to head on back. About halfway to London, we spotted a disabled vehicle pulled off to the side. The closer we got, the more it looked like Johnny's Daimler. "Holy shit!" we exclaimed in unison. "It's Johnny!"

Immediately we turned around and went back to help. Not only was the car disabled with a flat tire, but there was a tussle going on between Johnny and the driver. Each was grappling for control of the lug wrench in order to change the deflated tire. The instant Johnny saw me, he said, "I'll pay you twice what you paid for the Aston Martin if you give me your sonofabitch car right now." Not waiting for a reply, Johnny snatched the wrench. "Get back in the car," he commanded the driver.

"Please, sir, I can change the tire."

"The hell you can!"

"Sir, please — I have been trained."

"Trained to do what? Trained to keep us baking in a steel prison while you try to figure out how to work a jack? Now I know how Alec Guinness felt in *Bridge on the River Kwai*!" He stripped off his shirt and went to work. "Anybody here know how to whistle the 'Colonel Bogey March'?"

Meanwhile, I quietly ushered Judy, Joanna, and Tim into the air-conditioned Aston and sent them back to the air-conditioned hotel rooms, while I went back and observed the biggest TV star in America spend his vacation as an amateur mechanic.

Once Johnny conquered the flat, we headed back to London, three men in a rolling oven, the disgraced driver sulking in the backseat, a Yank lawyer hanging his head out of the window like a terrier, and a steamed and steaming chain-smoking TV star behind the wheel. The arrival of the shirtless Carson at the door of the august Dorchester was a sight to behold.

Just a few months after that trip to London, Johnny and Joanna received an upsetting gift: what appeared to be a live hand grenade was found near the front gates of the Carson home. The note that was attached said, in effect, that unless Carson put a laundry bag full of $250,000 in hundred-dollar bills in a trash container at a specified location in the San Fernando Valley, harm would come to Johnny's family. The line I remember vividly was "Do not insult our intelligence by dismissing this matter."

As it turned out, the grenade was a fake, but the threat was treated as real. The kidnappings of Frank Sinatra Jr. in 1963, John Paul Getty III in 1973, and Patty Hearst in 1974 were still vivid in everyone's memories. The decision was made to go through with the drop in the hopes of catching the would-be kidnappers.

Although the note specified that Johnny make the drop personally, the authorities were staunchly against the idea. It was possible that this was an elaborate ruse designed to lure Johnny into a place where he himself could be kidnapped or placed in physical danger. "Please, Johnny, leave this to us," urged the Feds. "We'll put an officer in your car, and he'll make the drop. It will be safer that way."

"Safer for me," said Johnny, "but riskier for Joanna and Tim. The note specified that I make the delivery. I don't see any point in pissing him off over such a minor point. Don't you think the son of a bitch will know what I look like? It's not as if he hasn't seen me before."

"I'm sorry, but we can't allow that."

"Allow?" Johnny raised a skeptical eyebrow in the way that usually caused laughter to break out in millions of America's homes, except no one here was laughing. "Look, here's what we're going to do. I'll deliver the money. You concentrate on catching the asshole."

The plan was hatched. Johnny was to drive his car with his trusty .38 pistol by his side (Johnny had a carry license for the gun; I never asked, but I bet Arthur helped him get it). A helicopter was stationed four thousand feet overhead to watch him every second. At that height, the aircraft could not be heard or seen. Instead of cash in the trash bag, there was cut-up paper stacked and wrapped in 125 bill-sized bundles.

At an appointed time, Johnny received a phone call at the NBC Studios in Burbank. He was instructed to take the cash up Lankershim Boulevard, then turn left on Oxnard Street and pull into the parking lot of a Spanish-style apartment building and leave the suitcase in a phone booth in the front of the self-service laundry. Johnny followed the instructions to the letter and then drove away. Within minutes, the bag was picked up by a twenty-six-year-old German national named Richard Dziabacinski, who was immediately arrested. Very soon after, the cops apprehended his wife, who was waiting at a local motel. He eventually pled guilty to a charge of attempted extortion and was sentenced to a year in prison and five more on probation.

As luck would have it, a young couple named Richard and Linda Culkin had just finished doing their laundry when they saw Carson dropping the bag at the phone booth. Hoping to get an autograph, they ran after Carson, if only momentarily, because the same team of police who captured Dziabacinski immediately arrested the Culkins. The mistake seemed pretty funny at first, but then it became clear that the poor Culkins were abused by the police. Eventually they were released with apologies, and Johnny made some gesture of regret, although I do not know what it was. I hope it was more than one of Dave Tebet's televisions.

The police not only hid Carson's role in the drama, they, in fact, denied it; the official statement said specifically that Carson was never in the car. But he did take part without a moment's hesitation. "He's got brass balls," one agent said in admiration, and he did.

I don't think Joanna ever forgot how fearlessly Johnny put himself personally on the line to protect her and her son. When things soured between them, her gratitude for his unquestioning love for her during this time nonetheless did nothing to keep their marital dispute on a fundamentally respectful plane.

Johnny was a little more cautious after this incident, most notably refusing to eat any food that had been sent to him by fans. Indeed, a few years later, his secretary became extremely ill after eating some homemade taffy sent in by a fan; it turned out that some laxatives had been added. After John Lennon was murdered in 1980, police found a hit list of targets among the belongings of the assassin, Mark David Chapman. Carson's name was second on the list. Naturally Johnny shrugged it off, along with the suggestion that he hire a bodyguard. But thereafter, whenever he was in the car, he carried his gun.

A memorable example of the way Joanna reciprocated Johnny's affection took place the following year, when Johnny was invited to Harvard University to receive the Hasty Pudding Man of the Year award from the school's famed theatrical society. I'm not sure why Johnny accepted; the weekend promised a student-written-and-produced comedy as the crown jewel set among a series of speeches, banquets, conferences, seminars, and receptions, all taking place in Boston in February. In short, it was not the sort of thing that usually appealed to him.

Still, it was Harvard, and the previous recipients included Bob Hope, Paul Newman, Bill Cosby, Robert Redford, Jimmy Stewart, Dustin Hoffman, Jack Lemmon, and Warren Beatty, so it wasn't as though he'd be slumming.

In honoring a celebrity, the group was, of course, trying to attract publicity and attention, and with the choice of Carson, they surely exceeded all hopes. Wherever he went on campus he was trailed by a horde of students, regular citizens, and news media. Every Hasty Pudding event was filled to bursting, and no matter where we turned, there was nothing ordinary: self-conscious Harvard boys tried to impress him with labored repartee; erudite dons tried to figure out who he was; and inquiring reporters, student and pro alike, pestered him with such questions as "What is Charo really like?" and "Why have you switched from wearing a Windsor knot to a four-in-hand?" The banal Q&A did yield one memorable exchange: a journalist asked, "What would you like your epitaph to be?" Johnny paused for a moment, then replied, "I'll be right back," his standard commercial-break hand-off. His answer got a big laugh. (Alas, since Johnny was cremated, the epitaph never got chiseled into stone.)

It would be an overstatement to call this experience an ordeal, but for Johnny, who generally suffered fools not gladly (or almost not at all), sustaining fake sociability and bonhomie for hours and hours was taxing to the max. I saw it and tried to help, as did Dave Tebet. But it was Joanna who was aware of every tiny tic in his mood, who stood close to him and stroked his hand and touched his back, who deflected the most gauche comments and deflated the biggest boors.

Some years later I was reading an article in which Joanna's friend, the actress Ruta Lee, observed that "Joanna's very accomplished at being a woman. I admire her femininity — her accommodation to men. It's as if she made a study of how Josephine handled Napoleon. She just has a wonderfully sensitive approach to men." When I read Ruta's comments, I thought of how Joanna supported Johnny so lovingly at Harvard.

In between the close of the daytime schedule and the start of the ceremonies in the evening, there was downtime, and I saw

Johnny and Joanna strolling arm in arm back to their rooms at Eliot House on the campus. They looked very happy. That night, after receiving the award, Johnny delivered one of the funniest monologues of his career, one that kept all the bright kids and brilliant professors of Harvard in stitches. "Thank you," he said, expressing his gratitude for the award. "This was the first time I've scored on a college campus since 1949."

The audience laughed, but their eyes then drifted to Joanna, who seemed oblivious. Slyly smiling, she had eyes only for her man.

Was this the high point of their relationship? It might have been. The generosity of her feelings was entirely clear, and he reciprocated not just with warmth but also with evident gratitude. In their years together, Johnny had grown: he became more confident, more assured. Part of that was his maturation, as a man and as a talent. But during their relationship, Johnny became more polished. She exposed him to fine wine, and he became a connoisseur. She taught him about art, and he became an astute collector. She arranged a trip to London and the Riviera, and he returned to those locations eleven straight years. It was as though part of him played up to Joanna. I'm not sure that before he met Joanna that Johnny would have even gone to Harvard or that he would have handled himself with such éclat.

And yet they always fought. Two years after they married, they had a three-month separation. For a while the relationship survived its upsets. When critical moments came, Johnny expressed his remorse and then demonstrated it with an appropriate gift, like a diamond bracelet, or a Picasso. But there came a point when that wasn't enough. There came to be too many moments when Ruth Carson's chilly influence abruptly took over his disposition, when he would be indifferent to Joanna's efforts and immune to her exertions and resentful of her emotional needs, and Joanna was simply too intelligent to suffer that behavior. And yet Johnny wouldn't have ended it if things had only maintained this low level of aggravation. Johnny needed a cause for war — his own casus belli. In the case of Joanne, it was her infidelity. In the case of Joanna, it was her desire to attain independent status through her charity work and then by starting a fashion consultancy. The rule that he applied to agents and managers and lawyers also applied to wives: he had to be number one, without a meaningful number two.

When we went to Harvard, Kenneth Tynan, the British journalist, critic, playwright, and producer, accompanied us. Known best today for *Oh! Calcutta!,* an all-nude review that became one of the longest-running shows in Broadway history (for a long time, it was number one), Tynan was a daunting intellectual with a wicked wit. He was present because he was writing a profile of Carson for *The New Yorker,* and never was there a better match of author and subject. Tynan and Carson had much in common, including excessive smoking, drinking, and an appreciation of Joanna, which Tynan, with his references to her "flashing eyes and quill-shaped Renaissance nose," did not attempt to disguise. There were differences: though both were witty, Tynan was more malevolently so; though both had numerous amorous adventures, Tynan was more open about it. He may have been the one man on earth Johnny Carson envied, if only because Tynan, a man who was famous but who did not have a household face, was free to do anything, anytime, anywhere he wanted.

Tynan's profile of Carson appeared in the February 20, 1978, issue of *The New Yorker.* Smart and insightful, the article made me think about Johnny in ways I hadn't before. Having been present during much of Ken's reporting and having been interviewed for the piece, I found it fascinating to see what Tynan selected and emphasized and left out. But one short line stood out among all the rest. "When you're at home," Tynan asked Johnny, "whom do you entertain?"

"Henry Bushkin," Johnny said, "my lawyer, who's probably my best friend."

This answer left me profoundly touched and somewhat astonished. We were certainly friends, but although we socialized together frequently and although our wives were close, never did I think of him as my best friend. I was always working when I was around Johnny, thinking of what he needed. Guys whom I could just relax and hang out with — that's who I'd call my best friends.

It had simply never occurred to me that he thought of me as his best friend.

SIX:
1979: NBC — SEE YA

As I learned outside of the Mancinis' house, Johnny Carson had, at some point in the beginning of 1979, during his sixteenth year captaining *The Tonight Show,* decided to bail on the most coveted spot in television, abandoning with it a compensation package in the neighborhood of $10 million a year. He'd had enough. He wanted out.

We did not explore this subject when he first revealed his decision to me at the foot of the Mancinis' driveway. Instead, as he and Joanna drove off, I picked my jaw up off the asphalt and headed home. First thing in the morning, though, even before we began our tennis match, I pressed him for an explanation.

"I'm done," he said. "I'm tired. Seventeen years is enough. I'm fifty-four years old. I don't feel fifty-four, but that's not the point. Can you imagine me doing this when I'm in my sixties? That would be absurd!"

I was shocked. This was entirely unexpected, entirely out of character. "Johnny, you can't quit like this. You have a contract that they won't let you out of. They will never let you walk."

"Make it clear to them that I'm not leaving so I can work somewhere else."

"Be that as it may, your show is the most profitable show on the network. They'll come after you for all the money they'll lose in advertising revenue."

"That'll never happen. They wouldn't do that. Tell them I'll do a few specials. Maybe after some time off I'll do a weekly prime-time show."

"Fred Silverman has got a million problems at the network. You're the only thing he can count on. He'll go nuts."

"I don't care. It's not his ass in front of the camera every night, and it's not yours, either. Nobody can force me to work."

That was the end of the debate about the future direction of Johnny Carson's career. From that point on, the only question under discussion was not whether to proceed, but how.

We agreed that we would give NBC six months' notice. Johnny's last night as host would fall on Monday, October 1, 1979, seventeen years to the day, and on the very same day of the week, that Groucho Marx stepped in front of the camera and introduced Johnny to the late-night audience, inaugurating his lengthy reign. "I'm telling you, the network will go fucking nuts when I tell them you're quitting. They have no one to replace you."

"Oh, bullshit, they'll figure it out. What was that line Charles de Gaulle said? 'The graveyards are full of indispensable men.' " Johnny had absolutely no fear about the consequences of his decision. But I did. That's one of the reasons we worked well together.

The fact is Johnny had a lot more experience fighting with NBC, which was probably the source of his confidence. Almost from the beginning of his tenure, he butted heads with the network about salary, the length of the show, and the ridiculously tiny dressing rooms at 30 Rock. The arguments came to a head in May 1967, when the American Federation of Television and Radio Artists went out on strike. The issues in the dispute mostly had to do with newsreaders and studio announcers and nothing really to do with Carson or *The Tonight Show,* but AFTRA was Johnny's union, and so he got on a plane and flew to Florida. The network countered by running repeats of *The Tonight Show,* not only without Johnny's permission, but also without paying him. Johnny was irate.

"What is the price that should be paid for a rerun when it's used while your union is on strike?" he asked in a press conference. He then sent a letter to NBC canceling his contract.

The network wasn't worried. By their reckoning, *The Tonight Show* was a profitable and popular program without Johnny Carson before, and it could be profitable and popular without him again. They put out the line that Carson's stand was all a smoke screen for his real demand, which was more money, and they began bringing in guest hosts like Bob Newhart and Jimmy Dean (not the actor, the sausage pitchman). ABC took a look at the subs and figured that a *Tonight Show* without Carson was a wounded wildebeest that could be plucked from the herd. They started a late-night talk show starring Joey Bishop.

The Tonight Show audience, having grown to appreciate the work of the master, tuned out the substitute hosts, whose obvious un-Johnnyness opened the possibility that NBC's domination of late night could be shaken. Moreover, the executives knew that they would be making the mistake of their careers if they let Carson leave NBC at the top of his career. Soon the network sued for peace. Arnold Grant then came in and negotiated the clever contract that gave Johnny a big raise but still left him broke. The network also agreed to give the show, which in some markets began at eleven-fifteen and at eleven-thirty in most others, a uniform starting time across the country, with Johnny's monologue front and center in the program, right where he liked it.

The man who paid the price for the network's stupidity was the veteran producer of *The Tonight Show,* Art Stark. Johnny valued Art's experience when he began as host, but Carson had long outgrown the unimaginative producer, and for some time had wanted to replace him. Johnny made it clear to the network that he wanted someone new, and the network didn't care. As Johnny later told me, he called Art over to the UN Plaza apartment.

"Art, I want a new producer on the show, someone who isn't currently affiliated with the program."

"All right, John," said Stark. "When do you want me to leave?"

"Right now," Johnny replied.

"Well then, fuck you," Stark said, slamming the door on his way out. Like it would make a difference.

When Johnny came back, *Time* magazine marked the occasion by putting him on its cover. "His viewers are mostly urban and at least high school educated, young enough to stay up late with ease, or successful enough not to have to show up too early for work. Jimmy Stewart watches; so do Bobby Kennedy, Ed Sullivan, Nebraska Governor Norbert Tiemann, Robert Merrill, and Nelson Rockefeller." *Time* then reported that CBS had tried to buy Carson away, a story that Carson dismissed without quite denying it. "I would feel as out of place on another network as Lurleen Wallace giving a halftime pep talk to the Harlem Globetrotters."

Now, more than a decade later, it was even more inconceivable to think of Johnny on another network. I was still amazed that he was ready to leave it. Knowing what he was thinking, I watched him more closely, studying him for signs of fatigue, impatience, and irritation. I saw none. But by this point, Johnny had hosted *The Tonight Show* twice as long as his two predecessors put together. Who knew what he had been feeling inside? Who knew what Joanna had been whispering?

Frankly, I felt bad about having to deliver

Johnny's news to the executives at NBC. He'd had a terrific run at the network, but from their point of view, the night was still young and the party was just getting started. Carson was an unrivaled asset who earned the network immense profits. During the first six months after taking over *The Tonight Show* in 1962, Carson's audience averaged 7,458,000; in 1978, the nightly audience averaged 17,300,000. Shows usually hit a peak after a couple of years and then start losing viewers; Carson had more than doubled the audience. In 1978 alone, Carson's show was earning the Peacock between $50 and $60 million in revenues, which constituted an enormous percentage of all of NBC's earnings. Moreover, his status continued to be unassailable. There had never been credible competition from any quarter, and there was none on the horizon. NBC knew perfectly well how to cancel programs; killing off favored old warhorses that had gone gimpy was what these executives lived for. But Johnny's intentions baffled them. Who the hell quits in his prime?

But that wasn't all that was in NBC's head. Replacing Carson at any point after 1967 would have been a big challenge for them, and lightning almost never strikes twice. The best they could have hoped for was an announcer who held most of Carson's audience; the worst couldn't even be measured because NBC was not a strong, healthy network in 1978: it was alarmingly weak. *The Tonight Show* was the cornerstone of its strategy to win the ratings wars, which were up for grabs for almost the first time since the popularization of television. It would also be a sturdy lifeboat that was keeping the well-paid suits in NBC's executive offices from sinking into oblivion. When NBC looked at its game plan, Johnny was both the offense and the defense.

Since the mid-fifties, CBS had always won the ratings wars, and with that primacy the right to charge a premium rate for advertising on its programs. NBC had always seemed content to be a prestigious number two, and ABC just seemed happy to be alive. But in the mid-seventies, up became down, white became black, and the entire universe was stood on its head: not only did CBS tumble out of the top spot, but it was replaced, not by the longtime runner-up, the gentlemanly NBC, but by the perpetual loser, ABC. Aggressively pursuing a younger demographic, ABC programmed such shows as *Happy Days, Three's Company, Laverne & Shirley, Mork & Mindy, Charlie's*

Angels, and *Starsky & Hutch,* and finished first as a result.

And NBC came in last, a humiliation that began to have immediate ramifications. Lower ratings meant less advertising income, for one thing. Lower ratings also meant that the top producers took their best programs to the other fellows first. Lower ratings also meant restless local affiliates. In Atlanta, Charlotte, Indianapolis, Jacksonville, Minneapolis-St. Paul, and San Diego, local stations with strong management and aggressive sales staffs and far-reaching signals dumped NBC and signed with ABC, leaving NBC with a weaker partner in each metropolis. The network still had strong assets, most significantly *The Today Show* in the morning and *The Tonight Show* at night. But ABC was actively gunning for *The Today Show* with *Good Morning America,* and Roone Arledge, the network's brilliant, ambitious head of news and sports, sought to expand his domain as avidly as a shark.

The man at NBC who was destined to receive the arrow Johnny had directed me to fire at the network was Mike Weinblatt, president of NBC Entertainment. Mike was a decent guy and a good executive who would one day make the bold move to cable and become one of the key figures in the development of CNN. I'm sure I must have ruined his day when I called him out of the blue and asked for an appointment. He had to have known something was up. His suspicions must have spiked somewhere into the stratosphere after he asked me if he could get a broad sketch of our contract renewal terms, and I told him it would be better if we spoke in person. I'm guessing that when Mike heard that, the very next action he took, unless he paused to down a shot of Scotch or Pepto-Bismol, was to share this conversation with his boss, Fred Silverman.

After a couple of years of pathetically failing to emulate ABC's young-audience strategy, NBC decided to stop trying to copy ABC's success and went out and bought it. Fred Silverman — widely heralded as the genius behind the miraculous ABC transformation and credited with the triumphs CBS enjoyed in the early seventies with *M*A*S*H, The Mary Tyler Moore Show,* and *All in the Family,* nicknamed by admirers as the "Man with the Golden Gut" — was hired in 1978 to be president and CEO of NBC.

And so far, he hadn't made a damn bit of difference.

Silverman had arrived at NBC like a tornado, ordering an astonishing forty pilots be made, and while he waited to see which, if any, would be worthy of prime time, he shocked the industry with a last-minute revision of almost his entire fall schedule, covering it with stunts and specials that would fill the air while his pilots gestated. He may as well have said, "Please watch this crap while we figure out what to do."

In January came part two of his stunner, called the "Slaughter on Sixth Avenue." Facing a certain last-place finish in the ratings, Silverman decided to go for broke. He canceled all of his predecessor's remaining programs and debuted his own slate. (Quipped Johnny in his monologue: "NBC now stands for Nine Bombs Canceled.") Among Fred's new shows were *Brothers and Sisters*, about three fraternity brothers meant to remind viewers of *Animal House; Hello, Larry*, starring McLean Stevenson, who had been purloined from CBS's successful *M*A*S*H; Mrs. Columbo*, where the never-previously-seen wife of Lieutenant Columbo solves crimes; and *Supertrain*, a kind of *Love Boat* on wheels, in which a super-duper, atom-powered, New York–Los Angeles train (complete with swimming pool) carries a load of guest stars from coast to coast in what was the most expensive series ever produced.

I arrived in New York about nine episodes into the new slate's run, at a point when it had become evident to everyone that they were all flops, although to be fair, we did not yet know that two of the shows, *Hello, Larry* and *Supertrain,* were such monumental flops that in the coming decades they would regularly have prominent slots on lists of the worst programs in terms of both quality and ratings in television history. What was also clear, however, was that until NBC managed to program some hits, *The Tonight Show* was still the network's Rock of Gibraltar.

My meeting in New York with Mike Weinblatt was scheduled for Saint Patrick's Day. Every time I pass through the magnificent art deco portals at 30 Rockefeller Center I experience the sense of occasion that I felt when I first went there to see Johnny with Arthur Kassel; even if you go to work there every day, I don't imagine it is ever quite just another day at the office. And on this day, there were 25,000 sons of Ireland parading by, with bagpipes.

Knowing the message I carried, I felt something like a diplomat delivering a declaration of war to the state ministry of a powerful foe. Of course, they were not foes, at least not yet. They certainly weren't going to be happy; in fact, as I ascended in the elevator to the floor occupied by NBC's top brass, I prepared myself for a range of possible reactions not dissimilar to Elisabeth Kübler-Ross's five stages of grief: denial, anger, bargaining, depression, and acceptance. Any or all of the first four were possible. I didn't really expect the last.

Mike Weinblatt greeted me affably, but there was an undercurrent of tension. I could tell he harbored apprehensions about my visit, and we rushed through only the minimal requirement of polite chitchat before I felt obliged to get down to business.

"Mike, Johnny has had a long run with NBC. Far longer than anyone else has presided over *The Tonight Show*. And he's spent the entire time at the top."

At that point Mike might have been expecting a demand for a big increase in pay for the best-paid man in television. But then I dropped the bombshell. "Johnny wants out. I'm here to give you a full half year's notice. He intends to make his exit the same day and the same month he started, October 1."

Mike was stunned. Whatever he had

guessed, even if he had guessed right, to actually hear the message was devastating. Finally he responded. "I can imagine there's a burnout factor. But there ought to be a way we can make adjustments Johnny can live with. He can't really want to leave now. He's still at the top of his game."

"He didn't come to this decision lightly, as you can imagine, Mike. But he's been thinking about it for a long time. The decision is as final as it can be. He feels that this is the right time to go. You know as well as I do, Mike, that Johnny could do anything he wants. Go fishing for a year or take a place in London for a year. But six months is what you've got to work with."

"This raises a lot of issues, Henry. It impacts our business from several angles. And six months is not a lot of notice for a deal like this. Look, Fred's in the office. I should let him know what's at issue here before you leave." Mike stood up and headed down the hall to alert Silverman. Minutes later — and not at all to my surprise — Fred Silverman burst into Weinblatt's office.

Fred Silverman was no smoothie. There was a time when network executives were men in starched white collars and Brooks Brothers suits who were cool and professional and drank martinis and never seemed ill at ease. Today network executives are guys with tans and tennis sweaters who are cool and friendly and who drink green tea and do yoga and never seem ill at ease. But Fred Silverman always seemed on the edge. Silverman was overweight, rumpled, damp, with dark circles under his eyes, and his success seemed to be driven by neither personal nor boardroom finesse. He got where he was by knowing better than anyone what viewers wanted to see. But lately his gift had deserted him, and he seemed like a man who had no idea where to find it.

"HelloHenrygoodtoseeyou," he rattled. "Mike says you're carrying an important message from the coast that I ought to hear directly from you."

I knew better than to squander any time on pleasantries. "Johnny's calling it quits, Fred. He's had a helluva run and he wants to sign off smilin'. I'm here to give you six months' notice. His last day will be the same date as his first day on the show, October 1."

"Henry, we all want our guy to be happy, but you must think me nuts to let this fucking guy go. But you're an attorney. You know it doesn't work like that. We've got a contract. And it's got two more years to run. If Johnny wants to go, he can go in '81."

Apparently they had enough of an inkling of the message I carried to do some homework, but it wasn't quite enough. "I'm afraid not, Fred. We've had a law in California for thirty-five years that says you can't keep somebody under a personal contract for more than seven years. Johnny's is well over that now. He's been working for NBC since 1962. It's now seventeen years and counting. Any way I look at it, Fred, Johnny can walk today."

"That's not true, Henry. You know as well as I do that in seventeen years there have been more than eight different agreements. Carson's signed at least three different contracts with us over the last several years. Don't expect us to roll over because of some technicality. If we have to tell our sponsors Johnny is leaving, we'll stand to lose $50 million a year. We'll go after Carson for that, Henry. We'll sue his ass for $100 million."

"Really?"

"Yeah. Really. Even for Johnny Carson, $100 million is real money."

"You're going to sue the most beloved entertainer in America for $100 million? Even if you win that one, Fred, you lose. And you're not going to win. Ask your lawyers." For the record, at this time the state of the law in this area was uncertain.

There was no point in swatting this topic back and forth; we certainly weren't going to resolve anything, and somebody might say something regrettable. Smiling affably and touching my forehead in a good-bye salute, I departed.

"Mike, sorry I had to bring you bad news. Fred, I'll send Johnny your regards." There would be plenty of opportunities to argue the legalities later.

Riding down John Rockefeller's elevator. I thought about what lay ahead. It's a lawyer's job to always appear confident of his case. I believed we had the law on our side. And we had a lot of other leverage on our side. But you never know how a judge is going to decide. They really might nail us for that $100 million.

I called Johnny from my room in the Waldorf Towers.

"How'd they take it?" asked Johnny.

"Like being drop-kicked in the balls."

"They'll calm down in a few days."

"I don't think so, Johnny. Silverman says this is going to cost him $100 million in advertising. He'll probably make Weinblatt be the one to tell the affiliates."

"So what are we lookin' at?"

"Silverman says he's going to sue you for the $100 million. But that would be terrible publicity. I think they'll just sue to enforce the contract."

"You said it wasn't enforceable."

"It's not, but we'll have to have a judge agree. The core issue that will decide everything isn't the $100 million they're talking about. It's the contract. California law says they can't hold you past seven years. If we show that we're past the seven years, you will be a free agent."

Flying back to LA, I reviewed our situation. Johnny was tired and frustrated, but what I really didn't know was how much of those feelings was due to the accumulation of the normal day-to-day bullshit that everybody experiences in any walk of life, and how much was due to the situation at NBC — the network's low ratings, the tension that affects everybody when the network is suffering, and, in particular, the special aggravation that results from encounters with the boss during difficult times. I don't know if Fred Silverman was a genius, but I do know that Johnny and Fred got off on the wrong foot and never quite managed to get in step.

There was bound to be some friction:

Fred was hired to shake NBC up, and it was perhaps inevitable that the network's reigning success story was going to get shaken up a little in the process. In one interview, Silverman made the mistake of pointing out the obvious: "You don't have to be a mind reader," as he said, "to see that the network as a whole performed better when Johnny was hosting his show." It shouldn't have been a problem for Fred to express his wish that Johnny would help out more by taking less time off, but saying it in public imputed that NBC's problems were Johnny's fault and were therefore within his power to rectify. Silverman also pushed Johnny to invite more NBC stars to appear on *The Tonight Show,* even stars of flops, in hopes of promoting the programs. It was an absurd idea; McLean Stevenson could have taken up permanent residence under Johnny's desk and it wouldn't have drawn an audience to *Hello, Larry.* It only would have hurt *The Tonight Show,* which I'm sure even Silverman would have admitted. A lot of this was nonsense that would have been smoothed over if Dave Tebet was still around, but he retired in 1978, and now there was nobody in New York that Johnny could turn to when he was feeling aggrieved.

Carson was also not particularly impressed with Fred's programming ability. Despite Silverman's stunning record of success, Carson felt that he possessed very peculiar judgment. The year before, Silverman invited us to a meeting and announced that he'd had a brainstorm. He was going to create a new program in the time slot right after Carson, and to host it, he was going to bring back to NBC none other than Steve Allen.

Johnny thought this was one of the more boneheaded programming ideas he'd ever heard. For one thing, *The Tomorrow Show,* starring Tom Snyder, was getting pretty good ratings and doing some interesting stuff; there didn't seem to be an aching need to replace him. More important, Johnny didn't think it made much sense to bring back Steve Allen. "You're going to bring back the first host of *The Tonight Show* and put him on behind me? In what, *The Second Tonight Show? The Good Old Tonight Show? The More of the Tonight Show?*"

"Well, whom would you have on after you?" Silverman asked.

Johnny suggested the name of a bright comedian he admired — David Letterman. And, indeed, several years later, Letterman was given a show in the twelve-thirty a.m. time slot following a now hour-long *Tonight*

Show. By then Silverman was long gone.

There is no denying the tremendous success that Fred Silverman had at CBS and ABC, but he was a piece of work, and most of the stories people told about him seemed to evoke his eccentric diligence. Typical was the tale once told by an NBC executive who was a regular visitor to Silverman's magnificent Central Park West apartment. The visitor discovered that Fred kept a high-powered telescope on the terrace. Was he an astronomer? Or a Peeping Tom?

The truth was either more or less lurid, depending on how you look at it. Fred liked to look through the telescope into the apartments of other people who lived along Central Park to see what they were watching during prime time. He didn't like waiting to see the results of the overnight ratings. He did his own survey, window by window. Perhaps this was the secret behind his golden gut.

There were no public announcements of Johnny's decision, but reports of his intentions inevitably leaked out. By April the entertainment world was filled with discussion and speculation. By then everyone knew that NBC's fortunes had not been revived by Silverman's bold gamble and that the network's earnings, apart from *The*

Tonight Show, had fallen precipitously. This only increased the already hefty percentage of NBC's revenue that was delivered by Carson.

For Silverman, the problem was becoming very personal. Hired to be a miracle worker, the only miracles he had accomplished were to make money and viewers disappear. If he were to lose Johnny on top of that, it was a very good bet that he'd lose his job, too, along with much of his reputation. With so much at stake in the case, he couldn't let Carson walk.

In a dramatic testament to the seriousness with which he took this issue, Silverman reached beyond NBC's in-house lawyers and hired one of the biggest guns in Hollywood, Milton "Mickey" Rudin, to serve as outside counsel. Famous as Frank Sinatra's longtime attorney and legendary for the loyalty he engendered from clients, Mickey had represented many of the very biggest names in the business: Elizabeth Taylor, Lucille Ball, George Burns, Liza Minnelli, Norman Lear, as well as such clients as the Aga Khan and Warner Bros. Studios. Rudin was not only brilliant, but he was also a people person who knew how to ingratiate himself in a way that propelled his career. A man who by instinct and experience understood the psychology of Hollywood, he was an astute attorney. And like nearly everyone else in town, I knew, liked, and respected Mickey.

All of which meant that my competitive juices were now on high boil. We never expected NBC to resist us so strongly, but once they did, we had only one choice. Together, my partners, including John Gaims and Ralph Jonas, and I determined that our only alternative was to fight back every step of the way. The stakes for Johnny — and for me — couldn't have been higher: would Carson be forced to continue working for NBC — with, admittedly, an enormous salary — or would he win his freedom?

I had an idea that I cleared with Johnny and then proposed to Rudin. Rather than subject NBC and ourselves to the enormous circus of civil litigation in a public trial, I offered the alternative of private litigation.

This option would allow the two sides to hire a retired California superior court judge and argue the case before him in private proceedings in a secluded place like a law office or living room. There would be no reporters, no television, and no insanity. For Carson, an enormously private person as everyone involved in this process knew, the benefits of this proposal were evident, but they were no less so for NBC, which would suffer a public relations disaster and incur a loss of goodwill by suing one of America's favorite stars. They had every reason to take the private trial option.

There was only one downside. Under the rules of this private litigation, the ruling of the judge would be binding and final. It was agreed that there would be no appeal. Although this represented one gigantic roll of the dice for both sides, the immense advantages to keeping our contentions private made the decision easy. Rudin and NBC accepted our proposal almost immediately, and together we selected the retired jurist, William Hogoboom, to preside over our private court.

What was in the offing had the makings of an epic trial, one where the fates and fortunes of one very famous star and one iconic corporation would be at stake. And it would take place in a hatbox, with the audience of a stenographer.

SEVEN:
1979–1980: FREE AGENCY

Once word got out that Carson had given notice, he was "in play." It didn't matter that Johnny was saying that he was tired and looking forward to a good, long rest. Nobody believed him, and suddenly, all over town, projects that had seemed moribund were leaping to life, dead meat turned into Sleeping Beauties, invigorated by the kiss of Carson's possibility. Most interested of all, of course, were ABC and CBS, the two networks that for nearly seventeen years had lived in awe and envy of *The Tonight Show* money machine. At various times I was accused of staging this move. Not true. When Johnny told me his plans, he was deadly serious.

Meanwhile, whatever Carson was planning to do with his upcoming leisure time, he had filled his 1979 calendar with a whirlwind of work — hosting the Oscars, playing dates in heartland cities in the South and Midwest, performing ten weekends a year at Caesars Palace in Las Vegas, and taking his customary vacation to watch the Wimbledon Championships in London, followed by a sojourn in the South of France. Throughout all of these events, we were together.

Somewhere in the midst of these events (by the way, we were also attempting to buy a bank in California, buy the Aladdin Hotel in Vegas, and prepare for the crucial trial before Judge Hogoboom), Johnny received a call from Edgar Rosenberg.

As anyone who has ever seen Joan Rivers on a talk show knows, Edgar was her husband, whom she enjoyed portraying as reserved, if not distant. However he behaved with Joan, he was an affable, friendly sort with the rest of humanity. For a while in the sixties, he specialized in producing films that were underwritten with funds from the United Nations. These films dealt with very important themes and had large international all-star casts. (For example, *Poppies Are Also Flowers*, about the international drug trade, starred Senta Berger, Stephen Boyd, Yul Brynner, Angie Dickinson, Georges Géret, Hugh Griffith, Jack Hawkins, Trini López, Marcello Mastroianni, Gilbert Roland, Harold Sakata, and Omar

Sharif — performers representing at least nine nationalities.) He now served as the manager of Joan's mushrooming career.

Joan was a favorite of Johnny's. Not only was she his discovery and therefore part of a very special few that included Bill Cosby, Richard Pryor, George Carlin, and others who got career-making breaks on the stage of *The Tonight Show,* but he also liked her humor, that weird mix of nastiness and neediness that could nonetheless be so endearing. Joan was his number one substitute host while he was on vacation, and she would enjoy a special status until their famous falling-out after she accepted an offer from Fox to mount her own talk show opposite Carson. Until then, he trusted her on confidential matters that required her profound discretion.

This high regard extended to Edgar, a gentlemanly Englishman who seemed to derive much of his persona from the cool hipster personality Peter Sellers projected when he wasn't projecting the personality of one of his dozens of characters. But he also had this odd fondness for intrigue, secrets, dramas, and surprises that really tickled Johnny. Edgar was one of those people who enjoyed being in the know and would try to gin things up to be in the know.

He amused Johnny, who thought he was a real character.

"Henry," said Johnny, "Inspector Clouseau just called. Says it's important."

"If Edgar's involved, it must be."

"God, he loves this secret agent bullshit. Anyway, I told him that he should call you. Be nice to him. The son of a bitch means well."

"Did he tell you what it was about?" I asked.

"No, he was in full James Bond mode. Everything is top secret. He's probably worried about wiretaps."

I phoned Edgar, who, in a hushed voice, said, "I'm acting today in my capacity as an emissary of the alphabet people, who want to discuss a possible post-Peacock throne." Edgar's code was transparent, and he accentuated every key syllable so much that you could practically feel him nudging you through the telephone receiver. Johnny, of course, was forbidden to talk with NBC's competitors while the contract was in effect. I hoped no one was bugging this conversation; I couldn't possibly testify with a straight face that I didn't know what Edgar's gibberish meant. ABC, Edgar revealed, would not only make Johnny much wealthier but they also promised to treat him with more respect than NBC did, and they would give Johnny opportunities to produce programs he was interested in.

Well, I thought, here was a subject that was worth the subterfuge. ABC began flirting with Johnny as soon as he agreed to host the Oscars, as though saying, "You may have been NBC's top talent for seventeen years, but in one night with us, we're going to show you what it feels like to be a star." All their promotion featured Johnny, the little gold man, and the ABC logo, as though this was their dream come true. Now they were going a step further, showing that they at least had the imagination to think of offering something Johnny might possibly want. After all, being a star in Hollywood was a fabulous thing, but the real money and power went to those who owned the companies that produced the programs. The average American could rattle off the names of people who starred on *Charlie's Angels, Dynasty, Fantasy Island, Hart to Hart* — the Farrah Fawcetts, the Joan Collinses, the Ricardo Montalbáns, and the Robert Wagners — but it was Aaron Spelling who called the shots and raked in the dough and lived like the sultan of Brunei. (Or to put it another way, Merv Griffin, who was a rival of Carson's but never his peer, was so much richer than Johnny because he owned the game shows *Jeopardy!* and *Wheel of Fortune.*)

Naturally we were curious about what ABC had in mind, but there was no way that Johnny was going to allow himself to be caught flirting with another network. However, if one afternoon I just happened to be driving through Bel Air and just happened to turn onto Ambyzack Road and just happened to find myself outside the English Tudor home of Joan Rivers and Edgar Rosenberg and just happened to drop in to say hello, well, who's to say who else might be there?

Well, as it happened, I did go out for a drive the following Saturday, and I did pop in on Joan and Edgar, and lo and behold, I found Fred Pierce, the head of the ABC network; Elton Rule, the chairman of ABC; and Tony Thomopoulos, the network's chief of programming.

"Henry!" Edgar said. "What a pleasant surprise! You know, the fellows here were just telling me about a rumor they had heard about some sort of dispute between Johnny and NBC."

At this point, Joan entered the room. "All right, fellas, just relax — the floor show will start in a minute. Elton, take off your jacket.

Ease up. In fact, take off your pants if you want to; we're all family here. Now, I know this is top-secret shit that you guys are going over, real hush-hush atomic secrets kind of stuff. I let all the staff off, everybody except the gardener and the maid, Edgar's cousins Julius and Ethel. No one else is in the place, so feel free to talk about your secrets — how much Barbara Walters makes, how much you have to pay plastic surgeons to keep Joan Collins's boobs off the floor. Can I get anybody a drink?" When she came back with the drinks, she had changed into a short, black, spangly dress, the sort of thing a cocktail waitress would wear in the high-roller room at Caesars. "Don't worry," she said, "it's from a prop house, not Edgar's closet." Everybody laughed as she sashayed around, served the drinks, and then disappeared.

"It's never easy following a headliner," I said a moment later, "but before we go any further, just let me remind you Johnny has an existing contract with NBC that contains a clause that prevents him from negotiating with any third party while that agreement is still extant." Simply put, I was telling them it might put Johnny in breach of his deal if I began negotiating with them. Our position with NBC was there was no agreement, and

I was dancing on the head of a pin. None-theless, I agreed to hear what they had to say.

"First, we just want you to know some-thing," Pierce said. "Our dream is to build a network that is full of the best people at what they do, and to do that from early in the morning until late at night. We don't think that achieving a dream like that will come cheap. None of us here knows what Johnny makes, but even in our dreams, we think we'd have to double it."

"Interesting," I said. "Here are some of the things Johnny dreams about. One is a more productive work schedule, one where he gets more money per show and does fewer shows than the four per week that he does now.

"Uh-huh."

"In his dream, he's on the air four nights a week, but perhaps three would be original shows and one a rerun."

"And the fifth night?"

"There could be a guest host, perhaps someone like our lovely cocktail waitress." Sitting in the corner, Edgar beamed.

"Uh-huh."

"Also Johnny dreams of working just thirty-seven weeks a year, with three of his fifteen weeks off coming in June so that he could enjoy his customary vacation at Wimbledon and the South of France."

"Sure," Pierce said. "That sounds like a reasonable dream."

"Interesting," I responded.

I then threw out the wild card. "I'm sure all of you know that the thing Johnny really dreams about most often is starring in a show that he owns and produces himself."

Everyone was quiet for a moment, and then Elton Rule finally spoke. "Well, Henry, you've heard our dream of a network full of stars. I haven't heard anything today that would make me think that dreams can't come true."

As the meeting drew to a close, I was handed a rather large book by one of the ABC contingent: a deal proposal, three inches thick.

"This is so you know we're not just jawboning here," Pierce said. "These are the concrete specifics of the deal we want to make with Johnny. Everything you laid out for us today will be folded into this."

Although I was impressed with their preparation, I refused to even touch the thing. "Thanks, guys, but right now we're in a dispute with NBC about what our contract obligations are to them. There is no way I can receive a document that could be construed as interfering with a contract."

All in all, it was not a bad little meeting. I had managed to approach the line of propriety without crossing it, and the intelligence I had gathered was priceless. I now knew just how much ABC was interested in acquiring Johnny and just how much they were willing to pay for the privilege. And although ABC's overture was fairly meaningless until the question of Johnny's free agency was established — and it was completely meaningless if Johnny was serious about intending to retire — I at least knew that we were holding better cards than NBC. If Johnny won, he was facing his choice of some highly interesting opportunities. If NBC won, all they would get is two more years of an increasingly disgruntled host. Viewers would tune in night after night just to hear Johnny mercilessly flaying the network executives who had haplessly hoisted themselves on their own petard.

But by then, Fred Silverman or someone else in the NBC high command had begun to figure out that even if Carson and NBC had to be adversaries, there was no point in becoming enemies, and they began trying to make Johnny happy. Brandon Tartikoff, a young executive Johnny liked and admired, was named the network's director of comedy, a move designed to fill the Dave Tebet gap and give Johnny a voice and an ally among the decision makers. And Silverman himself began to adjust his game, showing up from time to time to watch *The Tonight Show* and to offer support, admiration, and encouragement. Carson, though polite, was immune to the campaign.

There was one gesture that Johnny couldn't help but appreciate. When the New York Friars Club honored Carson as Entertainer of the Year, Silverman manfully took his place next to Carson among Lucille Ball, Kirk Douglas, Mike Douglas, Barbara Walters, Jack Benny, Roberta Flack, Jann Wenner, the ambassadors from Egypt and Israel, and the rest of the fifty-one eminences on the dais.

Although Johnny was ostensibly on hand to be toasted, not roasted, the Friars Club was not known for earnest, sober paeans to its honorees. And with Carson and NBC locked in battle, the 1,500 platinum-plated paying guests were expecting at the very least a deliciously dangerous evening.

The emcee for the evening was Bob Hope, the only celebrity of that era whose prestige as a master of ceremonies could be said to be in the same realm as Johnny's. Both had played before the most prestigious audiences, with Hope enjoying the advantage of having performed for FDR and Churchill. Both preferred the rapier to the broadsword, knowing it was better to sting than to smash, and both knew they could get away with going a bit too far if they made themselves the butt of some of the humor.

"All NBC's top brass are here," said Hope. "I'm sure you've seen them refilling Johnny's wine glass, cutting his steak, kissing his ring. None of them ever did get to eat dinner. They kept ordering and canceling, ordering and canceling." He then praised Carson. "You really have to hand it to Johnny. I can't help but admire a man who can do what John has done to his network — as many times, as many ways, and in as many positions." Hope's best line was about Johnny getting paid more to work less. "Next year he's got a sweeter deal: $43 million, and all he has to do is come in once a week and pick up his messages."

As things turned out, the evening was far more a tribute than a roast. Maybe there was too much worry about alienating either Carson or NBC with remarks about the sensitive situation between them. There was no more important venue on which one could promote a movie, a book, or a new

TV show than *The Tonight Show,* and *The Today Show* was a pretty close second. I suppose more of the crowd was rooting for Johnny, but what they really wanted was peace. Hope noted the presence of the Israeli and Egyptian ambassadors sitting next to each other so soon after their nations had signed a peace accord. "They're here to show Silverman and Johnny that it can be done," he quipped, generating more nods of agreement than laughter.

In general there was far more gentle joshing and outright sucking up than I had expected. The only real tension came near the end, when Fred Silverman finally got up to speak, and the crowd grew quiet in anticipation of a possible disaster.

As it turned out, one of the best things Fred had going for him that evening was me. Described in the *New York Post* the next day as "the least recognizable, but perhaps most significant man on the star-studded dais" — there's a line guaranteed to boost an attorney's ego — I was a target he could attack with impunity. "I recently learned that Henry Bushkin's dream has long been to perform in the Olympics," said Fred, "and I immediately made arrangements to have him participate. I'm happy to announce that in Moscow in 1980, Henry will be a javelin catcher. It's the least I can do for Bushkin after all he's done for me."

I couldn't have enjoyed that more. It's always good news to find out that you've become an irritant to your adversary.

Having taken his little shot at me, Silverman turned to Johnny. Anyone who was hoping for or expecting any poison darts or even little zingers walked away disappointed. Somewhere along the line Silverman grasped that NBC might lose the contract battle with Carson, but that didn't mean they would have to lose him, and that meant keeping this contract dispute in the realm of a disagreement, not a war. As Silverman stood at the podium, he aimed his guns at the ripest target in the room — himself.

"I was watching *The Tonight Show* the evening Johnny announced that he had decided to stay on at least until the end of the year." Fred paused a beat. "I was so relieved I got down off the chair and put the rope back in the closet."

He continued in that vein for a joke or two more, but then he turned very earnest in his summation. "Johnny, you're more, much more, than Entertainer of the Year," waxed Fred. "You're the entertainer of our time. You're the best friend TV ever had."

Fred did about as well as he could do, but

it was going to take more than a few blandishments to mollify Carson. With a polite nod of thanks and a handshake, Johnny sent him back to his seat. "There have been a lot of jokes about Mr. Silverman here tonight," Johnny said, "but I'm delighted to see NBC's top executive on the dais. It reminds me for some reason of another dinner — the Last Supper." Who was Jesus and who was Judas was left to the biblical scholars in the audience to decipher, but it was a good line on which to send everybody home.

The next morning Johnny and I had breakfast in his suite at the Waldorf Towers. "Silverman actually seems like a nice guy. I thought he was pretty much of a schmuck with the Steve Allen bullshit he was feeding me. Give him a call and let him know that I appreciated his remarks."

As busy as we were, nothing was more important than the upcoming private trial of the civil suit against NBC in front of Judge Hogoboom. It's true that we had very little to lose. If the judge ruled against Johnny, he would have to spend two years working in the salt mines of Burbank, earning a salary pretty much unrivaled by anyone on the planet who was not of Saudi royal descent. NBC had much more to lose:

on the line for them were a signature star, a late-night franchise, and a programming anchor. And by winning, all they got was time — two years to figure out how to woo an insulted Johnny back into the fold or find a new king.

If we won, though, Carson's position would be elevated from the stratosphere into a full-fledged orbit. He would enjoy complete independence, and given the way the industry had been going, he would be positioned to become a veritable entertainment mogul. Merv Griffin, as mentioned, had done it; for example, he had, with his talk shows and game shows, built a very substantial business. Dick Clark had done the same, building a huge production business that did *American Bandstand,* the *Golden Globe Awards,* all sorts of specials, and even a bunch of well-regarded television movies. Neither man had the star power or the access to talent that Johnny possessed.

The entire trial hung on four little numbers: 2855, which was the applicable section of the California Labor Code of 1937, as interpreted by a ruling of the California Court of Appeals in 1944, the specifics of which were codified in a revision of Section 2855 passed in 1945. Known informally as the de Havilland Law (after the actress

Olivia de Havilland, whose successful suit against Warner Bros. over her contract resulted in the key ruling), Section 2855 imposes a limit of seven calendar years on contracts for service, unless the employee agreed to an extension beyond that term.

This decision was one of the most significant and far-reaching legal rulings in Hollywood history. It undermined the old studio system under which even the biggest stars could be tied to one studio for their entire careers, and it ushered in a new era of free agent performers who would take control of their own careers. The old stars like Tracy, Gable, Cooper, and Stewart may have been very highly paid and pampered, but until de Havilland, they were also something close to indentured servants, locked into personal-service contracts that could stretch for decades. The kind of independence and clout enjoyed today by stars like Clint Eastwood, Brad Pitt, and George Clooney to choose the films they want to play in and form their own production companies to create their own vehicles owes much to the effects of Section 2855.

There was no question that 2855 applied to the Carson case. The issue that Mickey Rudin and I would argue was whether NBC was in compliance or in violation of the law.

Had Johnny already labored more than seven years under his contract as we claimed? Or, as NBC contended, had he signed a new contract, which still had two years to run?

In early 1980, Rudin and I appeared before Judge Hogoboom. Sitting in the conference room of my law offices, a wall of West law books covering one wall, a view of Century City from the other, Mickey and I went at it for two days with all the lawyerly ruffles and flourishes, cases and documentation and precedents. But when you boiled it all down, the question before the judge was simple: had Johnny Carson been under contract to NBC more than seven years or not? Obviously, he had been in their employ, without interruption, since 1962, but the original contract was signed by NBC–New York. He had been in the employ of NBC–Burbank since 1972. It was now 1980. Whichever one of these dates you picked as the starting point, once you did the math, the only conclusion you could reach was that Johnny's seven years expired at the very latest on October 15, 1979, and that as of now there was no contract.

No, no, no, Rudin in effect said, you have it all wrong. Over those years, Carson and NBC had signed a series of shorter intervening contracts, the most recent of which was signed in 1978, a three-year deal that wouldn't expire until 1981. He was free to sign or not sign that contract in 1978, and he'll be free to sign or not sign one in 1981. But the fact is that he signed it, and NBC had made considerable decisions and investments based on his word.

Mickey was a very smart guy and a great attorney. He presented his case adroitly. But there weren't a lot of clever angles for either of us to exploit. The clock either started running in 1972, or it started over in 1978. After two days, the judge took our arguments under advisement and promised a decision soon.

While the drama with NBC was being played out, other opportunities were coming Carson's way. Most significantly, we were also involved in prolonged negotiations to buy the Aladdin Hotel in Las Vegas.

No other entertainer owned a Vegas hotel casino, and Johnny was the perfect candidate to become the first. His finances were platinum plated, and his reputation for integrity was golden. Given that the Nevada Gaming Commission was working very actively to separate Vegas from the wild and woolly days when mob interests pretty openly ran the town, Carson, with his own wealth, his status in Vegas as the King of the Counts, and his sterling reputation, was just the sort of person whose ownership would be welcome.

The Aladdin had a star-crossed history from its start in 1962, when Edwin Lowe, the inventor of the game Yahtzee, sought to prove that you could have a successful hotel in Las Vegas without a casino attached. His $12 million, 450-room, Tudor-style English Tallyho Motel, complete with thirty-two villas, four pools, six restaurants, and a par 54 nine-hole golf course, closed in eighteen months. Another owner came along and achieved the same result twelve months later. In 1966, Milton Prell bought the joint and spent $3 million losing the English décor and redoing the hotel with an *Arabian Nights* theme, part of which included the opening of the 500-seat Baghdad Theater show room. Prell introduced an innovative policy by offering three completely different shows twice nightly with no cover or minimum charges. He also apparently concluded that Edwin Lowe was nuts, because Prell acquired a gaming license. In the ensuing years, the Aladdin had many more facelifts, many more architectural improvements, and several new investors, many of whom ended up under indictment when it was revealed that they had ties to organized crime. Noteworthy was the fact that the Aladdin always claimed that the hotel was twenty-nine stories high, but they began numbering the floors at 11. That seemed to me to be an apt metaphor for the way business was done at the Aladdin, but the Nevada Gaming Commission seemed resolved to embark upon a new era.

Our plan was to rename the hotel Johnny Carson's Aladdin and leverage his commitment to appear at the hotel a set number of days every year to attract other investors. Hey, if he was working in town, why not own the hotel where he worked? The best potential partner to join Carson's effort was the National Kinney Corporation, a New Jersey conglomerate. Kinney came to the deal late but with plenty of money, and things looked very promising. But on the verge of completing the deal, Johnny and I were blindsided by events that seemed disastrous then but pretty hilarious in hindsight.

We met with Andrew Frankel, then the CEO of Kinney. Ed Nigro was to run the hotel and casino, Jack Eglash would become entertainment director, and Johnny would be the headliner and namesake for the moribund hotel. Many stories have appeared on the subject of Carson and the Aladdin Hotel. For Johnny the deal had to make sense or he would pass. As it turned out, it didn't and we passed.

Essentially National Kinney would put up all the money and Johnny would get 20 percent of the hotel. He would have to undergo the process required by the Gaming Control Board to be licensed, but he was prepared to do that.

Given that there were other parties that were interested in buying the casino, the details of our protracted negotiations were kept under wraps as much as possible, and National Kinney's participation was a closely held secret. We felt that we could freely discuss the subject at home, of course.

Indeed, Johnny and I went over the plans for the formal announcement one morning in his living room. We knew there were people around, but we surely didn't think anyone was paying attention. Were we wrong! Shortly after breakfast, Joanna Carson phoned her brother, Peter Ulrich, and told him about the casino plan. Ulrich bought 2,000 shares of National Kinney, which he sold over the next three months at a profit of around $5,000. Joanna also told another friend, who bought 1,000 shares of

National Kinney the next morning and then flipped them several days later for a small gain. Joanna, apparently the CNBC of her generation, also discussed the deal with Judy, who told her father, who bought 5,000 shares, which netted him a profit of about $5,000. A lawyer in my firm also bought about 5,000 shares of the stock. He was reprimanded and fired.

Today middle school children know about the laws against insider trading, but the stock market was a foreign country to most people in 1980, and neither Judy nor Joanna knew the rules, and neither Johnny nor I ever thought to talk to them about it. Trading stock had never been one of their interests. But after the average number of shares in National Kinney traded daily on the American Stock Exchange jumped from 7,000 to 100,000, the Securities and Exchange Commission thought a discussion was in order. None of the traders in our little circle bothered to deny what they had done. Why would they? They thought it was not only legal but also very clever. They had no idea that this was the sort of thing that led to prison stripes. Very quickly they settled with the SEC and returned their profits to the original stock owners after receiving a good slap on the wrist. Johnny found it galling to find his pristine national reputation soiled by such a boneheaded escapade, but in a way, it was lucky that it was so foolish; no one believed that Johnny or I could be involved in or sanction something so foolish.

In the meantime, a strong competitor for the hotel had emerged: the pop singer and Las Vegas stalwart Wayne Newton. Newton had a large and loyal following. Known as Mr. Las Vegas, he symbolized every aspect of the desert destination: the glamour, the glitz, the flash. What's more, Newton filled theaters every night for forty weeks a year (Johnny filled theaters, too, but he performed only on weekends). Prior to this point, neither Johnny nor I thought Newton was a serious competitor. The sellers and their partners would be carrying the note for the sale, which obviously meant that they wanted to turn the project over to the buyers who had the soundest finances and the most promising upside. Johnny's name on the hotel and his commitment to play there every year carried enormous weight. When we realized that Newton's group was as strong a contender as Johnny's, we worked very hard to finalize the deal with the bankruptcy trustee.

Over the years, Johnny had been the

subject of threats, and in the course of reporting them, we developed a rapport with some special agents from the FBI. At around that time, one of them called and asked to meet me. Johnny happened to be performing in Vegas at the time, so I invited the agent to come up from LA to talk and stay for the show. We met in Johnny's dressing room at Caesars.

"Do you know who Vincent Alo is?" the agent asked. "Jimmy Blue Eyes?"

I didn't really, but I was beginning to form a hunch, based on my observation that members of the bar, the medical profession, and the clergy seldom attracted such colorful nicknames. Soon I realized that I was more on target than I knew. Alo was a prominent member of the Genovese crime family in New York. He was a close associate of Lucky Luciano, and he later ran casinos in Florida and Cuba with Meyer Lansky. The Manhattan district attorney, Robert Morgenthau, called him "one of the most significant organized crime figures in the United States."

"Did you ever see *The Godfather Part II*?" the agent asked me. "The character Johnny Ola? He's partially based on Alo, except Johnny Ola got whacked."

Alo was in his mid-seventies and supposedly semiretired, the agent told me. "But not really. Alo is lurking behind the scenes at National Kinney."

"How? What's he doing?"

"If I were you, I'd find a way to get Carson to back out of the deal with them."

"I don't know," I said. "We're pretty far along. We're ready to name the interim CEO."

"Look, let me be clear. You could name the Reverend Billy Graham as interim CEO, and the Gaming Commission's never going to give Kinney a license," the agent assured me. "Never. And Johnny will be embarrassed when the deal is rejected."

Of course, the agent was right. And it was the sort of stain that could never be removed because Johnny could never prove that he wasn't associated with criminals. And in Johnny's case, the absurd insider trading case would only fuel the flames. "Fuck it," Johnny said when I described the details of our meeting. "I don't need the press to pick up on this. Call Kinney and tell them we're out!"

When Newton and his group later acquired the Aladdin, news reports held that they beat out Carson for the hotel. Not true. Wayne and his group were the only bidders;

Johnny had withdrawn with no hard feelings. As time went on, however, Johnny became increasingly annoyed that he was being portrayed as having lost out to Newton. He then started doing lame, stupid Wayne Newton jokes. Newton called me on numerous occasions to get Johnny to cut the jokes. I felt Johnny was unfair and I understood where Newton was coming from. However, the jokes became a recurring monologue that didn't end until Newton confronted Carson. In a story he has related many times over the years, most recently on *Larry King Live,* Newton says he went to Burbank without an appointment and barged into Johnny's office. "Freddy de Cordova was in the office with him," Newton says. "I walked in, unannounced. I said to Freddy, I said, 'Would you excuse us, please?' He was so shocked that he did get up and leave. And I said to Mr. Carson, 'I don't know what friend of yours I've killed, I don't know what child of yours I've hurt, I don't know what food I've taken out of your mouth, but these jokes about me will stop and they'll stop now or I will kick your ass.' " According to Newton, Johnny responded, "I'm your biggest fan!" To which Newton replied, "Don't give me that crap. I am here to straighten out whatever your problem is. And whichever way you want to straighten it out is fine with me." After I left Carson's employ, I ran into Wayne, who told me of his NBC visit. Newton is a big guy, and Johnny was not in the best of shape at that time. It would have been no contest had they scuffled. But regardless, I don't blame Wayne for being pissed. Eventually the jokes stopped but not soon enough to soothe Wayne's ego.

As it turned out, Johnny never did work in Vegas again.

After the Hogoboom hearing, weeks passed in silence. At first, I was in agony waiting for the decision. Johnny, with his shows and his performances to fill his mind, never seemed to think about it. No doubt he calculated that whatever happened, NBC needed him more than he needed them. Maybe he felt that worrying was what he paid me to do for him. Eventually it passed into the back of my mind. Then Judge Hogoboom called.

We convened at the Hillcrest Country Club. Adjacent to Beverly Hills and Century City, just a few blocks from Fox Studios, the club is the headquarters of the Westside Jewish establishment in Los Angeles. Among its Jewish and non-Jewish members were movie moguls like Marvin Davis; major agents; performers like George Burns, Jack Benny, as well as Frank Sinatra, and Sidney Poitier; prominent businessmen such as Bill Belzberg and Bob Recht; and bankers and attorneys, including Fred Richman.

We convened in a small private dining room, sitting around the table, the same four people who had attended the trial. After a career of litigation involving so many lawsuits that reached their climaxes in courtrooms designed to awe, it continues to strike me as ironic that the most momentous decision of my career was handed down in an airy dining room. Pleasantries were briefly exchanged, and then Judge Hogoboom began to speak.

After summarizing the facts and the opposing arguments, he got to the point. "I recognize that Mr. Carson most recently signed a three-year contract with NBC. Under the terms of this contract, it unambiguously has two years to go. However" — when Mickey heard that word, he visibly sagged — "under the law as delineated in Section 2855 of the California Labor Code, the seven-year statute is inviolate. Mr. Carson had no contractual obligation to NBC after October 1, 1979, which marked the end of his seven-year contract for personal services."

By the time the judge completed the short recitation of his ruling, Rudin's face had gone completely white. I have a strong competitive instinct and, for a lot of reasons, I was thrilled to win. But admiring and respecting Mickey as much as I did, I can't say I relished his distress.

The announcement of the verdict had taken only a few minutes. It was near lunchtime at Hillcrest, and it put on an excellent spread. Under the circumstances, though, breaking bread might have been a little awkward. We thanked Judge Hogoboom, and we hurried back to our offices to share the news.

Johnny was, in his low-key Midwestern way, elated. He knew that a whole new world of opportunity was opening up for him, but it was going to take a while to fully sink in. I suppose I expected some sort of World Series moment, complete with champagne. Instead he thanked me and resumed his routine.

Fortunately, five minutes after I got off with Johnny, and entirely by coincidence, Edgar Rosenberg called. He didn't know and couldn't have known that the decision had been announced, but he knew the general timetable of things and had been checking in regularly, if only to keep reminding me of ABC's ongoing interest.

"Edgar," I said, "this is in strictest confidence. You're the first person besides Johnny to know. As of an hour ago, Johnny Carson is a free man. And a free agent. Let Fred and Elton know that we can now talk."

"That's fantastic!" Edgar responded. "You've pulled off the coup of the century. Carson has got to be very grateful to you."

"Gratitude is a rare commodity," I replied. "Let's just say he's having a nice afternoon."

Then Edgar delivered a message I believe he'd patiently been waiting to deliver for weeks. "Look, ABC knows that you and Johnny are going to Wimbledon and then the South of France. When you and Johnny are near the Mediterranean, they'd like to take you both for a cruise on their yacht to discuss in detail the proposal they outlined at my house."

"Sounds great," I said. "Why a yacht?"

"They think it will be better to have the meeting in international waters," Edgar said.

"International waters? Edgar, what's all of this cloak-and-dagger crap? We could meet in Macy's window if we wanted to."

"Maybe ABC's lawyers specialize in maritime law," said Edgar.

We didn't hear immediately from NBC

after the Hogoboom decision, which, upon reflection, was pretty smart on their part. There was no contract now in effect, but Johnny had made a commitment to remain until the end of 1980. One of the few advantages the network had was that it could lay back and wait to see what we wanted or what their rivals were offering.

Besides, Johnny was starting to feel better about NBC, even before the ruling. Silverman and the other execs were putting a lot of effort into recultivating their relationship with Carson, buttering up the king with gifts and considerations and perks that amounted to state-of-the-art superstar treatment. Silverman's shrewd appointment of the affable, intelligent Brandon Tartikoff to be NBC's point man in dealing with Carson began to pay off. Like all executives who achieve this rank, Silverman had a very healthy ego, but he didn't let it get in the way of success. He saw that he and Johnny were not a congenial pair, and he found somebody who could do the job. Johnny's feelings about the network began to soften. Now that he no longer had to stay, it was starting to seem possible that he would.

But there was still that Mediterranean cruise in the offing.

EIGHT:
1979–1980: CLEAR SAILING

With a contractual obligation to NBC no longer hanging over his head, Johnny's resentment toward his *Tonight Show* duties was swiftly evaporating. Now that he was not actually compelled to do the show, much of his old gusto returned. He was also tremendously excited about the plans we were formulating about how to organize the new Carson enterprises. But there was no hurry on our part, and as June rolled around, everything was taking a backseat to the upcoming holiday.

Vacations had never been that important to Carson, but he loved the experience of his first trip to London and the Riviera in 1976 (the heat notwithstanding). Afterward, whatever else was happening in the life of Johnny Carson, those three vacation weeks in late June and early July were sacrosanct. One might think that having successfully experimented with foreign travel, Johnny might have been open to other destinations, but that was not the case then: the man who valued familiarity in his social life extended the principle to his vacations. All the trips were substantially the same, with only minor deviations: the first week spent in the South of France at Hôtel du Cap in Cap d'Antibes, a hotel that has represented the height of elegant seaside luxury since the 1870s. During the second week, we would fly to London for three to four days to attend the semifinal and final tennis matches at Wimbledon. Once a champion was crowned, it was back to Hôtel du Cap. And he always insisted that I, as his lawyer and friend, come along, and that I, like he, bring my wife. Yeah, it was brutal. But for eleven years in a row we toughed it out. The biggest change came about halfway through the eleven summers, when each of the married couples divorced.

Among the aspects of the holiday that Johnny most loved was the annual novelty of becoming a face in the crowd. In the States, he was one of the most familiar people in the country, easily among the most recognized. This meant that he was frequently approached and always watched, and there is a fair amount of discomfort that comes from the feeling of never being alone. In France or Britain, though, only Americans knew who he was, and they usually were polite and kept their distance. Europe allowed Johnny to remember how a normal American (admittedly, a normal American with a ton of money) was able to live his life.

This year was different, if only in one respect: our business with ABC. In order to get us into international waters for our meeting, which they felt was advisable — again, I'm not sure what admiralty lawyer offered that opinion — ABC had chartered Lord Lew Grade's yacht *Cartigrey*. This yacht had been described by one guest as "not larger than an aircraft carrier"; it was designed to impress the natives — of whatever country — and it did.

Johnny was a free man now, so there were no limits on how ardently he could be wooed, and ABC was making damn sure they were doing it in style. Getting on the *Cartigrey* at the port of Antibes felt more like arriving on the deck of a naval vessel rather than a mere civilian boat. Crew and captain were handsomely uniformed, fitted out to what seemed like British Navy standards. Guests were piped aboard.

It was early afternoon, and Johnny and I were greeted topside by a small delegation from ABC. It was the same group that I had met at the Rosenbergs' home. At its head was the network's president, Elton Rule, a near legend in the television industry for having hauled ABC out of last place and onto the top, increasing the network's earnings twelvefold along the way. An army officer who had fought at Leyte and Okinawa, the bulbous-nosed Rule had a kindly face, a hard-charging personality, an acute intelligence, and a reputation for extraordinary effectiveness.

Joining Rule were three other major figures in the company: Fred Pierce, the head of the television division, who had a wide beaky nose and an intense manner; Tony Thomopoulos, the son of Greek immigrants who had worked himself up to become the head of ABC Entertainment; and Gary Pudney, the energetic, eager-to-please vice president in charge of talent and special projects. Gary held the same portfolio of duties that Dave Tebet did at NBC, meaning that his job was to charm, to schmooze, to entertain, and to always, always, always keep the talent happy. In this case, Pudney took the job a step further and devoted a tremendous amount of attention to Joanna as well, no doubt hoping that in the midst of pillow talk, she might throw her favor toward ABC. Rule, Pierce, and Thomopou-los also took time to court her, something no NBC executive with the exception of Dave Tebet had ever bothered to do. Judy and I were carefully looked after but the main draw was the Carsons.

We cast off and sailed into the Mediter-ranean, cruising along the Côte d'Azur to Monte Carlo. The wooing part went on for more than an hour and then Rule and his cohorts made their pitch. The particulars were the same as those kicked about earlier in the year at the home of Joan Rivers and Edgar Rosenberg. But with no contract over Johnny's head now, we could discuss any-thing and everything freely. As we talked, it became clear that as a business opportunity, the sky was no longer the limit.

- ABC would double Johnny's salary — whatever it was.
- Johnny would have carte blanche to do as he pleased.
- He would own his own show.
- He would control the time slot im-mediately after his show.

As the presentation concluded, Fred Pierce handed me ABC's proposed contract with everything memorialized in detail. This time, with no contract in place that I could infringe upon, I accepted the document; negotiations would follow at a later time. But as grateful as we were for ABC's attention, what we had in our hands now was not a contract but a lever. At minimum it would be a convenient template for whatever we might decide to ask for from NBC or whomever we decided to talk to, but it could also be something more powerful: a minimum bid that would spur further largesse. Our party debarked at Monaco, enjoyed some of the pleasures of the principality, and then cruised back to Antibes by moonlight. It couldn't have been a more pleasant outing.

After we returned to Los Angeles in early July, my life quickly grew more complicated. My many years as Carson's one-man entourage had taken its toll on my family life. Many of the heady, heedless pleasures that come to kings as a matter of course also fell in my lap. I had enjoyed many adventures in Vegas and on the road that did nothing to reinforce marital bonds. Unlike Joanna, Judy did mind the other women, and as a consequence, Judy and I split up that summer. Separations are always difficult and traumatic, and especially so with children involved, and I can't pretend to have been the blameless party. The fact that Judy and I still cared for each other and our children caused us to prolong the process, and at various times we tried to save our marriage. Even now it is hard to say whether we were wise to do so.

I rented an apartment in a new building on Spalding near Olympic, across from Beverly Hills High. The neighborhood may not have had quite the cachet of Whittier north of Sunset, but it suited me. As anyone who has been through this process will tell you, there are moments of terrible pain when you miss your family and hate your loneliness, and there are other moments when rediscovering your uncoupled self can be quite exhilarating. Certainly I knew both feelings. I also grasped more clearly than I ever had before the toll that being Johnny Carson's entourage had taken. It had enriched and enlivened my life beyond all imagination, but it had also been one of the factors that led to my separation and divorce.

And here's the kicker: because I was alone more, I was available to Johnny more.

One of the changes that arose from my new solo existence was my new role as host at my new place of the regular *Tonight Show* poker game. This game had been played every couple of weeks since the show moved to LA, usually in somebody's home (and usually to the regret of somebody's wife). We got deli platters from Nate 'n Al's, drank a little too much, smoked cigars, and generally relaxed. It was not a particularly expensive game, especially by today's standards; on an unusual night, somebody might go home up or down a couple thousand, but the stakes seldom got very high. Although attendance was elastic and participants would come and go, the core group consisted of me; Carson; Fred de Cordova; Bud Robinson (a song-and-dance man who with his wife, Cece, had opened for Carson on the road, and who eventually became Doc Severinson's manager); Fred Kayne, who was Johnny's stockbroker and the manager of his portfolio; Bobby Quinn, who was the director of *The Tonight Show* and one of Johnny's closest friends; and Pat McCormick, a comedian and writer for *The Tonight Show.*

Pat was one of the funniest people who ever walked the planet. A six-foot-seven-inch oaf of a man adorned with a bushy red moustache, Pat had an off-the-wall sense of humor that Carson adored. In one of his most memorable moments, Pat wrote and performed in a sketch for one of the show's New Year's Eve broadcasts in the seventies. Pat came onstage as Baby New Year, suitably naked except for a humongous diaper, and Carson interviewed him.

"So New Year's baby, what do you see for the New Year?" Carson asked.

"I have a new way to clean out your system."

"How does it work?"

"Sit on a piece of cheese," Pat replied, "and swallow a live mouse."

It was at one such poker game that Pat McCormick made me famous. We were playing seven-card stud, the game where players have four cards face up on the table and three others hidden in their hands. I had three aces face up, and I could see McCormick had a king high. I thought it highly unlikely that he had in his hand the makings of four of a kind, which is what he would need to beat me. Still, he kept raising and I kept raising back, and on and on we went, with everyone else dropping out. He was making kind of a bold play, and everyone at the table was captivated. When it came to show his hand, he had nothing, just that worthless king high.

"Ah," he seethed. "Bombastic Bushkin has done it again."

Everyone doubled up in laughter, roaring at the line, his timing, and knowing that he had deliberately played out a losing hand and threw away a lot of money just so he could deliver a line that he had been saving in his pocket for the right moment.

The next night, the moment went from hilarious to priceless as Johnny used his monologue to introduce America to his crack financial advisor, Bombastic Bushkin.

Johnny had called that afternoon to alert me and make sure I wasn't offended. Offended? No way! I instantly called my parents to tell them to make sure they watched the show that night because something big was going to happen.

You'd think that the moment I became a pop-culture footnote would be indelibly recorded in my memory, but honestly, I cannot remember the first surefire money-making deal that Bombastic supposedly brought to Carson. There were a lot of them over the years, including Roto-Rooter tampons, Orson Welles designer jeans, Mike Tyson charm schools, Krazy Glue toothpaste, a skinny and sweet diet drink (you won't even taste the rat poison!), Club Med Beirut, a doggie-bag factory in Bangladesh, and a five-star restaurant in Chernobyl.

What I do remember most clearly was that

minutes after Johnny delivered the Bombastic joke, my mother called, crying bitter tears. "Are you all right?" she asked. "Are you going to get fired?"

"No, Mom! Why would you say such a thing?"

"He called you bombastic!"

When I told Johnny about Mom's reaction, he laughed and said, "I thought your mother had a sense of humor. Look, call my secretary tomorrow and give her Mary's number. I'll surprise the hell out of her. Tell your dad to make sure she's available at five-thirty tomorrow."

Dad not only made sure Mom was available, but he alerted the entire condo building. Johnny called promptly at five-thirty and reassured Mom that he thought I was a good guy and one of his best friends. "Watch," he told her, "Bombastic Bushkin is going to become a household word."

Johnny was true to his word. Bombastic Bushkin became a running gag, and my mother became Johnny's biggest fan.

Years later, I learned that when he was in college, President George W. Bush's fraternity friends nicknamed him the Bombastic Bushkin. I only regret that I have but one nickname to give for my country.

I took this picture of Frank Sinatra and Johnny during the rehearsal for the 1981 Reagan Inaugural Gala. Two giants onstage at the president's first inauguration. Courtesy of Henry Bushkin

Sinatra and Dean Martin at the presidential gala rehearsal. Frank is ordering Dean off stage because of his intoxication. **Courtesy of Henry Bushkin**

Judy Bushkin with Dana and Scotty, 1977. **Courtesy of**

Henry Bushkin

The Aston Martin I bought in En-gland in 1977. Behind it is the Daimler limo that broke down while transporting the Carsons. Johnny drove the Daimler back to London, shirtless, during a horrible heat wave. **Courtesy of Henry Bushkin**

Johnny during our 1981 cruise to the Greek isles. The cruise with our wives did little to help our respective marriages. *Courtesy of Henry Bushkin*

Hôtel du Cap, Antibes, France, 1979. Bill Cosby and I played every summer for the "du Cap Cup." Looks as if I won. **Courtesy of Henry Bushkin**

Hôtel du Cap, 1983. Johnny and me on the court.

Courtesy of Henry Bushkin

Sammy Davis Jr. and friend watching Johnny and me play doubles at the Hôtel du Cap, 1980. **Courtesy of Henry Bushkin**

■ ■ ■ ■

Though things were going well for Johnny, his mercurial nature made him capable at any time of finding trouble in the bosom of pleasure. In 1979, *The Tonight Show* won its third straight Emmy, and Johnny took all of the show's insiders to Chasen's for a celebratory dinner.

At that time Chasen's was the most famous celebrity restaurant in town, the Spago of its day, renowned for the long list of movie stars and other celebrities who dined there since the days of Clark Gable and Howard Hughes. Chasen's had its special tables for special guests, and stars were generally seated in the small room to the right of the entrance. On this evening, Fred and Janet de Cordova, Ed and Victoria McMahon, Bobby and Tangley Quinn, Joanna and Johnny, and Judy and I comprised a table of ten.

As the evening progressed and the restaurant filled, more and more people approached the table to offer their congratulations on the award. I can't say that the award meant little to Johnny because it is always nice to be recognized, but deep in his Nebraska soul, Johnny was suspicious of flattery and the blandishments that all too easily came to people in his position. He knew audiences and was pleased when they liked his work. He knew ratings and took pride in what they proved about his appeal. He treasured the respect of his peers in the industry. Awards were all but irrelevant.

Sitting across the room was Tom Snyder, the host of *The Tomorrow Show,* the NBC program that followed Johnny's. Snyder, who was dining alone, sent our table a round of drinks. The polite thing on our part would have been to invite Tom to join us — after all, he was Johnny's network mate and a fellow laborer in the talk-show vineyards. The only problem was that Johnny had long harbored a serious dislike for Snyder, based on nothing but his performances on TV. He thought Snyder had no talent and was an officious bore, and after Johnny had his second glass of wine, we could see his anger bubbling just below the surface. Tonight, Bad Johnny was in the house.

Thankfully the food came and distracted Johnny, who was crazy for Chasen's chili and its hobo steak. Bobby Quinn diplomatically excused himself and went to sit with Snyder (a pal from the Bel-Air Country Club) in hopes of disguising the awkwardness, and everyone was striving to distract Carson's attention away from Tom Snyder. Still, Johnny kept eyeing him and finally said, "Why the fuck is he staring at me? I'm going to go over there and kick the shit out of that guy."

Once it became clear that Johnny's second drink had turned him into Mr. Hyde, our party was over. An embarrassed Joanna left with Judy, with Victoria McMahon, Tangley Quinn, and the de Cordovas hot on their heels. That left Ed and me sitting with Carson and Quinn standing guard with Snyder. Suddenly Johnny got up and went over to Snyder, with Ed and me close behind. Johnny peaceably enough took a seat, though it was clear that he was drunk.

"Whaddya say, fellas — let's have a round of drinks," Snyder said, knowing full well that this would provoke Johnny even more.

"Tom," a furious Bobby Quinn said, "I am going to punch you right in the kisser."

Before Bobby finished the sentence, Johnny lunged across the table and grabbed for Snyder's throat. He got nowhere close. Quinn got in front of Snyder and I pulled on Johnny's arm and McMahon moved his bulk in between. All of a sudden they were all best friends, and Ed shrewdly changed the mood by convincing us to take the party to the Beverly Comstock Hotel on Wilshire near Beverly Glen. It wasn't far away, but it would give Johnny a minute to clear his head.

We left Chasen's and arrived at the Beverly Comstock around two a.m. Richard Simmons was the maitre d' of the restaurant (he had yet to become a fitness guru), and he was going out of his way to showcase his flamboyant routine for the party of television personalities and friends who had been left in his care. ("Johnny and Ed!" he trilled when we entered. "Hello, boys! What brings America's favorite couple to our door?") Quinn and I were eager to split, but once again the drinks were flowing, and Ed and Tom and a suddenly jovial Johnny were ready to party on. I knew it would be risky to leave Johnny at this point, so I phoned Judy and asked her to call Joanna and let her know it would be a while before Johnny came home. Not until five a.m. did Quinn and I pour Johnny into the limo to take him home. McMahon and Snyder and Simmons continued to drink.

When we approached the St. Cloud residence, Johnny insisted that we stop the car outside his home. He decided that rather than wake the guard and have him open the security gates, he would scale the wrought-iron fence. Somehow he succeeded and found his way inside.

The next day Joanna banished him from the house, and he checked into the Beverly Hills Hotel. The next day I went to see him there and discovered that he had a guest, a lady whom I had met at various social occasions any number of times. She had always seemed to be a close friend of Joanna's. I had no idea that she and Johnny had a relationship. I was, of course, sworn to secrecy but shocked nonetheless. Perhaps in the only way he resembled a Boy Scout, Johnny was always prepared. A couple of days would pass until he was permitted to return home.

With summer over, it was time to focus on our options and make some decisions. ABC had made a compelling offer, but Johnny was no longer angry with NBC. I informed Brandon Tartikoff that regardless of what we ultimately decided, Carson wouldn't be packing up and leaving on the quit day we had given them.

To assist us in clarifying our choices, we recruited the hot, up-and-coming Creative Artists Agency for advice. CAA and its managing partner, Mike Ovitz, would become dominant figures in Hollywood for most of the next two decades (CAA is still quite powerful), and even at that relatively early point in its history, the work CAA did for us in scouting out and then negotiating opportunities for us was very shrewd. But for help in answering the key question — which network to select — Johnny turned for advice not to Ovitz, the man who was to become the most influential man in Hollywood, but to the man who already was.

Lew Wasserman, the respected chairman of the entertainment conglomerate MCA Universal, had for decades been regarded as the town's shrewdest, savviest, most insightful agent. Now close to seventy and at the height of his powers, Wasserman was credited with both building and destroying the studio system, and his ability to make money and steer careers had led to him being widely acknowledged as the "King of Hollywood." Johnny asked me to go visit with him in an effort to decide whether he should stay with NBC or go with ABC.

Wasserman had a sharp nose and a sharp chin and dramatic snow-white hair combed straight back from his forehead. What gave his face the most character, however, were his glasses, which had amber-tinted lenses encased in thick black frames. They made him look like some kind of raptor.

Like most oracles, Wasserman gave an opinion that was simple and sensible (but unambiguously presented, thank goodness). "It is not prudent," replied Wasserman, "to ask people to change their nightly viewing habits. Once they are used to tuning in a given channel, they find it hard to make the move, no matter how good an alternative is being provided elsewhere."

Was that it? All of our thinking and talking and arguing and agonizing came down to the belief that Americans won't change the dial? Somebody ought to find Dave Tebet and have him give this man a remote control. We walked out shaking our heads. We asked God, and this is the answer God gave us. It was as good a reason as any.

Wasserman's advice sealed our decision privately, but there was no reason to announce that. Negotiations for a new post-October arrangement began in earnest with NBC, even as we kept discussions going with ABC.

But by then something outside of our little Hollywood universe was going on: Iranian militants deposed the shah of Iran, and in late 1979 seized the United States embassy in Tehran and took fifty-two Americans prisoner. ABC had begun a nightly program in the eleven-thirty time slot called *America*

Held Hostage, which gave a daily update on the story.

As the hostage crisis went on, ABC became both Johnny's nightly nemesis and his ardent suitor. As the crisis wore on, Carson's ratings eroded in the face of the news coverage, even though there were days at a time when nothing of significance took place. After a couple of months of not much happening, it looked like viewers might resume their old reliable viewing habits, but ABC was smart enough to begin using the time slot to augment the network's Winter Olympics coverage in February and then to expand its coverage of an exciting 1980 presidential primary season, which featured a Carter vs. Kennedy contest in one party, and a Reagan vs. Bush, Baker, Dole, Kemp, and others in the GOP. Eventually ABC grew increasingly proud of the popular and profitable and critically acclaimed news program it had pioneered in that time slot.

Word began circulating that the powerful head of ABC News, Roone Arledge, was coveting that late-night period for an in-depth news program that would be hosted by his new star, Ted Koppel. The thinking was that the show could provide a real alternative to the same jokesters and song-stresses Carson was parading out for the umpteenth year. The ABC brass could read a ratings report as well as anyone, and they were paying attention.

And so Johnny made up his mind. On May 2, 1980, long before the embassy hostages were released, the NBC executives who'd themselves been prisoners of Johnny's decision-making process were finally let off the hook. A network delegation headed by Fred Silverman arrived at Carson's Bel Air home for the biggest signing ceremony since the Japanese met General Douglas MacArthur on the deck of the USS *Missouri.* They brought with them what was by far the richest deal ever offered to any single individual in the history of television, and of entertainment.

Carson's salary was set at $25 million a year. For that, he worked one hour a night from eleven-thirty p.m. to twelve-thirty a.m., three nights a week, thirty-seven weeks a year, with fifteen weeks off.

In addition, Carson and Carson Productions became the owners and producers of *The Tonight Show.* NBC still provided all the production support we needed; every week, Carson Productions' profits alone neared $50,000. Ceding Carson ownership of *The Tonight Show* was one of the more shortsighted of NBC's concessions. Carson also took ownership of all the show's episodes that had been made since his arrival in 1962 (to the extent that they existed; into the seventies, the networks routinely destroyed, discarded, or taped over much of their programming). We then created *Carson's Comedy Classics* (from old *Tonight Show*s), a series of 130 half-hour shows that Columbia Television's Herman Rush bought for $26 million. And he had zero cost for the material.

Carson Productions also would own the one-hour slot after Johnny's show, and own and produce the show that played there. David Letterman hosted that show. NBC also gave Carson Productions a commitment to air a minimum of five series that we would develop. And even with these commitments and relationships, we remained an independent entity, with full freedom to pursue any and all deals we pleased in movies, TV series, or any other business, with any partners we chose.

We now occupied a position that offered us almost limitless opportunities and had at the same time been launched on a trajectory that promised enormous success. And great success would indeed come our way. But in time we would learn that the Johnny Carson who loved what he did every night as an entertainer nonetheless possessed enormous ambivalence about acting as a businessman and taking on the mantle of entertainment mogul. We would also see that the friend and colleague who had helped Johnny attain that success came to be resented by him for securing him power he did not want.

But on that afternoon, and for the rest of his career, Johnny Carson occupied a position the likes of which had never before existed and has possibly not even been matched, except perhaps many years later by the estimable Oprah Winfrey.

NINE:
1980–1981: THE
INAUGURATION

A few months after the new contract was signed, late in 1980, Johnny received a request that was a singular honor, the kind of thing that would establish beyond any question his stature as a national institution. Ironically, the act of fulfilling that request revealed fissures and cracks in the foundation of the wonderful world of Johnny Carson.

The story begins in Matteo's Restaurant on Westwood Boulevard in Los Angeles, a classic old-style ristorante that serves southern Italian fare, very reminiscent of the restaurants in the Little Italy section of New York. The food was terrific, but one of the factors that helped to increase its popularity was that its owner, Matty Jordan (née Matteo Giordano), grew up in Hoboken, New Jersey, across the street from a kid named Frank Sinatra. Matty and Frank became lifelong friends, and when Matty opened a restaurant in Los Angeles, Frank made it a point to come by with people he met at work, like Dean Martin, Gregory Peck, and Sophia Loren, who in turn drew other famous figures, like Sam Giancana and Mickey Cohen, who added a certain edginess (funny how the same combination of celebrity and crime helped popularize Jilly's, that other spot owned by a friend of Frank's). Eventually, this Rat Pack in-spot became the place where the Hollywood establishment showed up on Sunday night to have dinner — other nights, too, but Sundays really seemed to draw the bold-faced names. Regulars included Kirk Kerkorian, who owned MGM Studios and the Beverly Hills Hotel, and Al Davis, whose Oakland Raiders were in the midst of a run that was going to lead to a Super Bowl championship, but who constantly talked about moving his club to Los Angeles. Getting a reservation on a Sunday evening was nearly impossible if you didn't know Matty or his brother, Mikey, who was the maitre d'. It didn't hurt the business that Matty had a gorgeous wife, Jackie, who made going into the joint a rather pleasant experience all by itself. As it happens, I knew the boys, but since I brought along Johnny, the whole point of a reservation was moot, because every restaurant in town had a table ready for Carson at a moment's notice.

Johnny and I were dining with good friends Bruce Singer and Michael Hattem, enjoying the atmosphere. As usual, the place was full of celebrities, most notably Frank Sinatra, who was dining with Jilly Rizzo and Mickey Rudin. I had been through a legal war with Rudin, but we came out of that battle better friends than before. Our conversation skipped around the usual events of the day: gossip, sports, politics. Ronald Reagan had just defeated Jimmy Carter for president of the United States. Given Reagan's longtime association with Hollywood, everyone seemed to have a distinct and personal view of this development, pro or con, based on some impression formed long before Reagan ever ran for office, and even before Johnny had come to New York, when Ronnie was still acting and working for GE and was just one of the crowd you'd see around town. Johnny liked Reagan personally, and while he was scrupulous to never share a political view with his viewers — "Why lose fifty percent of my audience?" — he was by instinct and upbringing definitely Republican, but of an Eisenhower sort that we don't see much anymore: strong on integration and civil rights, skeptical of the military and war, big on personal responsibility. Overall, you'd have to say he was anti-big: anti–big government, anti–big money, anti–big bullies, anti–big blowhards. We were waiting for dessert when Matty stopped by our table and surprised us all by saying, "Bushkin, Frank would like to talk to you."

"Me?" I had met Frank a number of times, but even so, this wasn't the sort of venue where I was asked to swing by Frank Sinatra's table. (The casino owner Steve Wynn once ran a hilarious television commercial in which he welcomed Mr. Sinatra to his casino. Barely taking notice, Frank peeled off some bills and said, "Here, make sure I get enough towels." In the back of my mind, I was always ready for Sinatra to send me for towels.) But before I could lift my jaw off my chest, Johnny jumped in and said, "I'll go and say hello and see what's up."

For whatever reason, Frank Sinatra had a special effect on Carson; he made Johnny uneasy, and that often manifested itself in a kind of obsequiousness. "He . . . makes . . . you . . . nervous!" a gleeful Don Rickles razzed Johnny when Sinatra made a *Tonight Show* appearance in November 1976. Rickles was thrilled because he had at long last spotted a flaw in Mr. Effortless's persona, but nobody laughed harder than Johnny, simply because it was so obviously, undeniably true. Who knows, maybe Frank was crooning over the radio during all of Johnny's formative romantic experiences. To Johnny, Frank was and would always be the Chairman of the Board. "With my luck," he once told me, "I'll be on a plane flight with Sinatra that goes down, and the headlines will read 'Sinatra and Others Perish in Crash.'"

Johnny popped up and went to see Frank. He didn't stay more than a few minutes, and when he came back, he seemed peeved. "Why don't you go over and speak with them? Frank wants to talk about the inauguration of Reagan. It was awkward for me to be cornered like that."

So I went over, feeling slightly more ridiculous because the cat was at least partway out of the bag. Frank was cordial but he cut to the chase. "I've agreed to produce the Inaugural Gala show for President Reagan and I'd love it if Johnny would emcee the event. Carson is the best in the world for this sort of thing, and if he does it, it will be a fucking great show."

Then Rudin chimed in, making it clear that if Johnny agreed to do the show, all of the costs of the trip, which would include me and Judy and Joanna, would be covered in full. It went without saying that none of the performers would be paid for the gig, but in addition to transportation, meals, and suites at the venerable Hay-Adams Hotel, the Republican National Committee would provide tickets for any and all of the inaugural events, including the swearing-in ceremony. Of course, I would have expected no less, but it was good of Mickey to make it all clear.

Then Frank closed the presentation. "Tell Johnny," he said, "it will be a personal favor to me if he does the gig."

I felt like I had been dropped into a scene from *The Godfather.* If Frank had been wearing a ring, I suppose I would have had to kiss it. "I'll speak to Johnny and call Mickey with his answer," I said, which everyone at the table correctly interpreted as a maneuver that would entitle Johnny to say no but that would entitle Frank, if I turned out to be the messenger of bad news, to behead me.

But Frank didn't want that. What was he going to do with a lawyer's head? "Should I phone Johnny tomorrow and go over it with him again?" he said, making it clear that while Frank was giving Johnny the chance to say no, he wasn't going to let him.

"No, Frank, I'll talk to him," I said. It would have been very uncomfortable if Frank phoned Johnny and put him on the spot. Johnny would have been forced to say yes, and Johnny never liked being forced to do anything. That left me no choice: I would talk to Johnny. Certainly it was his decision whether to do the show.

Singer and Hattem were impressed by my audience with Sinatra and pumped me for details, but I could see that Johnny was in no mood to talk about work. He was enjoying himself and began to tell jokes. "Have you heard the one about the mother cooking breakfast for her kids?" Carson always had the newest jokes, but comedians always ask if you have heard the joke to make sure their punch line is secure.

"This mom calls her three sons down for breakfast," Carson continued. "She says to the oldest, 'Son, what would you like for breakfast?' He says, 'I think I'll have some fuckin' French toast.' With that, his mother slaps him across his face and sends him to his room with instructions to never use that language again. She then asks the next-oldest boy, 'Son, what would you like for breakfast?' He replies, 'I'll also have some fuckin' French toast.' His mother grabs him by the collar and sends him to his room screaming at the boy about his language. Finally she asks the youngest boy what he would like for breakfast. He thinks for a couple of moments and replies, 'I'm not sure what I want, Mom, but I sure don't want any of that fuckin' French toast.'" We all roared.

Suddenly he got serious again and brought up the time Sinatra talked to him about sharing a week of dates at Radio City Music Hall, half with Frank getting top billing, half with Johnny. It had happened a few years earlier, only then we were at Chasen's. "Remember when Frank asked me to do that date? And I agreed. And Frank asked that you work out the details with Rudin? Remember?" Of course I did. "You called Rudin and he told you the date wouldn't work. And why? Because there wasn't enough money in it for Frank."

"Right, but money's not a factor here. Everybody's working for free. So either you want to do something for the president — and even more important, for Frank — or you don't." I was realizing that Johnny was more disappointed than he'd let on that the dream pairing hadn't come off. Perhaps playing on a bill with Sinatra was a dream he didn't know he had. Anyway, we left the matter there.

After talking with Rudin the next morning, I phoned Johnny with the lowdown. "It's just what Sinatra told you last night, except the request actually came from the new president. Sinatra's producing, but you are the choice of the president-elect to host the show."

"God, January in Washington," he said, "one of America's most charmless cities in one of its most charmless months. Ronnie does know that I answered my country's call once already, doesn't he?"

That the incoming president had requested him to emcee was not taken as a compliment by Carson. He looked at this as just more work. "Ah, you barely left Nebraska," I reminded him. "And besides, it's not like he's asking you to kidnap the ayatollah or anything. I think you have to do it."

Personally I didn't much care whether Johnny did it or not, but I didn't feel like telling Sinatra no. Besides, I had a new law partner in Washington. It would give me — and him — a chance to show off.

"Who else is going to perform?"

I didn't know, although I should have expected the question. In Hollywood, stars are willing to do things if their peers are also doing them, but nobody wants to be the biggest fish in the net; it lowers your stature. "I assume things will work from the top down," I told him, hoping and believing this to be true. "If you commit, others will fall into place." With Carson headlining the bill, I was pretty sure Frank Sinatra could put together a show.

"Don't be so confident," Johnny said. "This isn't 1960."

"He's still Sinatra."

"Okay, then he's got Dean. Big deal."

"Okay, look, do you want me to tell Rudin you'll think about it?"

"No, tell Mickey I'll do it — for Frank, as a favor to Frank. But no screwups like on that Radio City deal." He threw in that along with the condition that the Inaugural Committee would have to pay for two of his writers to prepare special material for the show. Johnny was always good about getting extra money for his guys.

Before lunch, I heard from Sinatra, who called to thank me for my help, and also from Charles Wick, the cochairman of the Inaugural Committee.

Wick was a veteran agent and an occasional movie and TV producer (he was the man behind *Snow White and the Three Stooges*), who had grown close to Reagan when he was governor of California. Reportedly in line to head the United States Information Agency, he would go on to become its longest-serving director. "I can't tell you how pleased and grateful the president-elect is that Johnny has agreed to this," said the slick Wick, who was famously fond of Savile Row suits and salty humor. "We're committed to making this the very best inauguration ever. Would you mind giving me Johnny's number at NBC? I'd really like to call him and thank him personally." Johnny later told me that he was pleased by the attention.

In mid-January, Johnny and Joanna and Judy and I flew to Washington for the big weekend that would culminate with the swearing in of the new president on January 20, 1981. Yes, Judy was with me. I had the brilliant idea that this weekend would be an opportunity to see if reconciliation was possible. I loved her, but I had not been the best of husbands. We had separated in August, but over the holidays, the family feelings and sentimentality ran high, and we both had second thoughts. Johnny's big crisis with NBC was behind me, and maybe with this new company, the demands on my time wouldn't be so personal, so hands-on. We both hoped the weekend would work to help the process of getting back together.

It was bitterly cold in the capital, even for ex-Easterners, who thought they remembered what winter was like. Johnny was especially uncomfortable because he never traveled with a coat. He never bothered to even own one, no matter the city or the weather; there was always the waiting car and driver. We were met by a military attaché and two military drivers with limousines who were assigned to our party for the duration of our stay in our nation's capital. We were impressed by the attention, but we all wondered how a group of private guests warranted military chauffeurs.

We were installed at the elegant Hay-Adams Hotel, which had been named for John Hay, who had been an assistant to President Lincoln and was later secretary of state, and Henry Adams, author and direct descendant of John Adams and John Quincy Adams. The men had had adjoining townhouses opposite Lafayette Square on the site where the hotel was built. Johnny and Joanna had been given a palatial suite on the top floor with an unparalleled view of the White House. We were all finding it hard to resist feeling a bit presidential ourselves.

Very quickly we entered a social whirl. That evening, the Carsons were invited to a small dinner hosted by Ambassador Walter Annenberg (publisher of the *Philadelphia Inquirer* and the enormously profitable *TV Guide*) and his wife, Leonore. Meanwhile, Judy and I had dinner with our good friends Connie and Donald Santarelli at their home in Alexandria, Virginia. Donald was one of the partners in my firm and an important figure in Republican Party circles. The next day, while Joanna was a guest of Nancy Reagan at an exclusive party, and Judy and Connie hit the historic landmarks, Donald and the Republican Inaugural Committee honored Johnny with a luncheon at a private club.

Donald had assembled many Republican senators and congressmen who were quite anxious to meet the host of *The Tonight Show*. I was enjoying myself, meeting all of these people whose names and faces I had known only from *Time* magazine and the evening news, and I was happy that Donald was enjoying a moment in the limelight. Unfortunately we forgot the first and by far the most important rule regarding Carson and social occasions: surround him with people he likes. In trying to give Santarelli a little boost, I neglected to tell Johnny how many senators and congressmen would be present at the luncheon, and there were dozens, every one of whom wanted his moment with Johnny. This is pretty much exactly the opposite of what Johnny wanted, and he was practically coming out of his skin. "This is a goddamn three-ring circus," he said. "We have got to get the hell out of here."

His next line was hardly a surprise. "No good deed goes unpunished," he snarled. In the course of eighteen years I must have heard that line a million times. This was pure Carson, and he was letting me know that I should never have talked him into doing this event. The spectacle of politicians jockeying for autographs and photos annoyed him far more than it flattered him. "I can make some excuse and we can get out of here," I said. "Santarelli will cover you. It is your choice." His ingrained good manners took over and he stayed, but as soon as possible I got him to a more secluded spot where there was less chaos. Looking down at the seventy-five people who were queuing to meet him, he shook his head and muttered, "Can you imagine standing in line to have your picture taken with one of these guys?" It was a rhetorical question but it made Santarelli and me laugh. It was a good sign; it meant Johnny was going to stop fighting and submit to the absurdity of the situation.

Ultimately Johnny was gracious and took pictures with everyone, but afterward, in the limo, he made his unhappiness clear. "Let's never do that again," he said. But he took immense delight in recounting the scene later that day, mocking the congressmen and aping their eagerness and generally showing how much contempt he had for the whole event. His irritation was disappearing, and I was glad, but I knew him well enough to know that it was bubbling around under a thin surface. The trip had not gotten off to a great start, and I hoped nothing else would go wrong.

The next afternoon we went to Capital Centre in Landover, Maryland, for the rehearsal of the upcoming gala. Carson went through all his paces, and I made sure to show him where Joanna would be sitting so that he could acknowledge her from the stage. For a time, Sinatra, Bob Hope, and Carson were all onstage together. It was quite a treat for a fan, although not everyone was entirely thrilled. You could see Johnny was bothered, and he kept coming over to me, complaining about the performers that Sinatra booked on the show. The list included Hope, Debby Boone, Grace Bumbry, Charlton Heston, Rich Little, Dean

Martin, Donny and Marie Osmond, Ethel Merman, Charley Pride, Mel Tillis, Ben Vereen, and the United States Naval Academy Glee Club. On the whole, Johnny felt they were a little too vanilla and a little too beyond their sell-by date. "Frank can still sing but he sucks at producing," muttered Johnny.

A green room of sorts was set up, and the big boys adjourned there to have a few drinks together in private. The prospect of a Carson, Hope, and Sinatra convocation struck me as a rare and exciting event, and I horned in. I was glad that I did.

Hope kicked things off by asking if we had heard the story about Jesus playing golf with Saint Peter. "They're teeing off on the 180-yard par-three sixth hole. Saint Peter hits a perfect five iron ten feet from the cup. Jesus then shanks his five iron out of bounds and it's heading over a fence. Suddenly an eagle flies overhead, and before the ball can land in the bushes, the eagle plucks it in midair and circles the green. A moment later, the bird drops the ball directly on the green. And it rolls right into the cup for a hole in one. Saint Peter looks at Jesus and says, 'All right — are you going to play golf or are you just going to fuck around?' "

The room erupted, and when things

settled down, Sinatra took his turn. "This guy is chugging beers at the Rainbow Room," he said, referring to the famous bar and restaurant on the sixty-fifth floor of 30 Rockefeller Center. "After he puts a few away, he gets up, walks out onto the terrace, and proceeds to jump off the sixty-fifth-story balcony. The guy who had been sitting at the bar next to him is in shock. He can't believe it. Guy's just jumped off the balcony! But he ain't seen nuthin'! Five minutes later, the elevator door opens, and there's the jumper! He comes over, orders five more beers, chugs them, and then — another shock — he goes up and jumps off the balcony again. Unbelievably enough, five minutes later, the elevator opens, and once more the jumper comes back to the bar. The guy who's been sitting there drinking finally asks, 'How the hell were you able to survive two jumps from the sixty-fifth floor?'

" 'Well,' the guy says, 'when you drink beer it creates these air pockets throughout your stomach. Pretty soon you become lighter than air, and you can float like a blimp.'

" 'No shit,' says the other guy. So he orders a few beers, chugs them, walks up to the balcony, and jumps. Seconds later —

splat! He crashes into the ground below.

"The bartender turns to the first guy and says, 'You can be such an asshole when you're drunk, Superman.' "

It was a special moment, and a good overture for the big event that was to take place.

Finally Johnny took his turn. "Once there was a young couple who were very much in love. The girl became pregnant and gave birth to their first child. It was a difficult pregnancy and there were complications, and surgery was required. When it was finished and the young woman came out of the recovery room, the surgeon met with the couple. 'I have some good news and some bad news,' the doctor said. 'The good news is that you are the parents of a seven-pound baby. The bad news, I'm afraid, is that there is an abnormality. Your baby is just a head. It was born without a torso.'

"Well, the young couple was very brave, and they took their baby home, and loved it, and cared for it, and played with it. And on the baby's twelfth birthday, the doctor called. 'I have amazing news,' he said. 'A torso has been found that would be a perfect match for a head. Come in immediately, for it is ready for transplant.'

"The couple was elated, not only by the

news, but that this amazing stroke of fortune should fall on their son's birthday. They ran to his room. 'Son!' the father exclaimed. 'We have the best birthday present a boy like you could ever dream of!'

" 'Oh yeah?' said the lad, looking up from the floor. 'Well, it better not be another fucking hat!' "

Even Hope laughed.

By the time everything wrapped up, traffic was at a standstill, and the two of us thought it would be safer to hang out backstage at the facility rather than go back to the hotel and risk being trapped in traffic on our return. Johnny and I killed time playing blackjack with a minimum five-dollar bet per hand. Las Vegas rules applied for the dealer, and I kept score on a notepad. I was getting hosed. Johnny started telling Bob Hope stories. His head writers, Hal Goodman and Larry Klein, had previously worked for Hope, who was known for being one of the cheapest stars in the business.

Carson told me, "At Christmas, Hope would invite Goodman and Klein over to his home in Toluca Lake in order to give them their gifts. Hope's idea of yuletide generosity was to lead the guys to a large room filled with all of the freebies that he had received from commercial sponsors and

266

then give them their choice of whatever was in the room. 'Take whatever you like, fellows,' said Hope." Carson loved that story and laughed all the while he told it.

From there, Johnny segued into doing "cheap" jokes that had me doubled up. "You want to know how cheap Hope is?" he asked.

"How cheap?" I obliged him.

"I'll tell you how cheap he is. When Bob pulls a dollar from his pocket, it blinks at the light of day! Do you want to know how cheap Hope is?"

"How cheap?"

"Bob is so cheap that he takes off his glasses when he's not looking at anything. Do you want to know how cheap Bob Hope is?"

"How cheap?"

"Bob is so cheap that he won't buy new clothes. He's worn his suits so long, they've been in style four times!"

He then began dishing about other notorious Hollywood cheapskates such as Cary Grant and Fred MacMurray. "You know the short seventh hole at the Bel-Air Country Club? One day, when Fred was a member, he had a hole in one there. Now, you know, it's tradition — Fred's supposed to buy a round of drinks for everyone in the club.

No way Fred was going to do that. Instead he marked down a two on his card and paid each of his three playing partners $100 apiece to keep their mouths shut.

"Can you believe how cheap that son of a bitch was?" Carson laughed. He mercifully gave Cary Grant a pass on the cheap jokes.

(Johnny, by the way, was never remotely cheap. Money was of very little concern to him, and he spread it around liberally. Restaurant and hotel staffers were never disappointed when he was eating or staying in their establishment. During that weekend in Washington, I know we passed out thousands in tips and gratuities.)

I have been privy to a lot of Johnny's jokes, and I have been the butt of a lot of them, but on this occasion I was getting a command performance as he played for an audience of one. And he was hilarious. All it cost me was about seventy-five dollars in blackjack losses. The president of the United States could ask for Johnny to perform, but I was the lucky son of a bitch who saw a comic maestro one-on-one.

We were alone for about an hour before the Secret Service guys came backstage to let us know the ladies had arrived, and I went out to say hello. That evening the bejeweled

Mrs. Carson looked quite regal, and Judy looked gorgeous as well. Satisfied that everyone was happy, I returned to the Capital Centre dressing area, which normally served as the visiting team's locker room. We spent the next twenty minutes reviewing Johnny's monologue for the show, which had been written by Mike Barrie and Jim Mulholland, the *Tonight Show* team he relied on for special material. Everything was cool.

But now, surprisingly, Johnny was beginning to get a little bit anxious, and he had been so relaxed just a little while before. "I think Sinatra could have done a better job," he said, returning to the misgivings he had entertained earlier in the day. "Look who he booked — Debby Boone! Rich Little!" Never a favorite of Johnny's, Little always seemed to bring out the worst in Carson. It was beginning to dawn on him that the gala was a three-hour show, and if things started to flop, people would blame the ringmaster. Now Johnny was acting pissed.

Dean Martin arrived backstage with his agent, Mort Viner, an old tennis friend of ours. Dean, it was clear, was thoroughly plastered, with no idea where he was.

"I'm sorry, John," Dean said. "A good friend passed away and I'm in mourning."

Carson thought of Martin as a friend, and he responded with concern. "That's awful, Dean," he said. "Who died?"

"My old driver," Dean mumbled, "but I can't remember his goddamn name."

"Dean, do you know where you are?" asked Johnny, half concerned, half irritated.

Dean looked at Johnny, not comprehending. Finally he murmured, "Do you have any lamb chops?"

"Dean, I'm not the goddamn maitre d'," Johnny sputtered. "I'm hosting, for chrissakes, not serving!" Then Johnny turned to me and whispered, "Speak to Viner because I won't introduce Dean. The son of a bitch can't stand up, let alone perform."

I called Mort over and delivered the news. Despite the obvious disaster in waiting that was staring us in the face, Viner assured me that Dean would sober up the moment the TV camera's red light came on.

"Are you kidding me?" I said, stunned. "Dean hasn't even got a clue where he is. There is no way Johnny will allow Martin to perform. Not tonight. Not before this crowd, on this occasion. He'll be humiliated."

"Oh, this happens all the time," said Viner, but he knew it was a lost cause.

I told Viner we'd see how things went, but

as show time neared, Martin reeled out of the green room, followed by a cloud of Scotch and nicotine; being near him was like opening the door to a bar opposite a navy base at three a.m. "Jesus," said Johnny, "I hope he doesn't vomit on someone during my monologue."

Next Charlton Heston came in. Here was the man known for playing epic heroes, and for once the man in the room lived up to the image on the screen; he strode into the room like Moses. Heston wasn't a favorite of Johnny's; he was a little too outspoken about his politics, too given to pontification. In truth, he was also a little too conservative for Johnny's tastes. Heston famously supported the NRA, which Johnny countered on *The Tonight Show* as the plaid-wool-hat-wearing Floyd R. Turbo: "If God didn't want us to hunt, He wouldn't have given us plaid shirts; I only kill in self-defense — what would you do if a rabbit pulled a knife on you?"

Heston's job was to be part of a relay: he would introduce President-elect Reagan after Carson introduced Heston. Like the good actor he was, Heston was focused on his part. Standing in front of the mirror, checking the fit of his tux, he saw Dean Martin slumped in a chair in the corner and then refocused on his appearance without batting an eye.

Johnny sensed an opening. "I think you have a tear in your tux," he said.

"Where?" asked Heston, twisting and turning.

"In the back," said Johnny. He kept Heston twisting and turning for a bit more until the actor ripped off the jacket in order to find the renegade rip. "I must have been seeing things," said Johnny, winking.

"Heh," laughed Heston.

At about that moment, Bob Hope arrived and right away started looking for Johnny. "Here," he said, handing Carson some papers. "I've written some lines that you might like to use." From Carson's point of view, this was a sign of disrespect, an indication that the older man didn't think Johnny was up to the occasion. I guess I could see that protocol was being violated here, but Bob Hope had been entertaining presidents since FDR; maybe this was just his way of coping with being bumped down the bill.

"Aw, thanks, Bob, that's really sweet of you," Carson politely said. "The material is all set, but thanks anyway." As soon as Hope was out of earshot, Johnny started griping. "Can you imagine the nerve of the man to think that I need jokes from him?" he seethed, sotto voce.

He didn't get to gripe long. A new crisis arose. Hope couldn't find his cuff links. Distressed, he loudly searched his overnight suitcase and then made everyone in the green room stop and look around. "Here, Bob, take mine," I said, to the old man's visible relief. I was rewarded the next day when Hope returned my cuff links along with an autographed copy of his latest book.

At long last, Sinatra arrived. "Frank's here!" said Martin, momentarily reviving. "Hey, can I have some chips for the casino?"

"We're not at the casino, Dean," said Frank, evenly. He then turned to Mort Viner. "Take him out. Have him sit next to Barbara. Every once in a while we'll put him on camera."

When Johnny agreed to first do the show, there was no mention of it being televised, which was one of the reasons he agreed to forego any payment for his performance. Late in the game, however — far too late for Johnny to back out — we learned that the Republican National Committee was putting the show on ABC and was making $6 million off the deal. Then came the news that really unnerved him: Marty Pasetta was directing the broadcast of the Inaugural Gala. He was a veteran of many broadcasts of special events, notably numerous Oscar telecasts, but Johnny hated him and thought he was a hack. When Pasetta directed the 1980 Academy Awards that Johnny had hosted just nine months before, he angered Carson with the way he edited Johnny's monologue during the show. That was one area that you did not screw with when it came to Johnny. So now, besides being unhappy with the talent that had been booked, Carson was distinctly not thrilled with the director, either. He insisted that I speak with Pasetta and make him promise that he wouldn't edit the monologue. Pasetta agreed, but Johnny was not mollified. "I still don't trust the son of a bitch," he barked, "but what choice do I have?"

The gala was just okay as far as Carson was concerned. His material was well received, his performance was sharp, and he had a number of memorable lines. "This is the first administration to have a premiere" was an opener that drew a big laugh. He went on, "Mr. President, if your movies drew crowds like this, you wouldn't have had to get into politics." He kidded the new VP: "George Bush gave up public life to become vice president." He was critical of the rest of the program, unfairly so, in my estimation. From where I sat, the other performers gave characteristic performances — they were who they were — and Carson's view was colored by his general regret for having become involved in the first place. Afterward, Don Santarelli arranged for an intimate dinner party where Johnny was the guest of honor. It was held at a fabulous Italian restaurant that Donald had taken over for the evening. The food was excellent, Santarelli had arranged for a bel canto singer to entertain, and the overall atmosphere was Washington-festive chic. President Ford and his wife, Betty, stopped by, as did the head of the CIA and several ambassadors, including Walter Annenberg. Fred de Cordova and his wife, Janet, came and they had invited Jack Benny's widow, Mary Livingstone, and her escort to be their guests. At one point I turned and saw that Mrs. Benny had just lit up a joint of marijuana and was passing the fat doobie to Janet de Cordova. I was amazed that no one seemed the least bit put off. Johnny seemed happy, or at least as happy as he could when he was at a social occasion outside his element.

There was only one problem. Joanna Carson was visibly upset, scowling in anger and very near tears. At first I thought she might be unhappy because she didn't go to some of the inaugural balls. The Carsons were invited to them all, but Johnny declined to visit the mad scenes. Joanna's anger increased, and she was getting out of control. Something had to be done, so Johnny took her by the arm and led her into a private area where she began sobbing hysterically.

She said, "I'm outraged — and embarrassed — that Victoria McMahon — had better seats than me."

If Ed McMahon's wife had better seats than Joanna, it would indeed have been humiliating, and it would have nothing to do with Victoria and everything to do with the fact that Johnny was a bigger star than Ed.

"It wouldn't have happened," she explained through her sobs, "if you really cared about me."

There you had it. Joanna was humiliated, and she blamed Johnny. Johnny was pissed about everything, and he blamed me. If I hadn't been so busy boosting my friend Santarelli and had done my damn job, Joanna would have had the better seats.

So now it was my fault.

It was nine p.m., and the cherry was about to be placed atop the shit sundae. Waiters wheeled in television sets so that we could watch the tape delay of the broadcast.

Within two minutes, it became clear that Marty Pasetta had edited Johnny's monologue.

"Turn it off," said a seething Carson. "That no-good son of a bitch. He swore to me he wouldn't touch my monologue and he did. Fuck him. Turn it off." The temperature in the room turned frosty, and Janet de Cordova and Mary Livingstone could have burned bales of marijuana without elevating the mood.

It was not a good night. We returned to the hotel barely speaking, where I found that Judy was angry with me. "You're up to your same old tricks, Henry," she said, not inaccurately. "We go somewhere, and all you can think about is Johnny, Johnny, Johnny." Now I was faced with a major situation: a client who had had a bad show, a very unhappy wife, and a director that he wanted to strangle. It did, however, make me think of a very funny remark that Johnny's brother, Dick, made a few years earlier. "Put it this way — we're not Italian. Nobody in our family ever says what they really think or feel to anyone else." I didn't know whether to feel grateful for that now.

Judy and Joanna, both polite and cool, joined me at the inauguration the next day. Joanna's mood gradually improved, and she apologized to Judy and me for her break-down. Judy was sympathetic to her but less forgiving to me, and now she jumped back into her blame Henry fest, expressing her aggravation that the weekend was so stressful. The main cause of the aggravation, meanwhile, remained in the hotel room; Johnny didn't want to deal with the crowds, but more to the point, he didn't want to have anything to do with any more of the inauguration, particularly if it involved me. It was just as well; it was so cold that he would have frozen his ass off had he attended the ceremony. The women, on the other hand, had major furs that they didn't get to display that frequently; it could have been twenty degrees colder with snow, and they would have paraded their pelts.

Happily, Judy and I flew home the next morning. We were too exhausted to do any more fighting. But all the warmth that had developed over the holidays was gone, and it was clear that nothing was going to bring it back. At the airport, I didn't even offer to drive her home. I just hailed a taxi, and she looked relieved to be by herself in the back of the cab.

Meanwhile Johnny and Joanna stayed in Washington in order to visit with the president at the White House. Perhaps Reagan would salvage this disaster.

When I arrived back in my apartment, I was greeted by five messages to call Mr. Carson. When I finally reached him, he berated me. "How the hell could you let all this happen? Joanna's seats were terrible. You should have made sure she would be happy."

"Look," I said, trying to defend myself, "I did everything possible to make sure your wife was comfortable. The Inaugural Committee provided the seats. Nobody consulted me. She had seats seven rows from the stage. She was sitting with ambassadors and senators. I thought they were great seats. Are you telling me that I was supposed to say, 'Hey, good job, but tell me, where have you put Vicki McMahon?' "

"And what about this damn tour?"

"What tour?" His visit to the White House, it turned out, was just a guided tour with about ten other people. "We stayed in Washington thinking we were going to visit with the new president, and instead we got to walk around the Reagans' house. I could have had my real estate agent do that for me in Los Angeles!"

As he was talking, I was trying to imagine what had gone wrong. I had played no part in arranging the White House visit. My guess was that Johnny spoke to Frank about arranging something nice, which resulted in the fuckup.

"Look," I said, "I'm sorry Joanna is upset, but I pointed out to you where Joanna would be sitting and you were fine with that. But now she's angry and so it's my fault. I didn't know where Victoria fucking McMahon was sitting! What am I supposed to do, get the identity of everybody in the first six rows? And now somebody arranges a White House visit for you and you don't like it, and I have nothing to do with it, but because you don't like it, it's my fault?" Somehow it was dawning on me in a way that it never had before that whenever something went wrong in this man's life, I was going to take some form of crap for it. I had the sense that one or the other of us was very close to saying something that would be very hard to forget. I paused a moment and then told him I would speak to him the next day.

In a panic, I called Mickey Rudin and told him what had taken place. "You got me into this, Mickey, now you get me out. I helped you guys out and now my ass is in the wringer."

Rudin had surely received more than a few irrational phone calls in his time, and he demonstrated appropriate concern for my situation. Still, I wasn't so sure he or anybody else could fix it. Carson wanted a dog to kick, and every time he looked at me, he saw a Milk-Bone in my mouth.

I was in danger of losing the number one television client in the world. He was right: no good deed goes unpunished.

Almost immediately Charles Wick called me. He was apologetic. He was appalled. He was distressed that things had gotten so far out of control. "Henry, I promise, we will take care of this." The following day he phoned me again. "Henry, I just wanted to let you know that the president of the United States has just phoned Mr. and Mrs. Carson and apologized for the mistakes. He also extended a personal invite to join the Reagans for dinner at their home in Los Angeles on their next return trip."

And so all was forgiven. Both the Carsons were now happy, or at least seemed so. Most important, as far as I was concerned, I was still his lawyer. But I had learned a couple of lessons. One was that in this crisis, my only friends were Mickey Rudin and Charles Wick, men like me, men who were highly accomplished at what they did, but who took it as part of the job that every once in a while, deserved or not, they had to swallow shit from somebody farther up the ladder. The other lesson was that while I was hoping to boost Donald Santarelli and please Judy Bushkin, I had forgotten the lesson that had been learned by Sonny Werblin, Al Bruno, Tom Shields, Art Stark, Joanne Carson, and others: Johnny Carson was client number one, and there was no number two.

When the newly inaugurated president of the United States made the aforementioned call to soothe the wounded feelings of a talk-show host and his socialite wife, he already had much on his mind — Soviets in Afghanistan, Sandinistas in Nicaragua, the well-being of the American hostages who had just been released, a prime interest rate that stood at 20 percent. It was truly a testament to the power and prestige that Johnny had by now gained as a performer and as a person that the president called him over a minor issue of protocol. It was also a reminder that Carson's ego had grown so large that only a call like this could pacify him.

A couple of days later, while we were playing tennis, Johnny brought up the weekend. "Look, Henry, I'm really sorry about the inauguration. Joanna pushes the right buttons and I go off. What the fuck do I do?"

I don't know if he wanted me to respond as his friend or his lawyer, but I still wasn't feeling that friendly. "It's totally fucked up between the two of you," I said, pointing out the obvious. "On again! Off again! A week at the hotel. A hunk of jewelry to apologize. Do you like the drama? You say you don't, but here you are. I thought Washington might be a new start for Judy and me. It was awful. I paid her no attention. And now, on Joanna's suggestion, she's retained that warmonger Arthur Crowley to file against me. The weekend was a complete disaster."

My words hung in the air without reply and eventually evaporated.

TEN:
1972–1980: VEGAS

This seems like an appropriate time to pause in the chronological telling of this tale, and the reason is simple: while Johnny and I enjoyed our usually friendly, sometimes stressful business relationship in Los Angeles and New York, we also lived in a parallel universe. Several times a year we left the real world and transported ourselves for days and sometimes weeks at a time to the fantasy world of Las Vegas.

Johnny Carson was the first person I ever met who lived in luxury. Even at first, when he was mired in bad deals and cut off from most of his income, he still lived in a splendid apartment, had a magnificent wardrobe, and dined out every night. Later, accessorized with the Rolls-Royce and the white Corvette and the luxurious Malibu mansion, he lived even more sumptuously. But never, and nowhere, was Johnny more pampered, more doted upon, more satisfied, and freer to explore and indulge the far boundaries of his Johnnyness than when he went to Las Vegas. It was his Shangri-la.

One of the things that surprised me when I first got to know Johnny was how often he went on the road. You might think that a television host who did five ninety-minute shows a week and earned a seven-figure salary would be content to enjoy some time off. But Johnny, like many entertainers, really preferred to work. He didn't want to go home. Domestic life bored him. His children challenged him with responsibilities that he didn't want. And for a while, until we undid the Werblin mess, he needed the cash flow. Besides, he didn't like relaxing all that much. Indeed, one of the challenges of vacationing with him was keeping him occupied.

He liked performing. He liked being onstage, being the center of attention, and doing something he did with supreme excellence. Doing stand-up was a different experience than performing on TV: no cameras separating him and his audience, no commercials interrupting the pace. Plus, there were other attractions. He liked hanging with the guys. He liked the excitement of being with new women. Being on the road stimulated him. It relaxed him. It freed him.

After he moved to Los Angeles, club dates around the country became a smaller part of his itinerary, and Las Vegas filled his remaining time. Most years he spent as many as ten weeks of his *Tonight Show* "vacation" working Vegas. And I use the term "working" pretty loosely: apart from some new jokes containing contemporary references that were fitted in, the act never changed, but Carson made the audience believe everything he was saying was fresh. There was, of course, no incentive to change: in all my years with him, there was never an empty seat in any show room where he performed. Johnny was the King of the Counts; of all the performers at the Sahara, Carson was their number one star.

Most people go to Vegas to pursue a fantasy: an ideal of glamour, luxury, easy money, entertainment, and forbidden pleasures. Sometimes they find it, sometimes they don't. But if you're a headliner in a premier Strip hotel, that fantasy is guaranteed to be fulfilled. For all intents and purposes, the indulgences are part of your compensation. When you headline Vegas, anything that is not explicitly in your contract is unmistakably written between the lines.

Once we redid Johnny's contract with NBC in 1971, Carson didn't need Las Vegas anymore, at least not financially. Most of the other entertainers who headlined the hotels and casinos did depend on Vegas as a primary source of income. The casinos could afford to be generous because entertainment was a loss leader, a cost that was carried as part of the business of separating gamblers from their money.

Johnny's original Vegas home was the Sahara. He would work the main room there six to ten weeks a year, doing two shows per evening. In those days he was making roughly $3,000 per show or $40,000 per week. That was a lot of money by early-seventies standards, but in time his pay would increase dramatically. Johnny appreciated the money, of course, but he paid little attention to it. Jack Benny might have been the comedian who had most influenced Carson stylistically, but the notorious skinflint had no effect on Johnny's attitude toward finances.

More than money, Vegas offered Johnny certain things you couldn't get at home in quite the same form. Pampering, of course. And a surprisingly controlled social atmosphere. Most places Johnny would go in Las Vegas had security that would isolate him from the curious and intrusive, but there were also a lot of places where Johnny could be in public in Vegas and be let alone. If he felt social, there were always a lot of comedians and musicians and other people in whose company he felt comfortable, and if he wanted to be alone, he was Batman in the Batcave, with all the privacy he could desire.

The house the Sahara provided was a good-size residence with multiple bedrooms, but Johnny never liked sharing quarters, so I stayed at the hotel. He liked his solitude, plus his visitors could come and go in privacy. There was never a shortage of women who visited.

Unlike a lot of Las Vegas headliners, Carson usually didn't mix in the social scene. Most of the entertainers lived in one of the sumptuous suites in the hotel where they were performing, and they could often be seen hanging with the high rollers and gambling at the tables. But Carson preferred to stay in a home owned by the hotel on the grounds of the Las Vegas Country Club. He lived something resembling a down-to-earth, regular domestic existence there.

Although the Sahara staff always stocked the place, there was usually something unexpected Johnny had a taste for, and off we would go to Smith's Food King supermarket on Tropicana and Paradise Roads, and stand in line with our groceries with the rest of the customers, who almost always were very cool.

Like Beverly Hills in the fifties and sixties, it wasn't unusual in Vegas to see the stars in department stores, buying ice cream cones, or taking their kids to school. The locals left the stars alone, and somehow most of the guests in the casinos grasped that they shouldn't ask for autographs. Once we were in line at the register at Food King, and the customer in front of us caught a glimpse of Johnny. "Oh my God!" she said. "What are you doing here?"

Johnny shrugged. "I needed peanut butter."

Life during show season had its routines and its rhythms. Opening night was always on a Thursday. Normally Johnny worked when *The Tonight Show* was on hiatus, but on rare occasions he'd be doing both and would commute by air between Las Vegas and Burbank. Headliners usually worked two shows a night, at eight p.m. and ten p.m. The time between shows was generally very boring. One of my "jobs" was to stay in the dressing room with Johnny during this interval and keep him occupied. Indeed, the only reason he brought me along on all these trips was to keep him company; I was like all those guys on *Entourage,* except there was only me. And while it usually wasn't hard to keep Johnny company, managing that one hour between shows was surprisingly difficult. I think it had to do with energy levels — he had been up for the first show; he would have to be up for the second show; he couldn't afford to relax in between or do anything that would tire him or take the edge off. If we were lucky, there would be something on television to watch. If not, I would try to get him something to eat from the House of Lords, the Sahara's gourmet restaurant. Sitting in a small dressing room with nothing to say can be a killer. "Let's not get like Dean Martin and Mort Viner," I said. "I don't know how those two guys can have dinner every night and not say a word to each other. They sit like two old ladies."

"If we get like that," he replied, "take out a gun and shoot me." But it never got that bad.

■ ■ ■ ■

Another regular who helped man the dressing room was Stan Irwin, a key figure in the Carson visits to Vegas, someone who knew how to drive away boredom.

Stan was the essence of old-time American-style show business. Born into a vaudeville family, Irwin had experience in every area of the business. He had been a writer, an actor, a comedian, and an impresario.

Early in his career, Stan worked the hotels and resorts in the Catskill Mountains — Grossinger's, Kutsher's, the Concord (where Carson performed), and Brown's (Jerry Lewis's old stomping ground). The Catskills were affectionately known as the Jewish Alps or the Borscht Belt. It was where all comedians of a certain age cut their teeth and honed their craft. It was where Irwin became good friends with another comedian named Jack Roy. Both struggled. The two were drinking one night and decided that things could not get any worse for them, so they traded acts. Jack Roy took Irwin's act and then changed his name to Rodney Dangerfield, the name of an obscure character on an episode of Jack

Benny's show. The rest is history.

Irwin produced *The Tonight Show* for two years in the mid-sixties before Art Stark, and then he left to become vice president and executive producer of the Sahara-Nevada Corporation, where he presided over the hotel's attractions for almost two decades. Knowing the requirements of every show business job helped him, but the real key to his longevity was that he recognized big talent when he saw it and had the guts to back it.

In 1964 every one of the Vegas resorts rejected the idea of bringing the Beatles to the Strip; they wanted patrons who were over twenty-one, not screaming teenagers. Never a victim of groupthink, Stan believed that a Beatles appearance couldn't help but benefit the Sahara, the Strip, and ultimately the city of Las Vegas. He booked the band into the Sahara's Conga Room. Very quickly the demand for tickets swamped capacity, and he switched the venue to the Las Vegas Convention Center, which ordinarily sat 7,000. Irwin promptly reconfigured the seating to admit another 1,400.

The band stayed at the Sahara, and the predictable pandemonium ensued, with teenage girls popping up everywhere shouting, "I love you, Ringo!" When the Beatles had to get into their cars to drive from the Sahara to the convention center, Stan and other Sahara personnel had to lock arms to form a human barrier between delirious fans and the Beatles. Only when he felt the surging humanity at his back did Irwin realize that they were holding back a pubescent tsunami. Stan and the Sahara profited handsomely from his gut call.

Another important member of Johnny's Vegas circle was Jack Eglash, entertainment director of the Sahara and Carson's bandleader. Jack was one of the major figures in the history of modern Las Vegas. Starting in 1950, Eglash played in dozens of bands and orchestras, and served as the conductor for many legendary acts. Eventually Eglash became a key lieutenant to Del Webb, one of the moguls who helped build Las Vegas. Jack handled the bookings and talent negotiations for all of Webb's casino properties in the United States. Noted for an off-the-wall sense of humor, Eglash, a big guy with drooping deep-set eyes, had the perfect personality and authority to manage the performers, their agents, and their families, all of whom Jack had to keep happy. Among the most demanding was the great Judy Garland, who often needed to be hypnotized before she would take the stage. Jack's hypnotist on call? Stan Irwin.

In general, Stan and Jack made it a point to be around during the break between shows. When the task was to keep Carson up for his next performance, the prescription was to pack the dressing room with friends. Civilians were seldom admitted, but headliners like Tom Jones, Dean Martin, and Sammy Davis Jr. were always welcome, if only for a few minutes. Stan Irwin was a master at managing these audiences, deftly ushering the celebrity in and then even more adroitly shuffling him out. Usually five minutes was the maximum even the biggest star would be permitted to stay.

The very first time I was ever in Vegas, I had flown in to talk with Johnny about the prenuptial agreement that Trugman and I had prepared for his upcoming marriage to Joanna. On my first night in town, Johnny arranged for a special booth for Trugman, me, and Bud and Cece Robinson to see Elvis Presley perform at the International Hotel, and I couldn't have been more thrilled.

The next night I caught Johnny's first show. Before the performance, he told me to come backstage right after the show, and I could meet Elvis. It seemed that Elvis would be catching Johnny's show from the wings, which was the only way he could ever see someone else perform. Think about it. No superstar could ever sit in a show room surrounded by unknowns.

Almost as soon as I got backstage, Jack Eglash announced that Presley was on his way. Amazing.

The King came up in one of his classic white rhinestone-encrusted jumpsuits with a matching cape. Without missing a beat, Johnny asked if he could try on the cape. "You know I've got this clothing line, right?" Elvis nodded in apparent agreement, being polite without quite knowing where this fast-talking Yankee was going. "We've never tried suits with capes before," Johnny said. "Can I have the name of your tailor?"

Elvis laughed. "Son of a bitch, Johnny, I can't do that. The cape is mine. How else will people know who I am?"

Johnny laughed, and then Elvis continued. "Hey, I hear Freddy de Cordova is now your producer. That son of a bitch directed me in *Frankie and Johnny*. I liked that cat a lot. Maybe I'll come visit the show one day."

"That would be great," said Johnny, "although remember not to come on a Thursday. That's my bowling night!"

"I'll keep that in mind." Elvis laughed and

then bid his adieu. "Hey, I loved the show. Got me a date with a casino hostess who my boys are keeping busy till I finish my visit here. Loved the show."

I don't believe Elvis ever made it on the show. Years later, Carson would make a remark that has become one of his most quoted lines. "If life were fair, Elvis would be alive and all the impersonators would be dead."

Johnny always had an opening act, usually a female singer. His favorite was the very pretty Phyllis McGuire. She and her sisters, Christine and Dorothy, became known as the McGuire Sisters, one of the top singing acts of the fifties, whose hit recordings included "Sincerely" and "Sugartime." Once a very close personal friend of the mob boss Sam Giancana, Phyllis was then the girlfriend of an oil wildcatter named Edward "Mike" Davis, who owned Tiger Oil Company based in Houston, Texas. One reason Johnny liked working with Phyllis is that she would fly to the site of the engagement in Mike's Gulfstream, and then send the plane to Los Angeles to pick up Johnny and me.

Johnny had other openers as well. One day, Johnny got the idea to ask the great drummer Buddy Rich and his band to open for him. Buddy was Johnny's favorite musician and, with his technique, speed, power, and ability to fashion incredible solos, was arguably the greatest drummer of his generation. Being a drummer himself, Carson was in awe of Rich's style and command of the instrument. A set of drums given to Johnny by Buddy was positioned prominently and proudly in his home for years — and when I was able to reach an agreement with Buddy's manager, who happened to be his daughter, Cathy, Johnny was thrilled.

Buddy opened and was as brilliant as always. He was delivering the goods for Carson's show, just as we had anticipated. And, better yet, Johnny got to hang out with him, a guy he greatly admired. There was only one problem. Johnny was slightly unhappy with the length of Buddy's act on opening night. The customary arrangement, which almost everybody seemed to understand, was that the opening act performed for about thirty minutes and the main attraction worked about ninety. Rich stayed on for forty minutes; Carson felt that was too long. "An opener is supposed to warm up the audience," he said, "not make people restless. See what you can do." I asked Cathy to speak with her dad to cut ten minutes.

During the runup to the second show, we were in the dressing room listening through the speakers to Buddy's hopefully shorter act. Johnny, always fastidious, abhorred creases, and never sat down once he got dressed for a performance. It took him ten minutes to put on his tuxedo and formal shirt with French cuffs and studs, and he and his valet, Jim Brown, had decided to use the start of Rich's *West Side Story* medley, which was his twelve-minute-long closing number, as his cue to get dressed.

We were sitting there chatting when Buddy began his set. The speakers were on low and we weren't paying much attention. Then after a few minutes, Jim said, "Wait — listen!"

"Holy shit," said Johnny, "he's opening with his closing number!" Sure enough, Buddy had cut the act — by more than two-thirds down to twelve minutes. Fortunately, Johnny got dressed and appeared on cue without missing a beat. After the show, we learned that Buddy, indignant at his reduced time, had quit. I'm told Buddy appeared several more times on Johnny's show, but the relationship was never the same.

With Buddy gone, we quickly needed another opener. As it turned out, the ideal replacement was right at hand. The Sahara Girls, a group of beautiful singers and dancers who had been performing as a lounge act, would certainly put the audience in a good mood for Johnny in the main show room. The girls were thrilled since Johnny decided to pay them double what they were making in the lounge. To be more precise, Johnny decided that the hotel would pay them double.

Another benefit to this change of acts was that Mr. Carson now had twelve gorgeous new friends. Joanna could not have been pleased with the nightly proximity of such dazzling temptation, but that was the thing about Vegas: there weren't a lot of limits on a headliner in Vegas, but there was one rule.

No wives or girlfriends in the hotel or casino.

You never saw a wife on the Strip. It never happened. It just wasn't done. Maybe Steve Lawrence got a pass when he performed with Eydie Gormé. Even if you were one of the headliners who lived in Vegas, your wife was provided with a sprawling mansion out in the sand to preside over, but she would never visit the hotel. Maybe the protocol was influenced by the old mobster tradition that is part of the DNA of Vegas, the one that dictates that family and work be strictly segregated, but it was made clear early, often, and explicitly that this was the custom on Las Vegas Boulevard: whatever you had to do, leave the wife out. Of course, special occasions were different. Wives and special friends were always expected to attend certain events such as important opening nights and charity events. But they weren't expected back.

By the end of the week, the Sahara Girls had so exceeded expectations that Johnny had me give the manager of the girls an additional $10,000 for their work. Meanwhile, he had taken up with one of the lovely young ladies, which put him in a tremendous mood. As for Joanna? "Out of sight, out of mind," Johnny said with a shrug.

By this time I had been Johnny Carson's consigliere for several years. He was still the star and the boss, of course, but the social disparity between us had considerably narrowed. I had been elevated somewhat, in the way Henry II of England had raised up Thomas à Becket. And as with Becket, the king wanted this Henry — Henry Bushkin — to join him in his frolics and his sport. Johnny encouraged me to pick a play companion out of the chorus line. And it was clear he wasn't going to be happy until I did. He wanted a partner in sin, and soon enough, I acquiesced. Thereafter, while on the road at the Sahara, there was feminine company constantly available for me. This was entirely normal for a star of Carson's magnitude playing Vegas, but it was not normal at all for a kid from the Bronx. If Johnny was conflicted by any of this, he never showed it. But while I won't claim I was having an entirely awful time gamboling with a few of the most beautiful women in America, the Faustian pact that this entailed put a serious strain on my real life and my marriage.

When the performances ended, the night began. For many headliners, that's when cards, dice, and roulette wheels joined the scene. But neither Johnny nor I liked gambling, so the casino presented little allure. Instead, most of the time after the second show we hung out at the lounge that overlooked all the action. These were some of our best times in the desert. A special table was always waiting there for Johnny, and the waitresses greeted him effusively. We considered them friends — friends whom we tipped generously.

Carson's arrival always ignited the room. You could hear the buzz rise and spread throughout the hall. Within minutes, you could see people in the casino edging closer and closer, trying to get a look at Carson and the celebrities who often accompanied him. The civilians would creep all the way to the rail to try to get his attention, and usually for the first few minutes he would be gracious and accommodating, chatting and signing autographs. Once this became a chore, security guards stepped in and prevented further intrusions.

At his lounge table, Johnny would hold court. Irwin, Eglash, and I were mainstays, with invited guests enlivening the mix. A few hotel executives might gain admission, maybe a few of the right NBC people, other stars who were performing in town, and most important, other comedians, both household names and less-well-known "comedian's comedians" as well.

The scene created at these gatherings was beyond anything I have ever experienced, even in Vegas, before or since. Everyone in attendance was supposed to bring new material, and Carson was no exception. Johnny told jokes brilliantly, and armed with great material and freed from television censors, he was hilarious, and he always held his own in the unofficial contest to see who could deliver the night's topper. Had someone chronicled these conclaves, they would be as celebrated as the witty luncheons that took place at the Algonquin Round Table. These were the funniest moments of my life, and I'm pretty sure they were among the happiest of Johnny's.

These sessions often lasted until three or four a.m. or however long it took Johnny to come down off the high of performing in front of a live audience. I was usually ready to drag my exhausted self to bed, but often Johnny was ready to soldier on. Even more than the company of comedians, Carson loved being around musicians, and he often invited everyone back to his house where he and some of the members of the band would play jazz — with Johnny on drums — often until daybreak.

The journalist Betty Rollin, writing in *Look* magazine in 1966, described Carson as "withdrawn, and wondrously inept and uncomfortable with people." And he often was. But I wish all those who only knew Johnny as shy or cold could have seen him at these occasions. They would have seen him enjoying the company of other people and having the time of his life. You probably can guess how Johnny and I whiled away whatever time remained between rising and show time: tennis. One late afternoon, we went to play on a court at Caesars Palace.

We were in the middle of a set when a couple approached to say hello. Johnny politely offered his greetings and went back to the game. As we played, we could hear the loud electric motor on the man's camera whirring away.

After a while, we changed sides, and Carson courteously asked the gentleman to finish with his pictures and move on. The couple left, but in fifteen minutes they were back, with the camera once again clicking away. Johnny walked calmy over to the guy — who happened to be quite a bit bigger — and said, "Look, I told you to cut out the camera crap. If you take one more picture, I'm going to take that camera and shove it up your ass — sideways." This time when the couple departed, they did not return. In all of our time in Las Vegas, this was the only unpleasant incident on the courts.

The other tennis venue that Johnny and I both loved was at Phyllis McGuire's house in Las Vegas. Her tennis pavilion was fully equipped with racquets, balls, and even tennis outfits. The staff was always available to assist. Phyllis was a great friend to Johnny and her house offered a refuge when he needed to "hide out." There were many rumors about a relationship between Johnny and Phyllis, but if it was true, both of them were too discreet ever to let on. Johnny really did like her, and many times he wound up staying at her house for the night. It had 65,000 square feet, featured a seventy-foot replica of the Eiffel Tower, and had steel shutters that could be lowered in the event of a nuclear attack. It was the largest home in Vegas at that time. There was plenty of space for Johnny to get lost in.

In 1976, after many happy years of Carson playing the Sahara Hotel, Cliff Perlman, the chairman of the board of Caesars Palace, called me and asked if Johnny was interested in making a switch. "Johnny should definitely come here," he argued. "We have a much bigger show room, and we're getting all the biggest acts. No reason for you to be the last of the Mohicans."

Johnny had played the Congo Room in the Sahara since the sixties, and he was its top draw. It had a capacity of about 700, and Johnny always sold out. "Look, Cliff, the Congo Room is known as a comedy room and gets all the best comedians because it is a great size for comedy. Your show room seats nearly 1,300. Carson is concerned about filling all the seats."

"Don't worry about that," said Perlman. "Your man is a major star. We will promote the hell out of the switch."

As predicted, when Johnny and I talked about the move, the size of the room was paramount among his considerations. "What do you think?" he asked.

In the meantime, I had done some research. "Sinatra and Bette Midler and Paul Anka are all doing well. I know they're not comedians, but Caesars is putting fannies in the seats."

After mulling over the move for a few days, Johnny came back to me with terms. "I don't want to play full weeks anymore, just three nights a week. And I only want to do one show a night. If they're agreeable and the money is right, I'll consider going." His idea was that he could fly forty minutes from Burbank to Vegas after the Thursday *Tonight Show* finished taping and play Caesars on Thursday, Friday, and Saturday nights. We also asked for Caesars to pay for Jack Eglash and his band, to provide the plane that would take Johnny between Burbank and Vegas, to pay for the opening act of Carson's choice, and, oh yeah, to pay Johnny $250,000 for each weekend. Perlman hemmed and hawed and rubbed his temples. "We've never done anything like this before," he said.

I wasn't surprised. The men who make

their living off the illusions of gamblers seldom take risks themselves. "Don't worry about it," I said. "Johnny has plenty of work at home to keep him busy."

"Aw hell, let's do it." Perlman wanted Carson. It was a sure thing.

I was pretty pleased with the terms — eight weekends a year for a tasty $2 million. But the money was not the deciding factor: for Johnny it was the challenge. "I might as well play at the best hotel on the Strip," Johnny said. "Let's see how I do against Sinatra's counts." In the end, the major regret was that he had to leave behind the Sahara Girls.

There was a sentimental aura surrounding Johnny's last gig at the Sahara. As was our custom, we arrived the night before in order for him to soak up the atmosphere. We were in high spirits when we arrived at the airport, but as soon as we saw Jim Brown in the car, we could tell that he was upset.

"There was a problem last night with Buddy," said Jim, referring to Buddy Hackett, who was preceding Johnny in the Congo Room. It appeared that Buddy, who almost always finished in second place behind Johnny in the counts, had dropped into third place behind Totie Fields. For those who do not remember, Totie Fields was a

short, stout, hilarious woman whose stardom was cut short in her fifties when she
died from heart problems and cancer.

"Buddy got wasted last night," reported
Jim. "Out of nowhere he pulled a .38-caliber
pistol and began shooting up the dressing
room. He shot Totie . . ."

"He shot Totie?!" Carson and I exclaimed.

"Well, you know, her picture . . ."

Johnny ended his run at the Sahara in
spectacular fashion. The crowds were wildly
enthusiastic, and there wasn't a seat to be
had. The Sahara Girls opened, followed by
Phyllis McGuire. Mike Davis asked Stan
Irwin to hold twelve seats for him and he
brought a group of oil execs up from Houston for the last show. Davis arrived and
tipped the maitre d' a cool $1,000. There
was a great party that the hotel threw for
Johnny at the Sahara house where he stayed.
The band came over. Johnny played the
drums and the Sahara Girls romped by the
pool. I left at five a.m. God knows when
Carson got to bed.

Several months later, it was time for the
opening at Caesars Palace. Acquiring
Johnny Carson was a major get for Caesars,
and to show just how pleased and proud he
was with this new arrangement, Cliff Perl-

man told Johnny that he could invite as many guests as he wanted, and the hotel would pick up the tab for their room, food, and beverages for the entire weekend. In addition, each couple or single guest was instructed to turn their airline receipts in at the casino cage where they would be given the equivalent amount in casino chips.

The occasion was a big deal for Johnny as well; he had invited more than 350 guests to what had become a black-tie event (the 900 or so paying customers who were going to attend would have to wear black tie as well). Carson's parents were coming, as were his brother and his sister and their spouses; so were important people from *The Tonight Show* like Bobby Quinn, Ed McMahon, and Fred de Cordova; Bud and Cece Robinson; many Hollywood notables; and even my parents and Judy's parents. It was going to be a very big night.

To make sure that everything was going smoothly, I went up to Las Vegas several days before the opening and brought my secretary, Carrie Becker, to help make sure that all of the invited guests were properly cared for. What I found was pretty close to perfection. The promotion was first-rate, and the town was buzzing. Cliff Perlman and the entire staff at the hotel had done a great job. But these black-tie events were hardly the norm, and even Johnny was nervous. After all, it was a new place, and the show room was much bigger. He still wasn't sure that his comedy would extend to its far reaches. He always said it was easier for singers to work big places than comedians.

The plan was for Johnny to fly up by himself the day before the opening; Joanna would come the next day with a group of friends. In those days, private jets were less common than today, and Johnny was coming in on a commercial flight. Ordinarily I would have gone to the airport to meet him, but I was busy in the show room dealing with seating details and watching Phyllis rehearse, so I sent Caesars' limo driver to pick him up at the airline gate. Johnny's plane was due in at one p.m., and when two o'clock came and went, I began to be concerned. This was long before cell phones, but the hotel had walkie-talkies that it used for communication, and I kept checking with the desk to determine if the driver had picked up its new headliner. Four times I called without the clerk being able to tell me anything. Now I was worried.

Finally I went out to the bell desk to see what was going on. To my surprise, I ran into Johnny, who had just exited a cab. He was standing at the check-in counter demanding the keys to his suite. "The driver completely fucked up," he fumed. "He went to the wrong goddamn gate and by the time he found me, I told him to get lost and I hopped in a cab."

At that moment, the check-in clerk advised Johnny that he would have to wait about thirty minutes before his suite was ready.

When this happens to you or me, we're expected to act like grown-ups and adjust. But when this happens to the biggest star in Vegas, who was arriving for his debut performance at what is supposedly the town's premier hotel, well, this, ladies and gentlemen, is what we call a catastrophe.

Carson went nuts. He started yelling at the clerk, who very politely excused herself and walked away. Later we learned that most of the hotel employees were of the Mormon faith and had been taught to walk away from rude behavior, but it struck Johnny as insulting.

"Damn it, Henry," Carson said. "Charter me a plane and get me back to Los Angeles. I will not work here."

"You know there are 350 invited guests on their way here," I reminded him. "Homer? Ruth?"

"I don't give a shit," he snapped. "I won't spend one minute more with these monumental incompetents."

The hotel general manager arrived and tried to make things right. A new suite was ready, a distressed and apologetic Jerry Gordon, the hotel's general manager, assured Johnny; the management could not be more anxious to please this unhappy star.

"Too late!" snarled Johnny. He was angry, but I also thought he was being self-indulgent. I was beginning to wonder how long he was going to continue to carry on. Then I got a call from Cliff Perlman.

"Henry, please bring Johnny up to my suite. I promise you I won't let him walk because of the fuckups of my staff. Please, please bring him up. Security will be there in a moment to escort you up."

"Okay, Cliff, but let me just say this: right now Johnny needs to feel as if he were the only star you have."

"Okay," said Cliff. "I get it."

I then talked Johnny into seeing Cliff. "That's the least you owe him." And up we went.

Once Carson entered the suite, the Perlman charm took over. He took Carson by the arm and showed him the apartment. Sitting atop the hotel, it was 10,000 square feet of opulence, with a rooftop swimming pool, Jacuzzi, wine cellar, health spa, six bedrooms, and a living room that was easily able to accommodate 300 people.

"Every time you come to Caesars," said Perlman, "this is where you'll stay."

"Nice," said Johnny, now notably calmer. "But I don't see a tennis court up here."

"No, it's downstairs. But you know that our head pro is Pancho Gonzales," said Cliff, invoking the name of one of the greatest players of the pre-Open era. "Any time you want to hit with him, it's on me."

"Thank you, Cliff."

"You know," said Perlman, closing the deal, "I've never let anyone stay up here, not even Sinatra. But I owe this to you as a show of my appreciation for your working here."

The grand gesture appeased Johnny, the weekend was saved, and from then on, whenever Carson came to Caesars, Perlman moved to a Motel 6 across town. Well . . . at least to quarters less grand.

Later that day Johnny met one of the casino hosts, Wingy Grober. Short, elegant, and very funny, Wingy was so named because he had a withered arm. "I'm taking you guys to dinner tonight," he said. A friend of Sinatra's and a former owner of the Cal-Neva Hotel in Lake Tahoe, Grober had been given Johnny as an assignment by Perlman, who felt Wingy could handle Carson's mood swings. Wingy soon became one of Johnny's favorites and was given the high honor of free access to the Carson dressing room. That night Wingy introduced Johnny to Jimmy Grippo, the legendary magician. Johnny became an instant fan of the eighty-year-old Grippo, a master of verisimilitude with his hands. Johnny pulled out all the stops with his own tricks in an effort to top the master. After a while, everyone was standing around watching all the fun at our table. A great evening was had by all.

Johnny's opening was magical. The reviews were first-rate, and the opening-night party was held in what was now known as the Carson Suite. The memory of Carson's tantrum evaporated in a haze of good cheer.

Several years later, the casino impresario Steve Wynn offered to double what Caesars was paying Johnny to move to the Golden Nugget. When I advised Johnny that Wynn was offering $500,000 a weekend, he was flattered but unmoved. "I don't need it," he said. "The room at the Nugget is very small, and I'll be playing to what amounts to an invited audience each show. Invited guests make for lousy audiences. Tell Steve thanks, but I'll pass." That was that.

By now you should not be surprised to hear that a major Las Vegas headliner, accustomed to receiving limitless perks and privileges, would conclude that among his entitlements is droit du seigneur. You may not be acquainted with this principle, but if you were alive during the Middle Ages, believe me, you would have heard of it. Allegedly it was the legal right allowing the lord of an estate to take the virginity of his serfs' maiden daughters. There is actually little historical evidence that supports the idea that such a legal right actually existed, but it has been strongly maintained in legend and, in many places, in practice. Johnny had for all intents and purposes exercised a contemporary version of this in his New York life when his *Tonight Show* stardom made him very prominent, and his separation from Joanne made him even more obviously available. Rather than just being a garden-variety hound, Johnny had the pick of the litter.

When home in Los Angeles, and now married to Joanna, he had to be much more circumspect. But in the environs of a Las

Vegas hotel, a free-fire zone where no wives were allowed, it was generally accepted that the bigger the star, the greater the latitude for indiscretion.

Early in 1980, Johnny was playing Caesars. Despite the fact that we were at that very time deep in the endgame of ABC-NBC negotiations, I still had to accompany Johnny to Vegas. Both of us were quarreling with our wives. I had by that point fallen into terrible habits. I was inattentive to Judy, I was routinely messing around, and we had separated several times. For this trip, as was often the case, I had arranged a date for the weekend, a young lady named Susan. I was far beyond being influenced by Johnny; I was by now well along into emulating him, and though I was conflicted and unhappy about where this was taking me, I made little effort to change.

The Thursday show, as usual, went off well, and afterward Johnny and I went to the Caesars lounge, where we were joined by Jack Eglash, Stan Irwin, his old pal Rodney Dangerfield, and Jimmy Grippo. Along with being a master of magic, Grippo astounded his audience with his apparent ability to read minds and induce hypnosis. By three in the morning our table had a large group of onlookers. Two of them were very good-looking girls, and Carson asked them to join our party. Soon we learned that they were from Nebraska, and they had come all the way just to see his show. Of course, Johnny invited them to come to Friday's show as his special guests. In his accustomed role, Stan Irwin made all the arrangements. He put them with my friend Susan and me.

Meanwhile, at home I had a son and daughter. And here I was in Las Vegas, blithely behaving like a complete shit. I was definitely Carson's protégé now. He loved who I was becoming.

The next day Johnny called to make sure the girls would be coming to the show. "Maybe they would like to join us at a small dinner party afterward," Johnny suggested, "up in my apartment." They were more than delighted to accept, and Mr. Carson attended to those details personally. Cliff Perlman had one thousand bottles of wine in his cellar, and Johnny availed himself of some of the best. The kitchen prepared a special menu subject to Johnny's personal approval.

After the show, I took the girls backstage for a few minutes to say hello to the star. They were then escorted to the suite while I sat with Johnny for forty-five minutes until he could descend from his performance high. Wingy Grober was with us. "If there is anything special that you want tonight," Wingy assured him, "the staff of Caesars Palace, as always, awaits your pleasure."

There were five of us at dinner. Susan and the Cornhusker girls soon became very drunk, while I was suddenly overcome by an excruciating headache. "Hold the fort," I whispered to Johnny. "I'm going back to my room for some painkillers."

Several pills and a hot shower later, I felt well enough to go back to the party. To my surprise, the three girls were skinny-dipping in the rooftop swimming pool, while Johnny, wearing nothing but an apron, served them wine from a silver platter. "Ze white is a 1968 Chassagne-Montrachet," he said in a cheesy accent plucked from the Mighty Carson Art Players, "and ze rhedd is a 1966 Pétrus." I was impressed; that Pétrus went for $3,000 a bottle.

"Come on, Henry," Johnny shouted. "Take off your clothes! Join the fun!"

Well, I did take off my clothes and I did try to join in, but something in the bacchanalian nature of the moment brought my headache back. Unable to enjoy myself, I had to leave. No one else did, not even Susan, the girl I'd brought with me, although I assumed she'd follow me back to our room soon enough.

My head had hardly hit the pillow before I fell asleep.

When I woke up the next morning, I looked around for Susan, but she wasn't in bed with me or in the room. She had spent the night partying with Johnny and the Cornhuskers.

I was humiliated. I was resentful. I was really pissed.

But it served me right. And besides, I wasn't sure if I was furious with Susan or myself. At that point, the difference was pretty much academic. When Susan finally came to my room I told her to get her things together and clear out. It had been the perfect way to fuck up a weekend and I had managed to do it perfectly. Johnny, who could rarely be accused of uncool behavior, never said a word about the previous night. But I had learned my lesson. You could ape Johnny's way of living. In fact, he pretty much insisted on it. But Johnny owned the game. The rules favored him. In Vegas, the house always won.

A few years later, something similar happened, although it came to a different conclusion. In the early eighties, Joanna

Carson introduced me to Joyce DeWitt, the vivacious and raucous dark-haired beauty who was then starring in ABC's hit comedy *Three's Company.* Joyce needed some legal advice, and Joanna recommended me. Some months later, Joyce, who had a background in musical theater, was looking to develop a nightclub act, and I was happy to send her to Jack Eglash, who began helping her create a song-and-dance routine in the style of Ann-Margret. As it happened, Joyce was in Vegas one weekend rehearsing with Eglash when Johnny came up to perform at Caesars.

By this time, my marriage was on its last legs, and Judy and I had again separated. (As Johnny was fond of saying, "Half the marriages end in divorce — and then there are the unhappy ones.") When Jack mentioned that Joyce was staying at our old stomping grounds, the Sahara, I gave her a call and asked her to come see the show. When she agreed, I was thrilled because I was smitten with her, and my instincts told me that she might be feeling the same way. I was holding out the hope that something would develop for me with Joyce. I let Johnny know I'd be sitting in the show room with Joyce, and she would be joining us for dinner. He knew her work and was all for it.

After the show, Joyce and I went to the Palace Court restaurant at Caesars for dinner. When Johnny came in to join us, it was as if the president had arrived. He was always slightly uncomfortable with that sort of reaction, but he handled it graciously. Johnny ordered the wine, and we soon were all having a lovely time.

"When are you going back to Los Angeles?" Johnny asked Joyce at the end of the meal. It was one of those questions that could sound innocent or invitational, depending on the interest of the recipient, but I certainly took it to mean that Johnny was expressing an interest in seeing her, or more likely, in not saying good night.

"Well," I said, "Joyce and I were thinking of going back to the casino to play some blackjack." I was certain that would shake him; Johnny would prefer a root canal over exposing himself to all the humanity in the casino. "Great idea!" Johnny said. "Mind if I come along and play?"

No, we said, the more the merrier. *Three's Company* ain't just a TV show, even if I was hoping to go to bed with the star. But actually I was angry. I knew what he was up to.

Johnny signed a "marker" in the casino

for $25,000 and immediately fifty $500 chips were placed in front of him. Joyce and I both played blackjack for $25 a hand, while Johnny bet $500 each hand. With Johnny in the casino, Wingy Grober was standing by, and after a while, Johnny called him over.

"Wingy, it's getting awfully late," said Johnny, the perfect gentleman. "Could you please arrange a room for Miss DeWitt here at the hotel?" Johnny knew, as I knew, that Wingy, being an old hand at facilitating assignations, would not only arrange a room, but would make sure it was stocked with toiletries and nightclothes in Joyce's approximate size. Anything was possible in those days, and I'm sure for some people it still is. Joyce was, of course, flattered and a little dazzled. Johnny then bid us good night.

Finally I was alone with Joyce, and things began evolving as I had hoped. "Why don't we check out my new room?" she suggested, which seemed like a very fine idea. Upon entering, we saw that the message light on her phone was flashing. Joyce wasn't expecting a message — she hadn't even expected a room — and she called the operator for the message. "It was from Mr. Carson," she reported when she hung up. "He would like me to call him."

It was now clear that Joyce had become the focus of his interest. We had a problem. And I knew what was coming.

Joyce phoned the operator and requested that if Mr. Carson asked to please say that the message had not been picked up. "We'll just pretend that it never happened," I said. But as we stood there pondering our next move, the phone rang again. Of course, Joyce didn't answer. It was now almost three a.m. Only one possible person could be calling.

"Let's go to your room," said Joyce. "At least the phone calls will stop." Wrong again. As soon as we entered my room, my phone rang. It was Johnny, and he was obviously drunk. "Hey, Henry," he said, "I just want to make sure you're okay."

"Oh yeah, I'm fine," I told him. "I just put Joyce in a car to take her back to the Sahara. And now I'm beat. G'night."

Joyce and I had our first night together, even though we were under the constant threat of "phonus interruptus." The damn thing kept ringing all night, and each time it was Carson calling to report that Joyce wasn't in her room. It might have been aggravating, but the predicament was so ludicrous that she and I started to laugh, and we would laugh together whenever we recalled the absurd situation. Soon afterward, Johnny realized that Joyce and I were an item, and the silly evening when the seigneur failed to enjoy his droit was never spoken of again.

One day, all of these high jinks came to an end. Johnny grew tired of performing anywhere other than on *The Tonight Show*. Anywhere else, the money just wasn't attractive anymore, and after 1980, he never performed in a nightclub again.

ELEVEN:
1980–1984: HOBSON'S CHOICES

The Carsons and the Bushkins returned from the inauguration in very different moods. Johnny and Joanna came back on an uptick. The blows to their egos, singularly and jointly, had brought them together and unified them. Johnny emceed the SHARE Boomtown event again in the spring without any recalcitrance, and the first part of the year passed with no known eruptions. But the attempt by Judy and me to launch a reconciliation went nowhere. I was too attentive to Johnny when we were in Washington, even before the slights and snubs, real and imagined, ever began to be felt. Once they started, Judy may as well have been a minor figure in the Carter administration for all the attention she was receiving. When we returned, I was back in my apartment.

Still, from where I stood in 1981, I had much to be happy about. In little more than a decade, I had gone from being a green associate in a small entertainment firm to one of the founding partners of a large practice that employed more than sixty lawyers in offices in Los Angeles, Washington, and New York. My principal client was not only one of the most popular entertainers in the country, but now, thanks to the deal I had negotiated, easily one of the richest, positioned to become one of the most powerful men in the entertainment industry. It's true that my personal life was a mess, that my marriage was on the rocks, and that the ordeal of a divorce loomed. It's also true that my willingness to devote more attention to Johnny's needs than to Judy's was the prime reason. But through my work I had reaped financial rewards, gained influence and respect, and met powerful men and beautiful women. I had attained a life beyond all imagining, and I suppose I thought the trade-offs, though regrettable, were worth it.

But if I could have looked forward in time with the same ease as I could look back, I would have seen that my tenure as Johnny Carson's lawyer was more than halfway done.

Joanna was now spending a lot of time in New York, having persuaded Johnny to acquire for her a one-third interest in the business of the dashingly handsome clothing designer Michaele Vollbracht. She was living in a splendid apartment in the Pierre that Johnny had purchased for her after one or another of his transgressions. It might have been bought after Joanna discovered a film of Johnny en flagrante with a comely young lady, after which she furiously shattered every vase, every picture frame, every single thing made of glass in her living room, creating such a dangerous mess that a hazmat team had to be hired to clean up. Or it may have been bought after she saw Johnny's white Corvette and Ann-Margret's Rolls convertible canoodling in a parking lot outside one of Johnny's friends' houses in the midafternoon. And if it wasn't the apartment in the Pierre that was purchased after such an event, then maybe it was her Rolls Corniche or her diamond brooch and matching pair of diamond earrings from Hammerman Brothers. After the divorce, Joanna seized the high road, telling interviewers, "When you are married to a man like Johnny . . . well, that goes with the territory. There were certainly times when you just look away." Perhaps there were, but often enough, Joanna then fixed her eyes on something with a big price tag.

Joanna became a habitué of the fine-art auctions in Manhattan. In May she learned that Sotheby's was going to offer an oil of Picasso's, *Homme et Femme.* Johnny and Joanna discussed bidding on it. Johnny loved the painting and was excited by the prospect of owning it. He authorized her to bid up to $2 million. The Los Angeles head of Sotheby's was recruited to accompany Joanna to New York and orchestrate the bidding. We happened to have dinner right before the auction, and he and Joanna kept rethinking the strategy. It was fascinating.

At the auction, Joanna successfully outbid her rivals and secured the Picasso. Johnny was delighted with her performance. Unbeknownst to him, however, she had purchased a second painting, a Kees van Dongen oil for an additional $750,000. Joanna bought the piece as a surprise gift for Johnny's birthday, which was still months away on October 25.

Her secret didn't last long. The auction house needed to be paid, and Johnny got the bill. Perhaps no man was ever so excited to receive an invoice: he was thrilled that she had bought the painting for him.

Weeks passed, and no paintings arrived. Johnny was surprised at how long it took to ship a couple of paintings from New York.

"They could have walked here by now," he griped. Eventually they arrived at the St. Cloud residence. The valuable art was kept in the crates in a secure part of the garage.

By spring, work at Carson Productions was well under way. We began forming the company early in 1980, even before Johnny had decided which network he would go to work for. We knew after our cruise with ABC that we would have a production company, and we didn't need to know where the underwriting was coming from in order to outline in broad strokes what the lines of authority would be. Johnny would be the boss, as if that was ever in doubt. In practical terms, that meant that he would have the ultimate say-so on things. Usually that meant ratifying the decisions made by his executives. Occasionally it meant that if he didn't like something, it would stop. Otherwise, he wasn't going to give orders or preside over meetings or, heaven forbid, read scripts, which is something that most people who produce television shows spend hours a day doing. "What the hell do I know about sitcoms?" Carson would say, aghast at the thought. "I don't have the foggiest fucking idea what would work." He would, however, control *The Tonight Show,* just as he had always done.

My role was to be Johnny's chief operating officer, his designee to oversee the running of the business. It would be up to me to negotiate the employment agreements with the key management personnel. After that was done, I would then deal with the president of the company whose job was to run the real business. Dealing with NBC was also my responsibility, but all the terms that I negotiated then had to be ratified by Johnny. One part of the arrangement took me by complete surprise. "I'm going to give you a 10 percent ownership stake in the company," Carson said to me one day. "I'm happy to do it. What the hell, that's how much I would have had to pay an agent. You earned it."

Naturally I was touched by Johnny's gesture and thrilled by its potential value as well. But the windfall complicated my life enormously. At a time when I was supposed to be focusing on negotiating contracts with our new hires, I had to think of what this meant for me. When Johnny made his offer, I had not fully decided that my marriage was over. Johnny's announcement forced me to make a decision.

According to California's community property law, Judy would be entitled to half of anything I made while we were living together, which meant that as soon as Carson Productions was formed, she would be entitled to half of my share. I had no problem with the idea of Judy getting her half of our estate and some alimony going forward. But if we were going to split, I saw no point in surrendering half my equity in a newborn company. Very soon my last hopes for our marriage disappeared.

Johnny was in the same position that I was, or at least it seemed that way to me. More than a year had passed since Joanna had decided that she and Johnny would have a very public reconciliation at the Mancinis' party, a method and an occasion that had very little to do with actually bringing the relationship closer and everything to do with cementing her status in SHARE. Since then, the relationship had more ups and downs than a castle jumper full of five-year-olds. From the inauguration and throughout the spring, things had been going well in the Carsons' marriage. So well, in fact, that in March, when the *National Enquirer* reported that there was trouble in the Carsons' marriage, Johnny was furious and wanted to sue for slander.

"You cannot be serious," I said, trying my best to capture John McEnroe's incredulous tone.

"Well, it's not true," he said. "We're getting along great right now."

"It doesn't matter," I said. "If you sue, they'll subpoena everyone who you were ever rumored to have gone out with. They'll subpoena the desk registers at the Beverly Hills Hotel; they'll call all the clerks and bellhops. You may as well hand them a proctoscope and invite their investigators to crawl up your ass."

But Johnny kept at it, and gradually it occurred to me that there was something more there than was meeting my eye. Maybe he was feeling gallant and wanted to prove something to Joanna; maybe she was feeling needy and wanted him to make a reassuring gesture. Eventually, we decided that he would make a statement on *The Tonight Show,* refuting the article.

"This is absolutely, completely one hundred percent falsehood," he said from his desk. "They said some very nasty things, attributed to her close friends and pals. But when they attacked my wife, well, I get a little bit angry.

"Now, I could sue the *National Enquirer,*" he said, but he explained that the length and stress of litigation made that an unsatisfactory choice and that he didn't want to put "my wife" through it. But because "our

332

friends, our relatives, our family, our children, and our parents" are troubled by the allegations, he felt obliged to respond.

"I'm going to call the *National Enquirer* and the people who write for it liars. Now [if that's false] that's slander. They can sue me for slander. You know where I am, gentlemen. Please accept my invitation [to sue me] for calling you liars. I've done it publicly now in front of fifteen or twenty million people, and I will be very happy to defend that charge against you."

The audience applauded vigorously, and Johnny's strong response won him a lot of attention and support. But I knew that their marriage wasn't the California redwood he purported it to be, and that even during the periods when things were going well, he had his moments of restlessness and doubt. In most relationships, a friend and counselor shuts his mouth and lets events take their course. But in this case, with Johnny about to begin his ownership of what we assumed would be the wildly remunerative Carson Productions, I wanted him to take a cold, hard look at the relationship and assess its prospects for longevity. If he was even thinking that the relationship might be over, then he owed it to himself to consider making a sharp cut.

"You have to face facts," I told him one day after tennis. "Once the production company starts operating, it will have income — value — that she'll be entitled to take half of forever. I've moved out — Judy won't have a claim on that asset. But even if you moved out right this minute, I think it would be a toss-up whether she would get a cut of the new deal or not. It's a Hobson's choice: the more we get, the more she's going to get."

"What should I do?" he asked.

"I don't know. Try to be happy in your relationship? Try to make things work? Get out while the getting's good?"

He shook his head. "I can't stand the thought of a divorce."

If nothing else, his reluctance meant that my job, which was principally about making sure that Johnny Carson was happy, would continue to include the obligation to make sure that Joanna was happy, lest her feelings infect his mood. In 1981 that meant making sure that none of the ugly violations of protocol that marred the inauguration for Joanna would take place at the 53rd Annual Academy Awards ceremonies, which Johnny was once again hosting, and which, in the world that the Carsons inhabited, was an infinitely more important event than any presidential swearing-in.

Carson, of course, is universally recognized as one of the great Oscar hosts, and he liked doing it, although I can only assume why. It wasn't the money; he was paid only $15,000, and the expectation was that he would donate that to charity (he did). Or was it the show, which he always groused was a three-hour program spread over four hours? Mostly I think it just reinforced his sense of his own eminence. In presiding over this event, he was the ringmaster of the ultimate show business circus. Five times between 1978 and 1983, he emceed the Academy Awards ceremonies and never broke a sweat. In 1981, however, I did enough sweating for both of us.

That year, since I was without a wife or a date, I escorted Joanna. I arrived at their home in the limo at four-thirty p.m. to collect the wife of the host; Johnny was, of course, at the theater, going through rehearsals. The show began promptly at six p.m. That left us an hour and a half to get to the Dorothy Chandler Pavilion at the Los Angeles Music Center, which under normal conditions is no more than a half hour away. Except Joanna wasn't anywhere near ready. She was in her robe waiting for José Eber, the hairstylist to the stars. He had wall-to-wall appointments and was running late.

"Joanna," I said, pointing at my watch and falling straight into sitcom-character panic, "we gotta go!" She refused to budge. I began doing time-and-traffic calculations in my head. *Sunset to Palm,* I was thinking, *that'll be crowded, but moving. But Palm to Beverly Boulevard could be tough, and where it changes into First Street . . .* If we were not in our seats in the second row when Johnny started the show, he would undoubtedly notice and would be supremely pissed. Of course, if we were in our seats in the second row and Joanna didn't think her hair looked right, she would be extremely pissed. The image of Scylla and Charybdis came back to me from high school English class. I sensed I was in for a long evening.

Eber arrived right around four-forty-five. It took another forty-five minutes for him to work his magic and for Joanna to get dressed and hustle herself into the limo. Given the way traffic always clogged up around the pavilion on Oscar night, I didn't think we had a chance of arriving on time. "I'll give you an extra $200 if you get us to the show before six," I told the driver. We arrived just as the big hand was touching the twelve, and I tossed the driver his $200 as Joanna and I ran into the side entrance of the theater. We could hear the president of the Academy giving her remarks. We were going to make it!

Suddenly, there was a problem. There were people in our seats. Kids — Jane Fonda's kids! She was an Oscar winner and was attending the event to see her father, Henry Fonda, receive an honorary Oscar. She had only two tickets, but she didn't want her kids to miss this, and so she planted them in our seats.

"I'm sorry, but these are our seats!" I said, brandishing our tickets. "You have to move them!"

"I'm not moving anybody now!" she replied with all the tenacity of a Hollywood princess who had grown into an award-winning exercise-company millionaire and Hollywood-family diva. "The show's starting! Go sit down before you embarrass yourself on national TV!"

Sweat literally poured from me. There wasn't very much I could do, short of making a very nasty scene that would turn me into a footnote in Oscar history: "Hey, isn't that Henry Bushkin, the hysterical attorney who got into a fight with Jane Fonda?" The program had paused for a commercial break, the last one before Johnny was to appear. Then Joanna and I would have to slink away, and it would be the fucking inauguration all over again. Meanwhile Joanna was maintaining a ladylike calm. I'm sure she was just pooling lava to spew all over me later.

"Take Jon Voight's seats," an usher suddenly interjected. "He's not coming." The kids were hustled to the available seats, Joanna and I hurried to two empty seats in the front row, and the usher was substantially rewarded, all seconds before Johnny, looking even more elegant and debonair than usual in white tie and tails, took the stage. As the applause fell upon him, he and Joanna exchanged big smiles. I was ready for a Scotch, a Valium, a nap, or all three.

As it happened, in those days the Oscar ceremonies were held on a Monday, and on that particular Monday, March 30, 1981, John Hinckley Jr. had wounded President Reagan in an assassination attempt outside the Washington Hilton. The Academy immediately postponed the ceremonies indefinitely, but when the White House announced that the president had survived and was in good condition, the Academy rescheduled the show for the following night. Rescheduling the event had a big impact on a lot of people: caterers, dressmakers, babysitters, and others, including Johnny, since about half his monologue dealt with Reagan. All through Tuesday, he and writers Mike Barrie and Jim Mulholland rewrote the monologue. On the night of the event, Johnny did just one Reagan joke, but it struck the perfect balance between irreverence and concern.

"Reagan cut $85 million from the arts and humanities. This is his biggest assault on the arts since he signed with Warner Brothers." Carson waited a beat and continued. "That should get him up and out of bed."

Later that night, after *Ordinary People* beat *Coal Miner's Daughter, The Elephant Man, Raging Bull,* and *Tess* for Best Picture, I told Johnny the story about the seats. "That fucking Jane Fonda," he said. "She's never going to be on the show again." His vehemence lasted until we all arrived at Swifty Lazar's Oscar party at Le Dome, when Jane apologized for the earlier "misunderstanding" while seated with Johnny and Elizabeth Taylor.

Although we had done a lot of planning, it took some time after Johnny signed his three-year deal with NBC before we could get Carson Productions up and running. Early on, Johnny casually dropped into a conversation a fact that had the potential to change everything. His financial handler, Fred Kayne, mentioned that the value of a new company is never higher than when it first opens its doors, when its potential is limitless, and everything about it has a rosy hue. "This would be the time to get yourselves acquired," Fred wisecracked, "before the two of you do anything to fuck it up."

I mentioned that I had read that Coca-Cola had just bought Norman Lear, Bud Yorkin, and Jerry Perenchio's company, Tandem Productions/Embassy Television, and were making further acquisitions in the entertainment field.

"Oh, well, then you ought to talk to Don Keough," Johnny said.

"Who's Don Keough?"

"He's the president of Coca-Cola," Johnny said. "He and I go way back. We were in radio together back in Omaha when we were kids."

A few phone calls later, I was on a flight to Atlanta to meet with Don Keough and Roberto Goizueta, the chairman of Coca-Cola, who, as it happened, was also a big fan of Johnny's. We had a terrific conversation. They thought Carson Productions, with *The Tonight Show* and a five-series guarantee, had amazing assets. They wondered if we might be interested in selling. "How about a swap?" I asked. "Carson stock for Coca-Cola stock." We talked about a deal that would have delivered us $100 million, with the stock swap providing considerable tax advantages.

"They have only one condition," I reported to Johnny when I returned to LA. "They want you to make a five-year commitment to host *The Tonight Show.* They feel that if you left after three years, NBC wouldn't feel any obligation to fulfill its commitment to buy five series, and with you gone, Carson Productions wouldn't have any more leverage with the network. They're probably right."

Again, the question of the divorce settlement raised its head. "Look, if I do a deal with Coke, does Joanna get half?"

It was a simple question, but there was no simple answer. "We can take the position that because you are required to perform services, the stock you will be receiving is actually being earned over a five-year period. If you separate, we will take the position that $20 million is earned per year. If we conclude with Coke and you split within the year, I don't think she'll get more than $10 million. But again, if the issue gets before a judge, there's no guarantee how the ruling will go."

There was one more thing, less a condition than a request. "Coke would also like you to consider being on their board of directors. It makes perfect sense: you're a prominent man, and you'll have a big stake in the company."

"Jesus, Henry, you know me better than that," he said, laughing that the idea had even gone this far. "There's nothing I would hate more. Make sure they know I'm flattered, but make some excuse."

Johnny thought about the offer for a long time, but the combination of a five-year commitment and the unsteadiness of his marriage was too much. We simply couldn't eliminate the possibility that by the time he was ready to split with Joanna, he would have locked himself into a five-year commitment, and that for all that time, half of his compensation would be going to a woman who was no longer his wife. Very soon after we said no thanks, Coca-Cola bought Columbia Pictures. Having whetted their appetite with Carson Productions, I guess they just had to eat something.

I can't say that I was entirely pleased with Johnny's decision. My 10 percent of the deal would have made me plenty rich. I couldn't see it then, but in retrospect, this was the beginning of the end of my relationship with Johnny. Had we each just pocketed our share, we probably would have continued on much as we had done. But we didn't grab the quick money. Now we would have to become moguls, and we would have to work together. Bit by bit, it would become evident that I was much more interested in succeeding at this than he was.

Early in 1981 we hired John J. McMahon, known as J. J., the former head of West Coast production for NBC. J. J. was a terrific guy and very talented, and perhaps most important, Johnny liked him; more than once I heard there was a resemblance, in style as well as in features, to Carson. In one of his first moves that had my blessing, J. J. hired Bill Haber, one of the three founders of CAA, to act as an agent for Carson Productions. Hiring the heavyweight agency certainly seemed like a crafty move on McMahon's part; we were CAA's first corporate client, and it stood to reason that in order to make us into a successful example of their clout, they would enlist their talent-rich client roster of actors, writers, and directors in our cause. With access to top talent, lots of money, and tons of support, Carson Productions clearly had it all.

The only thing it would ever lack was hits.

Carson Productions launched its first series on NBC's schedule in the fall of 1981. *Lewis & Clark* was a short-lived show in which a man from Queens, played by Gabe Kaplan, relocates his family to small-town Texas. It stunk. Airing on Thursday at eight-thirty against CBS's popular *Magnum, P.I., Lewis & Clark* was pulled off the schedule after eight episodes, with the last five episodes of the show's original thirteen-week commitment airing in the dead of summer.

With Fred Silverman still looking for prime-time winners, NBC was quick with the hook and quick to throw up midseason replacements. At about the same time we learned that *Lewis & Clark* had been shit-canned, we were told that two other of our productions were given the green light to go on the air in February. *Cassie & Company,* an hour-long drama starring longtime Carson favorite Angie Dickinson as a private eye, proved so unappealing to viewers that the network dumped it after only four episodes. *Teachers Only,* a sitcom starring Lynn Redgrave, achieved only modestly greater success. "Last season," wrote the television critic of the *New York Times,* "Lynn Redgrave departed from one situation comedy, CBS's *House Calls,* reportedly because the producers would not allow her to breast feed her new baby on the set. She is now back in another situation comedy, *Teachers Only* on NBC, and it would seem that she should come up with another unusual excuse to get out of this one." The show eked out eight episodes in 1982 and thirteen more in the spring of 1983 before being mercifully allowed to go to its unlamented rest.

"Jesus, what do we have to do to get a hit?" a frustrated Carson griped one day. Suddenly Fred Silverman's job didn't look so easy. But as Johnny said from the beginning, he didn't know what went into making a television series successful; he wasn't even a particularly enlightened viewer. Johnny Carson performed on television, but he didn't watch it all that much. And it wasn't as though there were any obvious flaws in J. J.'s approach that left him vulnerable to second-guessing. From what we could see, J. J. was playing the game by the numbers. We had a fish-out-of-water comedy starring Gabe Kaplan, who was a popular comedian, and whose previous series, *Welcome Back, Kotter,* had been a big hit for ABC. We had a workplace comedy starring Lynn Redgrave, an appealing actress who had starred on a series that was a ratings success on CBS. We had Angie Dickinson, who'd had a big following on her police show, now starring in a private eye show. J. J. had good people behind the camera, too — proven performers in proven genres.

It just didn't work. In the coming years, McMahon would double down. He got NBC to air a four-hour miniseries about a lusty studio executive called *The Star Maker* starring Rock Hudson, which received mocking reviews, and another series, *Partners in Crime*, about two female private detectives played by Loni Anderson and Lynda Carter, again two proven TV stars. The show, said the *New York Times*, "may be the top contender for this year's Dumbest-Show-of-the-Season award." Perhaps TV audiences had grown bored with these familiar approaches; before too many more years, Steven Bochco's ensemble shows, such as *NYPD Blue* and *Hill Street Blues*, would revolutionize TV dramas.

But in the meantime, everything we put out was DOA, and the name Johnny Carson was attached to every one of these stiffs.

Negotiating a landmark contract and becoming the unofficial head of a production company certainly elevated my status in most of the circles in which I traveled, but it was still the case that if Johnny called, I answered. During our annual Wimbledon trip in 1981, I caught some sort of a bug and got sick. For two or three days I just sacked out in my room at Claridge's. I missed the matches, and I didn't care.

And certainly Johnny didn't care. But what was on his mind was a tennis match he had set up, in which he and I were to face the team of Dick Enberg, the great sportscaster who was, as usual, covering Wimbledon for NBC, and Bob Blackmore, the network's head of sales. The match, months in the making, was to be played at the Queen's Club, the renowned private sporting club in West Kensington that is second only to Wimbledon in prestige in Great Britain.

Carson called the night before the match to see how I was feeling. He wanted to be sure I would play. Although I was improving, I still felt like crap, but I told him I would be ready for the match. Frankly, I thought it would be easier for me to say I'd play. If I said I wasn't feeling well enough, Johnny would summon the hotel doctor and subject me to a battery of remedies; all I wanted to do was sleep.

We arrived at the Queen's Club before the duo from NBC, Johnny in his customary white shorts (he never wore anything but white), me in sweats. We went through our warm-ups, but I was going through the motions. Johnny kept trying to pump me up, but I had no energy. Once the game started, though, I was running my ass off all over the court. Back for lobs, up for drop shots. As far as I could tell, the only thing Johnny did was shout the word "Yours!" We lost the first set 6–3, and I can't imagine how we got three games.

"We've got to do much better this next set," Johnny told me at the changeover. I was doing the work, and here he was telling me "We've got to do better." It was laughable, but on the court he had no sense of humor. On the contrary, he could become quite testy when he lost. All I wanted was for him to have a good time.

The second set turned out well for us. Johnny started to play good, smart tennis. He was in the right spots and making shots. Most important, he started to serve well. If Johnny was able to hold serve against the opposition when we played doubles, we always had a good chance, and we won the second set 6–4.

That, thankfully, was enough. We lost the

last set but it was because I was totally out of gas; Johnny continued to play great, and that was enough. He cracked jokes and bought drinks at the clubhouse. Later he held court in the NBC tent, an enclosed pavilion inside the Wimbledon Club grounds where celebrities could hang out. Johnny ruled the room. I was back in bed, exhausted, but happy that the boss had been appeased for another day.

TWELVE:
1982–1985: *HOMME ET FEMME*

Johnny may not have done much to save his marriage, but he certainly was upset about the impending divorce. I could hear it in his monologue. "I went to see my butcher the other day, Murray Giblets. I said, 'How do you pick a good turkey?' And he says, 'You ought to know. You're a three-time loser.' The audience groaned or tittered nervously. They weren't sure how to react. Johnny had become a fixture in their homes by being consistently light; he was never guilty of opening a vein. This one, however, he couldn't let go of. "My giving advice on marriage," he cracked, "is like the captain of the *Titanic* giving lessons on navigation."

Like boxers in their respective corners — she in Bel Air on St. Cloud Road, he at the beach house in Malibu — the Carsons prepared to duke it out. Until a settlement could be reached, the court ordered Johnny to pay $44,600 a month in support. Joanna, claiming her expenses were actually several times that, had requested $220,000 a month. "I heard from my cat's lawyer," Johnny reported in his monologue. "My cat wants $12,000 a week for Tender Vittles."

Personally, I was sorry to see them divorce. It was inevitable now that my relationship with Joanna would change, and I regretted that. From the beginning she had been one of my biggest supporters, and she was a great friend to Judy. And once Judy and I split, Joanna introduced me to Joyce De-Witt, with whom I enjoyed a happy relationship for several years. Ostensibly Joanna introduced us because Joyce was looking for a lawyer, but I don't think Joanna was that naive. I liked Joanna, and I owed her a lot, going all the way back to the time when she advocated my move to LA.

But once the Carsons' domestic situation soured, it was clear where my loyalties and responsibilities lay. Joanna and I became natural adversaries. If you work for the Hat-fields, you can't pal around with the Mc-Coys. I don't know if Joanna feels the same today as she did right after the divorce, but she was angry with me and blamed me for Johnny's decision. "We'd talk," she told the journalist Paul Corkery for his 1987 book, *Carson: The Unauthorized Biography,* "and as we started delving into his world, so to speak, he was very agitated and aggravated. I knew then that I was dealing with two personalities, his, and Henry Bushkin's." She said she "never knew who was calling the shots," Johnny or me, whom she describes as being "even angrier than her husband."

Was she right? I don't think so. From where I sat in the relationship, it seemed like Johnny always called all the shots in the end, although that's the kind of thing that I suppose can look very different from the outside. Surely Johnny took a lot of my advice, which may have made me look like his Svengali, and I'm also sure there were times when Johnny used me as a shield and allowed me to take the heat for decisions he made; I thought that was part of my job. But it's also true that Judy and I were going through a divorce, and Judy and Joanna had similar objectives, although Joanna's were on a far grander scale, just as Johnny and I had similar objectives. The women sought to value the new Carson companies at the highest possible amount in order to increase the worth of their community property and their portions of the settlements. Johnny and I had the opposite objective. Were there times when I said something that persuaded him to take a hard line after he had led her to believe he would be more accommodating? Very possibly. But I really did less persuading and more giving information. Johnny had generous impulses; I'm the one who often had to explain how much they would cost. He would then decide. I was genuinely sorry that they split up, but all I ever wanted, one way or the other, was for him to be happy.

Unlike Johnny's divorce from Joanne, there was never a possibility that I would handle the suit. I took care of the earlier divorce pretty well, but now the stakes were far too high and the situation far too complicated for a man of Johnny's wealth and stature to hire anyone other than an expert. Our first choice for representation was Miles Rubin, a very gentlemanly lawyer. We thought Johnny would work well with the low-key Rubin, and we thought the other side would respond well to quiet professionalism on our part. We didn't sense that a war was in the offing; Joanna wasn't going around town bad-mouthing Carson. The two of them were talking almost every day. "Johnny would talk about the issues," Joanna admitted in an interview after the divorce. "We just never resolved them."

But I suppose Joanna could afford to be

friendly to Johnny because she hired a bully to represent her. Arthur Crowley was a hard-nosed lawyer. The legendary producer Robert Evans hired Crowley when Steve McQueen and Evans's ex-wife Ali MacGraw wanted to adopt the son she had when she and Evans were married, and Crowley proceeded to build up a foot-wide dossier on McQueen that was apparently enough to derail those hopes. Evans called Crowley "the toughest Irish attorney west of Chicago." Fair enough, I thought, but why limit it to the Irish? Crowley, who had a bald dome like Adlai Stevenson and a five o'clock shadow like Richard Nixon, learned to play rough by staring down the studios in the *Confidential* libel trial of 1957. Crowley represented the notorious scandal magazine in a case brought by the State of California, no doubt at the behest of the studios, contending that the magazine was lying when it published articles about the stars who drank excessively, took illegal drugs, and slept around with members of the same or opposite sex. Crowley said fine, we'll see if the magazine was lying or not. He subpoenaed more than a hundred stars, including Elvis Presley, Clark Gable, and Maureen O'Hara, ordering them to testify about the behaviors in question. It's said that half of

Hollywood immediately went on vacation in Acapulco. The studios, thinking that maybe the lawsuit idea wasn't such a good idea after all, had a word with the prosecution, who essentially then dropped the matter.

Being hard-nosed was one thing; when I represented Johnny in his second divorce, I thought Joanne's counsel, Raoul Felder, was hard-nosed, but he also had a charming side, and I rather liked him. I think Crowley took pleasure in being a prick. Mel Tormé once called him "the meanest man I have ever met," and in this case, I think the Velvet Fog spoke for almost everyone I knew. Arthur was also sort of the house counsel for the SHARE ladies. One of his other clients was Judy. Soon it became clear that Miles Rubin was simply too nice to be in this fight, and we hired Norman Oberstein, who could be counted on to be as hard-nosed as he had to be.

This was a complicated case. Because there was no prenuptial agreement, a lot of issues, such as when community property ceased to exist and when separate property rules prevailed, had to be litigated. The entire matter was contentious. In a normal marriage, the day the couple stops cohabitating is the day when income ceases to be community property. Joanna naturally wanted a later date, while Johnny wanted an earlier one, but in this marriage, Johnny left and came back so often that it was difficult to fix a date. Furthermore, if he left and stayed at their Malibu residence, can that really be said to be leaving? An even more difficult problem involved valuing all of the assets that Johnny had built up over the years. Ownership of *The Tonight Show* was a tremendous asset, and Joanna was certainly entitled to her fair share. But was Joanna really entitled to a 50 percent share of something that had great value before she married Johnny? How were we to value Johnny's decade of stardom that predated their marriage?

Answers to these and other questions were eventually hacked out, but Crowley made sure that the entire process was a painful and acrimonious ordeal. A lot of the terrain that Crowley covered in his grueling depositions was expected and unavoidable; it would have been silly to think that private investigators hadn't vacuumed up every hint of Johnny's infidelities, and forcing Johnny to sit there and acknowledge so many incidents as they were monotonously entered into the record was part of the punishment. But there were uglier and more embarrassing moments — allegations of physical and emotional abuse, of drunken misbehavior, most of them deliberately exaggerated or maliciously misinterpreted, many of them baseless and false — that were raked over simply for the purpose of shaming or annoying Johnny. Crowley then went over financial documents relating to the various Carson companies, questioning him in numbing detail about the minutiae of the data that had been entered, stuff that Johnny hadn't personally prepared and probably didn't understand, but on the advice of counsel, had signed his name to, in precisely the same way you and I have blithely signed tax forms or mortgage papers that may as well have been written in Sanskrit. "This is all about Crowley padding his fees, isn't it?" Johnny ranted. "How much do you think this will cost me? Christ, he's going to have a field day dissecting the companies. Maybe you were right. We should have sold the goddamn thing to Coke when we had the chance." Mercifully, I declined to point out that had he signed a prenuptial agreement in 1972, he would not be undergoing this trial. But he knew. He knew.

Crowley's lowest blow came when Carson was permitted to return to the St. Cloud residence — still his property, remember, and something that certainly could remain so after the settlement — to collect some clothes and other personal items. When Johnny arrived, he discovered that Crowley had posted armed guards throughout the premises to ensure that he didn't try to take anything that didn't belong to him. None of them knew what was his and what wasn't; they were just there to crowd him. It was a nasty thing to do. Soon Johnny began to refer to Crowley as the Master of Misery. "Who the fuck does this prick go home to? He's such a lousy bastard." Crowley was getting inside Carson's head, which might have been his tactic all along.

It wasn't as though the fight was always one-sided. Johnny's counsel was able to make it clear that he would be happy to reveal at trial the understanding Mrs. Carson enjoyed with Hammerman Brothers, her jeweler of choice when an apologetic Carson needed to buy the aggrieved Joanna a sparkling something to make amends. After she pointedly wore the bauble a few times in his presence, she would send it back to the Hammermans. They would send her a check for the refund minus their percentage and sell the thing again. They profited, she built her own little nest egg, and Johnny was none the wiser. I'm sure Joanna was embarrassed when this was discovered. But then again, the money was all community property when these transactions took place.

But these small satisfactions didn't amount to a hill of beans. The divorce from Joanna was more harmful to Johnny than I thought it would be. I had never seen the man so disturbed. He was bitter and angry with Joanna, not because she wanted his money — she was going to get plenty of money under any settlement, many millions — but because she had effectively authorized her lawyer to torture him. The intensity of his reaction was alarming, and I wasn't the only one who was worried. One day Bobby Quinn asked me if I thought Johnny was capable of hurting Joanna. What could I say? I had seldom seen Johnny behave violently, but when he got drunk, he became unpredictable, and if he was willing to punch Tom Snyder for no good reason, what else might he be prepared to do when he was feeling so emotionally threatened? My mind flashed to the .38-caliber pistol that he carried on our raid on Joanne Carson's love nest, a gun he still carried in the glove compartment of his car, a gun he once actually pulled and waved at a shocked-shitless camera crew from a local TV station that decided it would be good fun to tailgate Carson's Corvette down Pacific Coast Highway. It made me sick to think about it.

Quinn and I worked out a plan. Bobby would hang with Johnny at the studio after the show until he was in a good enough frame of mind to go home. Later I would drive over to his home and make sure he was okay. This tag team approach worked; he seemed less enraged.

Less enraged, perhaps, but still different. Johnny changed during the divorce proceedings, and I don't know if he ever entirely changed back. He was always capable of being a miserable prick. The nasty remark, the stony silence, the surprising indifference — they had been part of his repertoire ever since I knew him, but they were usually interruptions in a generally more genial mood. Now these stormy moments came more frequently, and there was an overall harshness, an impatient intolerance, that wasn't there before. His profitable clothing business, for example, closed up shop, in part because it required Johnny to model the clothes in advertisements. Johnny no longer had the patience to spend a day or two modeling in return for the couple of million dollars the clothing deal earned him, and he no longer needed the dough. In one of the final sessions, which took place at the Playboy Mansion, the photographer said, "Now smile!"

"Don't ever say that to me again," snarled Johnny, walking off the shoot. "You're fired."

He became oddly imperious. For example, now that he resided in Malibu, he became determined to build a sea wall, which involved heavy construction and required the acquisition of a permit from the Coastal Commission before work could commence. Johnny had my firm prepare the application papers, but before the commission could even review the application, he ordered his contractor to start work. He ended up being fined thousands of dollars for his lack of patience, and although he was clearly in the wrong, he was angry at them.

It even got to the point where it seemed like he couldn't recognize a joke. Somehow we learned of an Ohio company called Here's Johnny Portable Toilets, which advertised its product with the slogan "The World's Foremost Commodian." Carson didn't think that was funny and ordered me to sue the company to make them stop. Ultimately we spent about $500,000 to win less than $40,000 in damages. The case went to the U.S. Circuit Court of Appeals for the Seventh Circuit, and the favorable decision for Johnny is often quoted on the subject of trademark protection. To me, it didn't matter that we won. I thought it made him look mean and small.

Nowhere was the change in personality more evident than on the tennis court. John McEnroe and Jimmy Connors are the most competitive tennis players I've ever seen, but Carson comes in third. He was always capable of indulging his petulant, sore-loser side, but during this period, his language became nastier, his anger more demonstrative, and his line calls more bold. Longtime tennis buddies now frequently found that their schedules were full.

One day we were playing doubles with Willie Shoemaker, who was not only a great jockey but also a tremendous overall athlete. Willie's partner that day was Bob Trapenberg, a former pro who now taught tennis. He was for a time one of Johnny's closest friends, and although Willie was all business, "Trap" kept setting Johnny up to look good. It was the definition of "customer tennis." On that day, however, Johnny wasn't finding himself able to reap Trap's largesse. After missing an easy forehand for about the third time, he heaved his racquet high into the air. It landed just inside the pool, about two feet from where Shoemaker's wife, Babs, was sunning herself. Needless to say, the match was over. Johnny offered a terse apology and stormed off in his Mercedes.

My friend Hank Greenberg, the Hall of Fame slugger, sponsored me for membership in the Beverly Hills Tennis Club. In turn, Hank and I sponsored Johnny for membership. Hank was as great a gentleman on the court as Johnny was not. He played with us on several occasions, but Hank very soon tired of Johnny's curses and self-serving line calls. Before long, when I would invite Hank to join us, he politely declined. That became typical of many members at the club. Johnny had such a mystique, though, that no one would ever question any of his line calls, no matter how egregious they seemed; people just didn't play with him anymore. After several years of membership and relatively few games, Carson resigned.

"My personal life has been exactly like this year's Academy Awards," joked Johnny during his monologue at the Oscar ceremony in 1984, the last one he would emcee. "It started off with *Terms of Endearment,* I thought I had *The Right Stuff,* it cost a lot to *Dresser,* then came *The Big Chill* and for the last month I've been begging for *Tender Mercies.*"

One by one, the dramas of those days came to an end. My divorce from Judy became final. She was awarded $23,000 per month and received the house in Beverly Hills. Valued then at $3 million, it's surely worth more than $10 million today. Like Joanna, Judy was represented by Arthur Crowley, whose flamethrower approach probably cost me $500,000 in fees. (By the way, I think Johnny was right about Crowley pursuing certain inquiries just to raise his fees, which were high anyway; he charged $500 an hour, and double on Sundays — like a plumber.) None of that money went to Judy, but it aggravated the tensions between us. For years after the divorce we did not speak.

After the failure of *Partners in Crime,* the fifth Carson Productions series to bite the dust, J. J. McMahon was fired. He was a friend and a good guy who worked hard and deserved better, especially from the supposedly omnipotent CAA, which instead of bringing us their elite talent as we had hoped, used Carson Productions as a dumping ground for the junk their clients couldn't get rid of. In fairness, it must be said that J. J. had some successes. During his tenure, *Carson's Comedy Classics,* 130 half-hour programs edited from old *Tonight Show* broadcasts, were sold into syndication for a sweet $26 million.

Also, Carson Productions was able to team up with Dick Clark Productions to produce *TV's Bloopers & Practical Jokes,* a hit that earned us a lot of money and no esteem. The big problem, though, wasn't the hits or flops that he did sell; it was the many, many shows he put into development that never sold, to NBC or anyone else. There was a sense that we were losing traction, that our big potential was dissipating, and that we were becoming just another production company.

"The big difference between us and Norman Lear's company or MTM is that they have their own people creating shows," I said to Carson one night. "We've been depending on CAA, and they've been bringing us dreck."

"Well, look around. Maybe somebody like Jim Brooks or Larry Gelbart is available."

Those two weren't, but J. J.'s luck ran out when we finally had a chance to hire someone of a similar caliber. Edwin "Ed" Weinberger was a true giant among sitcom writers and producers, and he seemed like just the sort of talent who could help us restore our luster. Everyone at the company had hoped it would have turned out differently for J. J., no one more than Carson. He found that he hated being a boss when being a boss meant firing friends, even in a case like this, when J. J. was sent off with a golden handshake.

For a man who actually fired a lot of people during his career, Johnny sometimes found it hard to do the deed. Once he summoned me to his offices at NBC — summoned, as in "drop everything you're doing and get over here." It turns out that Johnny, who never carried a wallet but usually kept $1,500 to $2,000 or so in cash on his person, had noticed that at the end of every week for the last month or so, he would be at least $700 to $1,000 light. "Get some surveillance cameras in here," he demanded. "I want to catch the son of a bitch who's stealing from me."

Michael Hattem of Brentwood Communications managed to conceal two cameras in hollowed-out books, and within days we caught his dresser, a union guy who was responsible for taking care of Johnny's wardrobe, pilfering the money. Johnny was very proud that he had solved the mystery, but he never fired the culprit. He liked him too much as an employee. Instead, he sat him down and told him that as long as he didn't steal anymore, Johnny would give him another $300 to $400 week. A complicated and strategic result: at once generous and lenient, but conflict averse. Johnny didn't want to lose an excellent valet just because he was an untrustworthy thief. He was not about to change things that worked.

Unnoticed among the problems of its high-profile but underperforming television division, the movie division of Carson Productions enjoyed a critical and box office smash straight out of the gate. We produced *The Big Chill,* Lawrence Kasdan's comedy-drama about members of the baby-boom generation feeling their first intimations of mortality. With a terrific, top-selling Motown-based soundtrack and a cast that included such present and future stars as Kevin Kline, Glenn Close, William Hurt, and Jeff Goldblum, it ended up receiving Oscar nominations for Best Picture, Best Screenplay (Kasdan), and Best Supporting Actress (Close).

Oddly, the picture almost didn't get made, at least not by us. When we first received the screenplay, Marcia Nasatir, who was running the company, loved it, as did I.

Mike Ovitz, head of CAA and the future king of Hollywood, hated it and argued hard against our involvement, but fortunately we managed to outvote him. The other person who didn't much care for the film was Carson. Johnny dutifully assumed the role of producer while the film was in development and went to screenings of the rough cuts and other meetings, but he did not like the process, and he did not like the film. He thought the movie was okay, but saw no greatness in it.

Coming off *The Big Chill,* I thought we had achieved an important success that we could build upon. We produced one more film called *Desert Bloom.* Like *The Big Chill,* it had an excellent cast featuring Jon Voight (my absent friend from the Oscars!) and Ellen Barkin. Although it enjoyed some critical success, it did no business. At that point, Johnny insisted that the film division be shut down. I thought he was crazy, but the decision was made. As I had seen when he declined to make a commitment to the Aladdin, when he declined to make a commitment to Coca-Cola, and when he closed the clothing business, making money beyond a certain point held very little interest for him. To him, making movies was a distraction. He didn't like it, he didn't want to try to get good at it, and he wasn't willing to hand it off to someone. He just shut it down.

The wrangling with Arthur Crowley continued, injuring both parties. Joanna was embarrassed after Crowley demanded that she receive a $220,000 monthly allowance; it made her look like a gold digger, although really, it was a normal-size request for a woman whose husband was as rich as Carson. Nor did Crowley do her much good when he demanded more than half of their community property, arguing the principle of "celebrity goodwill," in which he maintained that Johnny's brand was enhanced during and because of the marriage to Joanna, and that therefore she deserved more. More than the actual earner? The doctrine was specious and the PR aspect atrocious; all Crowley succeeded in doing was to make the classy Joanna Carson look grasping. She began to lose a lot of friends, even some SHARE women who admired her attributes but whose husbands' work was somehow related to Johnny. Her experience could be summed up by a run-in Joanna had one day with Joan Rivers.

"I hope we will still be friends after this is over," Joanna said.

"No, sorry, dear," the always candid Rivers replied. "My relationship with Johnny is far too important to risk it on a friendship with his ex."

Still, there came a day when Johnny finally threw in the towel. "This is too much," he said. "I've got to clear my head. Tell Norman to get me out. Fuck the cost." And so it ended.

Under the property settlement, Joanna received the house on St. Cloud Road in Bel Air; the apartment in the Pierre; a Rolls-Royce and other cars; some significant art and half of their stocks and bank accounts. Overall, her portion was worth $35 million. It was less than Crowley had demanded, but much more than the average on-again, off-again fashion model/single mother could expect to be awarded after a twelve-year marriage. It was also far, far more, tens of millions more, than Johnny would have paid had he not, in a grand romantic gesture, dispensed with a prenuptial agreement. Regardless of the amount, she did well for putting up with a difficult man during a difficult time. According to Joanna, when they signed the divorce decree, Johnny turned to her and said, "What I'll miss the most is being able to talk to you." As far as I know, they never spoke again.

Carson retained all the stock in Carson Productions and Carson Tonight Inc., their Malibu house, the Trump Tower condominium, assorted properties and automobiles, and his membership in the Beverly Hills Tennis Club.

When Johnny started dating Alexis "Alex" Maas in earnest in 1985, he called me aside and said, "Look, I'm not going through this bullshit again. If I ever get married again, put a .38 to my head, and if we don't have a prenup, pull the damn trigger."

THIRTEEN:
1982–1985: DAYS OF WEINBERGER AND NEUROSES

In the early sixties, Ed Weinberger was a newly minted graduate of Columbia University when he left Morningside Heights and went down to 30 Rock to write jokes for Carson's monologue. He went on to create material for Bob Hope, Dick Gregory, and Dean Martin before teaming up with the writer Stan Daniels. This duo then joined James L. Brooks, David Davis, and Allan Burns to form the legendary comic brain trust of MTM Enterprises, the hit factory that produced *The Mary Tyler Moore Show, Phyllis,* and *The Betty White Show.* Later the quintet moved to Paramount where they created the hit series *Taxi,* among other hits.

After all that success, Ed might have been content to rest on his laurels (and royalties), but he went back to working by himself. When we first began talking to him, he had just finished writing the pilot for a new family-based sitcom for Bill Cosby, *The*

Cosby Show, which would win Ed his seventh Emmy, and which would become one of the funniest and most beloved series in the history of TV. In other words, we were interested in Ed because he was exactly the kind of heavy hitter who would make people notice Carson Productions again. He was a creative force who knew what audiences liked, knew how to invent compelling characters, knew how to identify talent, and knew how to make people laugh. And he could develop his own material.

All that was to the good. On the other hand, given that he was already a heavy hitter and a creative force, he wouldn't be acquiring any new radiance by standing near Carson's glow. That might not be to the good. Johnny was accustomed to being a Star Among Stars, nowhere more so than in his own domain. Ed was nobody's second banana. Stocky and droll, he always spoke slowly and thoughtfully in a deep voice about whatever topic was at hand; listening to Ed was sometimes like watching a wave roll in and suddenly break with a funny line or a sharp rejoinder. He was famously passionate about his work, which is the way fans of a person describe an attitude that the critics of that person describe as stubborn, hardheaded, or uncompromising.

Either way, he was unafraid to butt heads with anyone whose vision did not support his own. How would the dynamic of the relationship work when Carson was the guy who owned the company that was adrift, and Weinberger was the savior who was being summoned to set things right?

Ed's attorney, Joe Horacek, suggested him to us, and Joe and I had very positive discussions about the advantages of bringing Ed aboard. Horacek was up-front about Ed's personality. "I know he can be difficult and demanding," Horacek said, "but he's a creative genius, there aren't many of them, and you need one. His attitude is not his problem, Henry — it's yours. This is how you're going to earn your money. Pacify him, mollify him, kiss his ass, or kick it — you figure it out."

I explained all this to Johnny, and he was not put off. "It's been a long time since I talked to Ed," said Johnny. "I'll have lunch with him, just me and him, and I'll let you know." I don't know exactly what happened, but after the two of them met at Roy's Restaurant in West Hollywood, Johnny was very positive, and we hired Weinberger for $750,000 a year for three years, plus all of the normal profit participations and perks that an executive of his stature commands.

One of the first decisions of the Weinberger regime was to move the company out of that lovely little building on Riverside Drive (wholly owned by Johnny) and onto the Paramount lot in Hollywood. He felt isolated in that building and wanted to be part of a creative community that got his juices flowing. That was fine with us, expensive, but fine. But soon other clouds appeared on the horizon, clouds that bore watching. Maybe Ed knew of his reputation as an iconoclast and was trying to be a good team player, but he called Johnny a lot and felt frustrated by Carson's inaccessibility. This happened often because Johnny didn't want him to call, he wanted him to make decisions. You could see the disconnect, like a severed power line crackling on the ground: Ed, who had never had this much responsibility and authority before, was seeking some reassurance for some of the moves he was making; Johnny, who had all the authority but who wanted none of the responsibility, was content to leave the issues to Ed. With Johnny uninterested in being CEO, Ed and I were forced into a working relationship, and generally, we did fine.

The first show that Weinberger developed for Carson Productions was called *Mr. President.* It was a sitcom about the family life of a president of the United States, Samuel Arthur Tresch — who was played by George C. Scott — and it aired on the brand-new Fox network. The program got middling reviews — the *New York Times* said that watching Scott in the show was "like watching an elephant trample a marshmallow" — but the adequate ratings made it the best-performing show on Fox. We were glad when it was renewed for a second season . . . sort of.

There were problems. George C. Scott was a drinker; more to the point, he was a distinguished Academy Award–winning drinker with a lot of opinions about the show. He thought it was too much of a kitchen-sink comedy and that it ought to bring issues like racism and the environment in through the side door, the way a Norman Lear comedy might. Weinberger wearied of dealing with him and shuffled responsibility for the show to colleagues.

A bigger problem than Scott, however, was the cost of the show. Television financing is difficult to explain because it is so illogical. In the 1980s virtually every network paid less than the cost of production to license a show. If a show ran for five years, however, it could be put into syndication, and the producers could expect to reap huge profits. Until that occurs, each show that is produced loses money. In our case, because we were paying George C. Scott $100,000 an episode, the highest sitcom salary in the business, and because Ed Weinberger had a fastidious, damn-the-costs attention to detail, we were losing piles of money. Our distributor, who was absorbing the deficits, was losing patience. Scott was in the bag half the time, and when he had a heart attack, production shut down. Johnny had been a big supporter of Scott's and had personally lobbied Weinberger to hire him, saying, "He's the only one who can pull this off." But when we concluded that this would give us a good opportunity to get out from under this pain-in-the-ass obligation, Johnny urged us to talk to Barry Diller, the bald, lantern-jawed broadcasting executive who was the head of Fox, and ask him to cancel the best-performing show on his network.

I had some concerns about seeing Diller. More than a decade before, there was a financial disagreement between Carson and Diller that turned into a lawsuit before it was resolved. It stemmed from a deal I had negotiated in the early seventies with Frank Yablans, then head of Paramount, to form a company called Carson/Paramount Productions. We set up shop on the Paramount lot in the vacated offices of Bob Evans, which were as good as you get and which Joanna did a marvelous job redecorating to suit Johnny's taste. A couple of made-for-television movies were produced by the company (the never-to-be-forgotten *Locusts* being one, starring Ben Johnson, Ron Howard, and Katherine Helmond). Despite this, I don't think Johnny was there more than two times throughout the entire history of the company.

The period when Yablans ran the studio is now usually referred to as the Golden Age of Paramount, the time when its movie division released *The Godfather, Chinatown, Paper Moon, Serpico, Death Wish, Lady Sings the Blues, Murder on the Orient Express,* and *The Longest Yard,* and the television branch had successes with *Star Trek; The Odd Couple; Mission: Impossible; Love, American Style;* and the pilot of *Happy Days.* The successes no doubt pleased Yablans's egomaniacal boss, Charles Bluhdorn, the chairman of Gulf+Western, parent of Paramount. Bluhdorn was known as the "Mad Austrian of Wall Street," but once the media began calling Yablans a genius too often, Bludhorn replaced him with Barry Diller, who had created a big success running

ABC's TV movie-of-the-week franchise.

New bosses often clean house; it's nothing personal, just business. You make some kind of settlement and move on. Diller, trying to avoid costs, was surprisingly calculating. He called Carson first, ostensibly to cancel the Carson/Paramount deal because it was too expensive. Diller then called me to say Carson agreed to the closure. I then called Johnny, who told me that Diller didn't cancel anything; he was just griping about the high costs he inherited from Yablans. "I didn't agree to anything!" insisted Johnny. Diller then proceeded to cancel the deal. We ended up having to file suit and begin taking depositions before Paramount settled the case with a million-dollar-plus payout.

That was years earlier, and although Carson and Diller now sometimes played poker together, I was still worried that this earlier episode would color our discussion. However, not a word of it came up. Diller was gracious and completely accommodating. "I love Johnny," he said. "We're poker pals. I'm happy to help." As time would soon tell, his love of Johnny was more specifically a love of Johnny's viewers, and what he was happy to do was dump an expensive and not very popular George C. Scott, who wasn't all that valuable to him. Later, when Diller decided he wanted to go after the King of Late Night, none of that poker-playing love stood in the way.

Around this time, Johnny began suffering heart problems. No surprise: the man smoked four packs a day or more. Everyone around him knew that he was a prime candidate for heart and lung disease. Yet, at the same time, he was so fit, so energetic, so lively, that disease seemed like a remote event, something to be reckoned with in the distant future. But little by little, those of us around him noticed signs of change: an ominous cough that would not go away or his sucking wind on the tennis court long before our usual match was finished. At one point he seemed so pale to me that I bought him a tanning machine. It was a big contraption shaped like a coffin that you had to climb in and out of, but it restored his color.

Johnny was too much the stoic Midwesterner to complain, but he must have felt tightness in his chest if not outright pain because he took himself in for a checkup. Very soon he was in Cedars-Sinai Medical Center, among the premier cardiac facilities in Los Angeles, undergoing an angioplasty to remove a buildup of plaque blocking one or more arteries to his heart. Everything was hush-hush — he used an assumed name at the hospital, but since the name he chose was Art Fern, the name of the "Tea Time Movie" announcer on *The Tonight Show,* I'm not sure he achieved much of a disguise. I assumed his recovery process would prevent him from his annual pilgrimage to Wimbledon, a notion that was confirmed by his physician, Dr. Robert "Bud" Foran, who told me Carson should stay home and watch this year's tournament on TV.

"Bullshit," responded Johnny. "Besides, Foran's partner was the one who actually did the procedure, and he said I was good to go." As it happened, we went and had our usual good time.

Not long after this, my father's chronic coronary condition worsened. Carson recommended that I take my dad to see his doctors at Cedars-Sinai. Dr. Foran examined my father and concluded that he needed the type of sophisticated vascular operation that was best done at Cedars because of its staff expertise. My dad thought about it but decided to have the operation done where he lived, in Florida. Taking the company plane, Scott and I flew to Miami to be with Dad during the surgery. We stayed three days, leaving only when it seemed Dad had weathered the operation and was on the mend.

Two weeks later, during spring break 1985, Joyce and my two children and I were vacationing at the Mauna Lani Bay Hotel on the big island of Hawaii when I got a phone call telling me that Dad had died. I called Johnny to tell him that I would be heading to Miami immediately and that naturally I was going to be preoccupied and largely unavailable for the immediate future.

Usually Johnny was not very good at moments like this, and I was surprised and touched at how consoling he tried to be. He reminded me that I was with him when his dad died and that he appreciated it, and several times he asked what he could do for me. When I told him that I was planning to get the morning flight out of Honolulu to LA and then catch a flight to Miami, he said, "Look, I'm going to arrange to have Bob Elliott meet you with the plane at LAX. It'll be faster, and you'll be more comfortable."

Even in my grief I was conscious of how uncommonly considerate he was being, but then he blew my mind. He asked for my mother's phone number. Normally when something unfortunate happened to someone he knew, he would have me call and express his condolences. To call my mother personally was a big deal for him, and it was a big deal for me.

And that wasn't all. When I arrived at my parents' apartment, I found that Johnny had sent a beautiful flower arrangement, as well as platters of food from the famous Sage Deli in Hallandale Beach. He knew it was traditional in Jewish homes to have this kind of food on hand to offer mourners, and he had his secretary track down the best place to order from. When I called to express my appreciation, my mother got on the phone and broke into tears as she thanked him.

Weinberger's second show for Carson Productions was *Amen,* a series set in a black neighborhood church in Philadelphia. It starred Sherman Hemsley as a deacon whose wacky and wily schemes often got him into hot water. Anna Maria Horsford played his daughter, an unmarried lady in her mid-thirties, and Clifton Davis played the new young pastor who developed an attraction for the daughter. Despite NBC's decision to bury the show in the nine-thirty time slot on Saturday night, *Amen* was a hit and finished the season in a very respectable fourteenth place, with a 19.4 rating and a 33 share. (To show you how things have changed, the top-rated show in the 2010–2011 television season was *American Idol.* It had a 14.4 rating and a 23 share.)

Unfortunately, Carson didn't like the show and never worked up any enthusiasm for it. He loved the concept but felt the writing and acting were subpar. His trouble began at the outset, during the making of the pilot. Johnny and I went to Paramount to observe the filming. He was not pleased with the dialogue and was determined to let Weinberger know of his displeasure. Little Richard was doing a guest spot in the pilot, and Carson did not think him funny. He wanted him cut or the lines changed. "Make Ed change this," he said, reading me his notes. "And change this line. And this one." His mood was not good, and what was worse, everyone could hear what he was saying.

"Johnny — Henry — I'm sorry, but we really need everyone to be quiet while we're rehearsing."

"I understand that, Ed, but you're rehearsing things that need to be changed. I don't see much point in perfecting dialogue that has to be changed."

Weinberger's face went through several shades of red, but to his credit, he stayed calm. "Why don't we all take ten?" he said, closing the set, and he came and sat down with us. He got right to the point. "What's the problem, Johnny?"

"The dialogue is awful, Ed," said Johnny.

"I don't agree, but there is nothing that can't be improved on. What should they be saying here?"

"I'm not going to write your show for you, Ed," Johnny replied. "I'm just here to say that what you've got here is a piece of shit. I don't know what you have Little Richard doing there, but somebody should tell him to stick to his rock-and-roll schtick and stay out of acting. The guy can't deliver a line, and he couldn't ad-lib a fart after a baked bean dinner."

This was going nowhere good, and it was getting there in a hurry. If Johnny left the stage without feeling that Ed had listened to him, Weinberger's days would be numbered and our problems magnified.

I managed to interrupt the discussion and separate the two men. "Look, he was in the middle of producing the show," I said to Johnny. "You know how you are when you're working. It's not the best time to give you suggestions, is it? Let me go talk to him. Please don't leave."

I then went to Weinberger, who didn't wait for me to begin. "He just doesn't get it," Ed said. "All he knows is live television and immediate audience reaction. I know episodic television and what makes a sitcom work and what doesn't. I know what the fuck I'm doing, and he doesn't have a clue. So what should we do?"

"Give him something," I said. "He has some suggestions; reshoot the scene the way Johnny wants it. Make him feel that he made a contribution. And then go and do whatever the fuck you want to. Agreed?"

"Whatever I want?"

"You're the producer, right?"

"All right," said Ed. He and Johnny went into the green room, and Ed dutifully wrote down all of Johnny's notes and reshot the scenes the way Johnny recommended. Feelings were soothed and the pilot was completed, with none of the changes included.

Amen went on to become a success, but Carson never warmed to the show. It was Weinberger's baby, not his. And after the confrontation at the pilot, Ed always thought of Johnny as a lurking threat, capable of exploding at any moment. Thereafter, any time Ed and Johnny had to deal with each other, I had to act as the go-between.

One morning at the office, I received a call from a reporter at the *Los Angeles Times*.

"Would you like to comment on today's announcement that Fox is going to run a late-night talk show opposite Carson, hosted by Joan Rivers?"

Lawyers are trained to repress involuntary reactions to unexpected news, but this one made me feel like a cartoon cat. "Whaaaat?" I answered. "Let me get back to you."

I immediately called Carson. "Can you believe this?" He was genuinely shocked, but not that *The Tonight Show* was going to be facing a new competitor. Networks had been running talk shows at Carson for years; even Fred Silverman, once NBC had its fill of his failures, ran Alan Thicke at Johnny on a group of independent stations. Johnny shrugged him off like a fly. If the infant Fox network wanted to stand on its tippy toes and take a swipe at the king, well, bring it on.

No, the shocking news was that it was Joan who was taking this shot and that she had never breathed a word to Johnny. This seemed like a huge betrayal and one quite out of the ordinary. What was ordinary was for Barry Diller to sit with a shit-eating grin on his face and profess how much he looooved Johnny and would do anything for him and then turn around and launch a show as a direct challenge to Carson's dominion. That was just business.

With Joan, it was personal. Not only did Johnny admire Joan as one of the very best comedians of her generation, he had a soft spot of affection for her. She was among a small, special group that included Bill Cosby and Richard Pryor who got their first big break from Carson. Moreover, Johnny and Joan's husband, Edgar, were friends, and Edgar and Joan had acted as intermediaries during the secret negotiations with ABC in 1980. Over the years, Joan had hosted *The Tonight Show* ninety-one times (second only among guest hosts to Joey Bishop, who logged a lot of time in the host's seat in the early sixties, between the Paar and Carson administrations). Johnny thought highly enough of the way she handled the throne that he named her his official stand-in, something that enhanced her value and gave her real cachet when she had to negotiate with the many bookers and agents and promoters she had to deal with.

And the feelings of respect and affection were completely reciprocated. "Johnny is one of the great straight men of the century," she once wrote. "He never cut off a punch line, and when it came, he broke up." Rivers has compared the sparkling comic rapport she and Carson displayed during her *Tonight Show* appearances to that of Burns and Allen.

And yet somehow she was able to turn around and blindside us. It was inexplicable. And despicable. Just days before, she had been a guest on *The Tonight Show* and presented Johnny with a copy of her book, *Enter Talking,* which she had dedicated to him, all the while knowing this announcement was about to come down. And just weeks before, Johnny had been sitting with Barry Diller at Swifty Lazar's Oscar party, with Barry being all sweet to his poker buddy, even as he was sharpening his shiv.

The moment Johnny and I hung up, I called the lawyer who had negotiated her deal. "What the fuck was she thinking?" I asked. "Johnny gave her every break in the book. Just tell her this: Johnny feels like he's been stabbed in the back. She will never appear on his show again."

"I think Joan would love to talk to Johnny and explain . . ."

"Forget it. Tell her not to bother to explain. Her actions have said everything there is to say." Then I slammed down the phone.

Looking back, I wish I had listened to her explanations, although I wonder if I would have been calm enough to hear them with an open mind. Later, in *Still Talking,* her memoir of this period, Joan offered a credible explanation of why she felt she had to act the way she did.

First, as Joan points out, being one of Johnny Carson's nearest and dearest show business friends didn't entitle you to much. For example, it didn't mean that he ever spoke to you, at least not off the set. Johnny almost never greeted guests in their dressing rooms before the show; he wanted to save all the energy and spontaneity for the audience. Beyond that, the list of people with whom he liked to socialize was short, and Joan's name wasn't on it. Instead, she spoke to intermediaries, and those conversations often made her feel insecure. Peter Lassally, one of the producers of *The Tonight Show,* told her that if her ratings as guest host dropped below a certain point, she'd be replaced, which was a cold thing to do and not the sort of discussion he ought to have been having with the talent.

Second, she was feeling insecure because of something I had done, namely, when it was time for her to sign a contract to become the permanent guest host of *The Tonight Show,* I offered her a one-year deal. But because Johnny had just signed a two-year deal, she felt endangered, although I do not remember attaching any long-term significance to the number, nor do I remember Edgar coming back and asking for another year.

Most serious, Joan was also feeling insulted, having been told that Brandon Tartikoff at NBC had worked up a list of ten comedians who could succeed Carson should he retire from *The Tonight Show.* Despite the strong ratings she generated as Johnny's replacement, the list did not include her name. Frankly, I would have been surprised if it had. Whenever Carson left the show, the only sensible thing NBC could do was to make a generational change. They wouldn't want one of Carson's peers; they would want someone like he was in 1962, someone who could endure.

Then Fox, the clever fox, addressed all those fears and insecurities, and offered her a talk show that would begin at eleven p.m. on the East Coast. It was a very tempting offer — good money, the prestige of having her own show, and being the first woman to do so in the late-night time slot; and with that half-hour's head start on *The Tonight Show,* a very real chance to put a dent in Johnny's numbers. The other attractive part of the offer was that Edgar would serve as the executive producer. This would certainly elevate the stature of a man who for a number of years had been best known as Joan Rivers's husband.

It isn't hard to spot evidence of Edgar's love of secrecy and subterfuge in what happened next. Joan says that she wanted to talk to Johnny, to discuss his feelings about the offer. She asked Edgar to set up the call, and Edgar later told her that he called me on two separate occasions, and a key NBC executive on a third occasion, to discuss her future. Edgar reported that he never received a return phone call.

I can't speak for anyone else, but I didn't get a call. My office keeps meticulous phone logs, and besides, talking on the phone is what I do. Joan was a friend and former client and someone with whom Carson Productions had a contractual relationship, all good reasons for me to pick up the phone. And even if human error caused us to drop a call, I seriously doubt we would have done it twice. The chance that we would have missed or ignored both calls and that NBC would have overlooked a third call from Joan on top of that was infinitesimal.

But is it possible that Edgar would have tried to deceive Joan and tell her that he called but that I never called back? Yes, I think it's possible. Edgar and Joan were certainly right to worry that she did not have a long-term future at *The Tonight Show* once Carson departed. She got good ratings, but in Johnny's opinion, she couldn't maintain an audience night after night; she was, he said, "too hard." Going to Fox might well have been her best opportunity to prove Johnny wrong, to show that she could carry a nightly program.

But Joan admits that she was deeply ambivalent about leaving Johnny and the security of *The Tonight Show* in favor of an unproven outfit like Fox. To me, it's entirely plausible Edgar feared that if Johnny talked to Joan and offered her any inducement to stay — a free oil change at Jiffy Lube, say — she would have rejected Fox and stayed with *The Tonight Show*. And in two months or two years or whenever Johnny retired, Joan would have nothing, and neither would Edgar, his dreams of validating his career by becoming an executive producer of a network talk show gone a-glimmering.

But here's one thing Edgar would have been wrong about: Johnny wouldn't have stood in Joan's way. Johnny told me later that had Joan called him before the decision was announced, he would have given her his blessing. He knew it was a good deal for her and, frankly, he really didn't fear her.

The Late Show Starring Joan Rivers debuted in October of 1986. It got reasonably good ratings at first, but then they sagged. In the spring, Fox decided to replace Edgar as executive producer. Joan declared that if Fox fired Edgar, they would have to fire her, so Fox got rid of them both. Three months later, Edgar committed suicide.

I remember talking to Johnny about this terrible news involving people who had once been friends. "I guess he kept pushing Joan," he said. "The poor son of a bitch — married to that woman. Do you think it was Joan or Edgar that fucked me?" Of course I believed it was Edgar who hatched the scheme. At the very least, he knew the details of ABC's offer to Johnny in 1980 — details to use in his negotiation with Fox.

Johnny then tried to change the mood. "Did you hear this one? When a woman's husband passed away, she put the usual death notice in the newspaper, but she added that he had died of gonorrhea. Once the newspapers were delivered, a good friend of the family phoned and complained bitterly, 'You know very well that he died of diarrhea, not gonorrhea.' The widow replied, 'Yes, I know that he died of diarrhea, but I thought it would be better for posterity to remember him as a great lover rather than the big shit that he really was.' "

In 1989 Joan got another shot at a talk show. It was a daytime syndicated program that ran for four years and earned her an Emmy. The award seems to prove that Johnny had underestimated Joan's appeal, although the relatively short tenure of four years seems to confirm his view that she was too hard to succeed on a daily basis. But the strength of her ongoing career certainly proves that no one is more resilient than Joan.

Johnny's mother died later that year. "The wicked witch is dead," he said when he called with the news. It was a bittersweet remark, jokey without being funny; in other words, it was true. He loved his mother as a son must. But he did not like her. He left the arrangements to his sister, Catherine, and did not attend the funeral. This did not entirely surprise me; a couple of years earlier, he had absented himself from his father's services as well, telling me, "The only time I want to go to a funeral is when I want to make sure the son of a bitch is really dead." According to his own criteria, I thought these circumstances might fit.

In my opinion, many of the difficulties Johnny had with relationships can be traced back to his relationship with Ruth. She was a difficult parent, the kind who inflicts consistent emotional pain on her offspring, pain that endures throughout their lives and grows. As Susan Forward says in her insightful book, *Toxic Parents,* "All of us develop our expectations about how people will treat us based on our relationships with our parents. If those relationships are, for the most part, emotionally nourishing, respectful of our rights and feelings, we'll grow up expecting others to treat us in much the same way. . . . But if childhood is a time of unrelenting anxiety, tension, and pain, then we develop negative expectations and rigid defenses."

From all that Johnny told me, his mother ignored his needs and burdened him with guilt. She was indifferent and lacked emotion. She really did damage Johnny — damage that manifested itself in adulthood in his difficulties with bonding, decision making, and depression. According to Truman Capote, who saw Johnny frequently when Capote and the Carsons were cotenants in the UN Plaza, Johnny once told him that his mother would throw herself on the floor and scream, "I bore you from these loins, and you do this to me! All that pain and this is what I get in return!"

"I met his mother once," Capote continued. "She was an absolute bitch. Despite everything he's done, she's never really accepted him, and he constantly wants her approval. That's what keeps him going."

In my opinion, Ruth Carson soured her son to the point where it was damn near impossible for him to be happy with any woman for any extended period of time — or with people in general, for that matter. The one thing he couldn't deal with was his heart. Perhaps Jody or Joanne or Joanna had it for a moment in time, but it didn't last. Surely he never really opened himself up to his children. It still impresses me how many times I saw him exhibit enormous heartfelt generosity. He bought a brand-new car for an old pal from his radio days. He sent Danny Stradella $100,000 when he was down on his luck. After Freddy de Cordova died, Johnny sent Janet de Cordova $100,000 with a sweet note that read: "I will always remember the great moments we shared. . . . I know Fred was not a great money manager, and you are no doubt encountering unexpected financial demands. Please look on the enclosed as a bonus for almost twenty-five years as *The Tonight Show* producer. Right now I have this strange feeling that Fred is telling Saint Peter how to do his job better." And this was after he and Johnny had a serious skirmish. He was enormously generous with me on numerous occasions, and no one was ever a better tipper. But if somebody close to him put pressure on him, like Joanna committing him to emcee the SHARE banquet, he was grudging, angry, and sullen.

And just as he had trouble giving love, he had as much difficulty receiving it. I'm certain all his wives made great efforts to keep him happy and centered, but he never really trusted happiness, and even when things were going well, he would find a way to stir things up and get all those around him upset. More than anything, and certainly more than his infidelities, I believe Joanna grew tired of seeing her very best efforts to build a home for him being met with indifference, if not hostility. He couldn't lead a normal life, nourishing people and being nourished in return. When I saw him with his sons, there was never warmth or affection.

I have been told that Johnny idealized his mother and believed that everything bad in his childhood was somehow his fault. I know that as long as his mother lived, he strove to win her love, and he never received it. He was the child of an emotionally abusive mother — no matter how strong and successful he became, he was a child whose trust had been betrayed. "She was selfish and cold," Johnny's second wife, Joanne, once told an interviewer. "No wonder he had trouble dealing with women. Mrs. Carson was cold, closed off, a zero when it came to showing affection."

Johnny's most successful relationships had a transactional foundation, one where his money compensated for a lot of bad behavior. I enjoyed Johnny's friendship, but I overlooked a lot, in no small measure because he put a lot of money in my pocket. His wives and his sons put up with many insults and disappointments, but the women always got their payments, and the boys received their stipends. Freddy de Cordova and Bobby Quinn and Ed McMahon and the others at *The Tonight Show* swallowed a fair amount of shit from Carson, but he was the man who signed their generous paychecks.

Ruth, however, was immune to his gifts: to his minks and his trips and so on. More to the point, Ruth was immune to all of his charms, all of his talents. Nothing this extraordinary man could do impressed her, and she let him know that from his childhood onward. Johnny Carson enjoyed the adulation of millions, but his mother could not love him. He carried that pain, and spread it, all his life.

FOURTEEN:
1987: DARKNESS FALLS

Tom Shales, in the *Washington Post,* wrote, "Johnny just gets better and better; everyone else gets worse and worse. He has probably been funnier longer and more consistently than any other comedian who ever lived."

And it was true. On *The Tonight Show,* Johnny just kept rolling on and on, never deviating, seldom surprising, seldom surpassing, but nearly always delivering. "You have to understand," Ed McMahon once explained. "Every day, no matter what else is going on in his life, he has to come out there and be Johnny Carson." Well, for the part of the day he had to host *The Tonight Show,* he mastered that challenge. But for the rest of the time when he had to be Johnny Carson, he accomplished that by making his world smaller, or simpler, or harder to reach.

Johnny began dating Alexis "Alex" Maas in

1985. She was a tall, lissome blonde in her early thirties, very pretty, who had once worked for Governor Michael Dukakis in Massachusetts. It's said that they met when she came wandering across his property in Malibu holding an empty wine glass, and he went out with a bottle of Montrachet and said, "Can I fill you up?" How she came to be on his property and where she was heading were details never explained, and it's just as well — all that would do was ruin a good story. The reality was that they met at a party on Carbon Beach, a few doors away from Johnny's home. It was at Irwin Yablans's leased beach home where Johnny dropped by to check things out.

Johnny was dating other women at the time — since the divorce, he'd been linked with Sally Field, Morgan Fairchild, Angie Dickinson, and many others — but after a few months, it became clear that none of the others mattered, and that the relationship between Johnny and Alexis was becoming more than casual. At that point, Johnny had me order a background check from our PI, Joe Mullen. The report was unremarkable, the information familiar to the point of cliché. In the series of positions she had held, one could read the signature of an attractive girl moving from job to job in the hopes of landing the right one. And Johnny was finally the right one. I suppose Johnny could be considered a job by all those who knew him. Every other wife and girlfriend he had had found him to be a handful.

It was not a surprise when Johnny announced that he wanted to marry again; Johnny was the marrying kind. No commitment phobia there, perhaps because commitment wasn't really part of the marriage package. It was, however, somewhat surprising that he chose to marry Alex, who was bright, amiable, and refined but nothing special. Had he, on that special day when they met, been doing something other than looking through his window, I don't think that his life would have been much diminished. In my estimation, he could have met someone very much like Alex an hour later seating guests at a restaurant, or two hours later managing a spa, or three hours later in a shop on Rodeo Drive. Johnny's previous wives were closer to being matches for him in temperament and interests and experience. Jody and he were two unformed college students from the Midwest, similar in age, upbringing, and expectations. Joanne was a television personality, younger and hardly a star of his magnitude, but from the same milieu; they were the same kind of fish swimming in the same waters. When he married Joanna, he was an established star and a grown man, but she was a complex and challenging woman who shrewdly built up her own stature to be worthy of his, maybe not entirely his equal, but more than his match.

But Alex was not his equal. She was a companion and a plaything, much younger, not as sophisticated or as intelligent or as experienced. Perhaps his marriage to Joanna had exhausted him and left him wishing for a relationship that posed less of a challenge, something that required less engagement. Often in those days we were present at the same occasions, but I can't recall a time when Alex made her presence felt.

It wouldn't be fair to say that Johnny was indifferent to Alex's wants, needs, moods, preferences, and so on. But after all, this was his fourth marriage, and even at his best, he never spent a lot of time thinking about others. There was a lot about the relationship that he seemed to conduct on autopilot. Their wedding, for example, on June 20, 1987, took place outside his home in Malibu, overlooking the Pacific Ocean. It was a beautiful setting, as any guest could have told you. However, there weren't any guests. Johnny wanted to avoid publicity, so there were no guests, just his brother, Dick, with Judge Hogoboom, the judge from Johnny's arbitration in 1979, presiding. I wasn't particularly upset at not being asked to attend — Johnny said that as long as he didn't invite me, he could get away with not inviting anyone. I suppose this made sense at the time; after all, not even Alex's parents were present, although a speakerphone was connected so they could listen from their home in Pittsburgh. Judge Hogoboom, I thought, assessed things perfectly. "It's a perfect spot," he felt, "but it felt a little bleak." In retrospect, I should have seen that not only had the marriage ritual been downgraded in Johnny's eyes, but so had our friendship. I was now among the people he was trying to get out of inviting to this wedding.

The honeymoon was, if anything, even less romantic.

Right after the wedding, Johnny and Alex headed to London for Wimbledon. The taking of vows is usually marked with the couple spending some time alone getting to know each other, but Johnny had gotten to know Alex plenty over the last two years. Besides, this was Wimbledon, which he hadn't missed in ten years, and which he wanted me to attend, just as I had done for ten years. Why let a new bride change things? I guess Johnny and Alex got some private time together, if only because he and I spent less time together than we usually did on these trips. I was dating Mary Hart at the time, and because her *Entertainment Tonight* commitments kept her from attending all but the last few matches, I spent more time hanging with the guys and was excused from some of the usual couples-only shopping and dining events that I and whomever I was with typically spent with Johnny and whomever he was with.

For the most part, we had a great week in London. There were no problems to deal with, and every night we had reservations at Annabel's or the Guinea Grill or Santini. We were there with our old tennis pal Bob Trapenberg, who had a new girlfriend from South Africa, Ruan Lowe, who was a kick. Bob was a former tour tennis pro, a good friend to Johnny and me. He stayed wherever we were and had a car and driver for the week, generally fulfilling the role of the gentleman tennis player. Trap dressed fastidiously and always traveled first class. I provided him with the Wimbledon tickets and the NBC passes and he paid for all the rest.

One day, when we were in the lobby waiting for a car to take us to the matches, a situation arose. Just us three guys, a sudden shortness of temper, no big deal. Johnny abruptly turned to me and right in front of Trap, making no effort to be discreet, asked if we were paying for Trap's room and his airline tickets. I responded that Trap always paid his own way. Johnny was satisfied, but Trap was upset. Here was a man who played tennis with Carson almost every day. They were good friends, and Carson chose to ask an embarrassing question that implied that Trap was freeloading. Like Carson paid any attention to money anyway! Years later, the thought that Carson suspected Trap was sponging off of him still bothered the old pro.

In truth, I didn't pay much attention to what seemed like a bit of garden-variety nastiness from Carson, who had always been capable of marring a nice moment with a cutting remark. Perhaps I should have sensed it might be a harbinger of what was to come.

After the Wimbledon finals, Mary and I left for a week in the French countryside, while Johnny and Alex left for Italy. We planned to meet at a yacht in a week's time. Mary and I had a great week, traveling through the Côtes du Rhône vineyards, which run for more than two hundred kilometers down the Rhone Valley from the south of Lyon to just south of Avignon. The wines of the region are brilliant, and the steep, vine-covered slopes of the region are breathtaking. At the end of the week, Mary and I picked up two cases of wine to bring to the yacht. We were looking forward to the cruise.

When we arrived in Ventimiglia — in those days, one always chartered a boat in Italy rather than France because the taxes were less and the paperwork was more efficient — we could see that the yacht, *Parts V,* was everything we had been told to expect, with opulent bedroom suites, Jacuzzi tubs, jet boats, WaveRunners, Jet Skis, inflatables, kayaks, and fishing and snorkeling gear. And as if anything else was needed to elevate our excitement, we would be spending the week cruising the incomparable Italian Riviera, the narrow coastal strip that lies between the Ligurian Sea and the mountain chain formed by the Maritime Alps and the Apennines.

The setting was idyllic, but as we quickly recognized, the atmosphere was not. One unexpected factor was that Johnny's brother, Dick, had joined the cruise. Dick's wife had recently died, and I guess Johnny felt the trip would be good for him. This was a generous gesture on Johnny's part, but on this occasion Dick was a fifth wheel if ever there was one, and a melancholy one at that.

As soon as we arrived, I could sense a chill in the air. I had no idea what had transpired during their week in Italy, but Johnny was not happy. He was irritable; something was bugging him. One could only hope that, as on so many previous occasions, the mood would pass.

Not that day. When we convened for dinner at nine p.m., we could see that Johnny was still cross. The chef on the cruise was reputed to be first-rate, and as dish after dish was presented to us, we could see that his reputation was justified. But Johnny was glowering. Alex then said something that he disliked, a remark so inconsequential that it didn't even register with me. But Johnny looked her straight in the eye and said, "We've been married for three weeks. If you say something like that again, this marriage won't last another three weeks." It was as nasty a rebuke as I have ever heard, akin to a slap, and I don't know why any of us remained at the table, particularly Alex. Dinner was, of course, ruined. We hurried through the food almost without tasting it, just to be able to escape the table.

My mind flashed to another dinner I had with Johnny and Alex some months earlier back in California. I was with Joyce De-Witt, and as we were eating, Joyce wondered why Johnny had never strongly pursued a career as an actor. "You'd be a natural to play Puck in *A Midsummer's Night Dream*," she told him. "I think people would love to see you do something like that." I knew Joyce meant this not as a mere compliment but as something she recognized in his presence and star power.

But Johnny thought that she was just flattering him, something he had always hated. Usually he just brushed it aside, but on that night, he reacted with real disdain. "You don't know what you're talking about," he said to Joyce, who obviously knew at least a little bit about what she was talking about. "My audience doesn't want that. They don't want to see me perform [that way], especially not Shakespeare." His speech grew heated. He began lecturing her, instructing her. I kept thinking that any moment he would stop, but he continued in this stern, didactic way until Alex mercifully forced a change of subject. We left early that night, too, before dessert.

The next day, sitting on deck, I spoke to Johnny. With a combination of concern and diplomatic chiding, I encouraged him to lighten up. "Geez, man, you're on a yacht in the Mediterranean! Feel the sun! I don't know what's bothering you, but throw it overboard!"

He laughed, although not very mirthfully. "You're right," he said. "You know I don't have much of a talent for happiness. I never have. My mother saw to that." Somehow, here on the Riviera, he was feeling a howling Nebraska wind.

"Well, come on — Ruth's not on the boat."

By now I'd seen this a thousand times. The man who was caring, empathetic, sometimes even sensitive, could abruptly become nasty, cutting, cruel, and sometimes even despotic. Here we were on a beautiful yacht, and four people were trying to make one man happy. We were all deferential to his mood swings, and we were all trying to cheer him out of an unhappiness that had no obvious cause. It was as if four adults were ministering to one child. Of course Ruth was on the boat. Ruth was always there.

The second day passed pleasantly enough. We stopped at a small island near Cannes for lunch and then headed over to the little town of Juan-les-Pins for dinner. Once described as "a pop-art Monte Carlo," Juan-les-Pins had a carnival spirit that drew a young and noisy crowd. For many years, Restaurant le Vésuvio was a favorite of ours here. It was in the middle of town, with lots of action that added to the festive atmosphere.

The yacht captain booked a table for dinner at nine p.m. The tender from *Parts V* brought us from the boat to the dock in town. As we alighted, the captain handed Johnny a walkie-talkie. "We will be waiting here at the dock at eleven-thirty to bring you back to the yacht," the captain said, "but if you have any change in plans, call us."

Dinner was excellent. After we finished, Johnny, Alex, and Dick decided that they wanted to go back to the yacht, but Mary and I wanted to enjoy the town a while longer. "Just tell the crew to come back for us at two o'clock," I told Johnny.

"Sure," he said, "but here, take the radio."

"No, you keep it," I said. But he pressed it into my hands, and not wanting to create some comedy routine on the sidewalk, I took the radio. Mary and I walked around the picturesque town for a couple of hours and had a delightful time.

We headed back a little before two. As we neared the dock, we could see several people standing by the yacht's tender. One was Johnny. *Holy shit,* I thought to myself, *what is going on?*

Before I could say anything, the captain of the ship was blurting his apologies. "Mr. Bushkin, I have told Mr. Carson that I was very sorry that I was six minutes late in arriving, but he refuses to accept my regrets."

"Fuck this," snarled Johnny. "I didn't pay $150,000 to have you late in picking me up. We will be leaving the boat tomorrow morning. Call your headquarters and have them arrange a flight from Nice to Los Angeles for the five of us. I will not stay on this boat any longer."

I was dumbfounded. We all were. Johnny had arrived at the dock at eleven-twenty-five, five minutes before the tender was due. At eleven-thirty-five he was so angry that he instructed Alex and Dick to leave the dock with him. Because he hated to shop and was not interested in going to a club, there was little for him to do while waiting for Mary and me. He refused all efforts by Dick and Alex to lighten him up, and he wouldn't return to the dock where the tender was standing by. He just sat and fumed for three hours. As we boarded the tender, Johnny continued to harangue the poor captain, who was soon offering to have himself replaced by a captain who would fly in from London to salvage the trip.

We spent the next few hours in the saloon of the yacht trying to reason with Johnny. By four a.m. he was willing to accept a new captain. At six a.m. he finally decided the old captain could stay, and we finally went to bed.

"He's insane," I said to Mary as I crawled into bed. "We've got to find some way to get off this damn boat."

I slept past noon. When I woke up, I found out that Mary had already taken the tender to town and back. "Henry, I have such terrible news," she said. "*Entertainment Tonight* called. There's an emergency at the show, and they need me back immediately."

If there was one excuse Johnny was bound to accept, it was that there was an emergency at the show. We packed immediately. I'll never forget the woeful look on Alex's face as Mary and I escaped.

This was the last vacation I took with Johnny.

In 1985 Johnny asked me to talk to Ed Weinberger about giving his son Rick a job somewhere in Carson Productions. In Rick's long up-and-down battle with alcohol, this was an up phase, and Johnny, who seldom interceded on behalf of his sons, hoped to encourage his progress. Weinberger took the request well and hired Rick to be the stage manager of *Amen,* which was just starting its run.

Being a stage manager is a substantial job. Effectively the director's right-hand man, the stage manager is in charge of schedules, scripts, props, and actors during the rehearsal process. He or she also records all of the director's decisions about blocking, lighting, sound, changes in set design, wardrobe, and so on, and follows up to make sure that all of these directives are fulfilled. It is a key position, and if it's not being performed well, the entire production notices.

Unfortunately, Rick was not up to the job. He was habitually late for work and was often drinking on the job. Weinberger spoke to me countless times about the problem. His message was almost always the same. "Please talk to Johnny. I'd have fired him long ago if he wasn't the boss's son."

I did talk to Johnny. And Johnny always promised to talk to Rick.

One day I got a call from Weinberger. "I

fired Rick," he said. "He came in drunk, and I threw him off the set. It's done."

My immediate concern was about Johnny. "Did you call Carson and tell him?" I asked.

"Hell, no," said Ed. "That's your job. You tell him. And make it clear — he is not coming back."

"Come on, Ed, you're not being reasonable."

"On the contrary, Henry, I'm the only one who is being reasonable."

This was a major problem. I immediately drove over to the Paramount lot to try to persuade Weinberger face-to-face. He was having none of it. "I put up with it for a long time, Henry. I gave Rick a lot of chances. If he was a stagehand who could just go fall asleep someplace, it wouldn't matter, but he's got responsibilities, and when he doesn't do his job, it really does screw up the entire show."

I waited to tell Johnny until after he had finished taping that day's edition of *The Tonight Show* and then drove over to the studio to break the news. Johnny's reaction was predictable. "That fucking Weinberger!" he said. "The nerve of that asshole to fire my kid without talking to me first! Well, he's gone. I'm firing him."

It took every ounce of diplomacy I could

muster to remind him that this wasn't Rick's first offense: there had been many prior incidents that had been brought to his attention. "You were going to talk to Rick, remember?"

The reminder quenched some of Johnny's fire. "Yeah, well," he said. "You know, it's not easy being the son of a person like me." I could see a sense of hopelessness overcoming him. It was clear that if he could have traded his entire fortune for a magic potion that would have cured Rick, he would have made that deal in a heartbeat. On some level, he obviously loved his son, but he had little ability to express it and certainly no capacity to help Rick fight the disease that had enveloped him in such a tight grip. "God, I wish I could be a better father. Tomorrow, I'll go see Weinberger and get him to give Rick another chance." I didn't see any point in that, but neither did I see any point in trying to talk Carson out of it.

The next morning Weinberger called Johnny and then told me how it went. "I told him that he was the boss, and he could hire or fire anybody he wanted. But I also told him that it was Rick or me. If he brought the kid back, I'd quit."

I don't think anyone who had a financial relationship with Carson had ever challenged him so directly. Weinberger won, but I don't believe the two of them ever spoke to each other again.

Some five years after this crisis, on June 21, 1991, Rick was killed when his car plunged down a steep embankment along a paved service road near Cayucos, a small town north of San Luis Obispo. The story is that he had been taking photographs, and the car started rolling. On the first *Tonight Show* after Rick's death, Carson used the last segment of the show to share with his audience some of Rick's photos. It had to have been difficult for Johnny to reveal a piece of his inner self, the sentimental side few were permitted to glimpse, and to do it while the pain of Rick's sad life was still so raw.

Later I heard that in the course of this difficult and emotional tribute, Freddy de Cordova, the longtime executive producer of *The Tonight Show* and Johnny's trusted captain, saw that the program was about to run over its allotted time slot and, as he no doubt had done several hundred times before, he gave Johnny the signal to wrap it up. Afterward, Carson, furious that Freddy had tried to rush him through his tribute, banned de Cordova from the floor of *The Tonight Show* set and never permitted him to return. This was like telling a captain that he was no longer allowed on the bridge of his ship; de Cordova finished out the last year of Johnny's tenure on the program as a nonperson. In his own twisted, dysfunctional way, Johnny was a very loyal father.

As time went on, being Johnny's lawyer meant playing a lot of roles and I became a business manager, overseeing not only Carson Productions, but also other investments (although not his stock portfolio) where Johnny took a position of equity in a company. Several of the deals, such as the television station we bought in Las Vegas, performed very well, and others were disappointing. Invariably, Carson's interest in these projects was highest at the beginning, and he was frequently quite willing to promise to commit not only money but also time, which was often more valuable. The possibility of seeing or meeting Carson was often key to enlisting other investors or making the venture work. As I came to learn, however, no matter what Johnny would promise, we couldn't depend on him to follow through. Although sometimes he surprised us.

In the late seventies, my firm represented a developer who was constructing a ninety-three-acre mall in northwest Houston called Willowbrook. When the developer ran out of money, the firm formed an investment group to take over the project. Johnny agreed to become a member of the group.

"Sure, Houston, I love Houston," he responded. "Aerospace. Oil. Mike Davis says Houston is going to surpass New York and Chicago."

One day I mentioned that a few of my partners and I were going to Houston for the initial unveiling of the site model, showcasing all its residential, commercial, hotel, and mall components. "Great," Johnny said. "You don't mind if I come with you, do you?"

How could I mind? How could I not be suspicious?

On the plane, Johnny surprised me again. "Listen, dinner tonight is all arranged, okay?" He ticked off the names of the six or seven investment partners who would be invited.

"Great," I said, thinking how unusual this was. "Who made the arrangements?"

"Remember Miss Texas?"

"Miss Texas from Houston-Dallas-Houston?" Houston-Dallas-Houston was our shorthand for an oddly scheduled trio of club dates Johnny played in 1974: Thursday in Houston, Friday in Dallas, and Saturday back in Houston. It wasn't an engagement he was too keen on keeping, but it turned out to be one of the best weekends in our entire time together. We had great accommodations, great crowds, and eager-to-please promoters. Phyllis McGuire opened for Johnny, and she is a very amusing person, especially when she has had a drink or two. It was on the trip that she introduced us to her then boyfriend, Mike Davis, who would become a lifelong friend of mine and with whom we would enjoy many adventures in Cap d'Antibes and other exotic locales. It was also during that trip that Johnny made the acquaintance of a nubile young lady whom we thereafter called Miss Texas. I don't remember if she ever officially held that title, but I'd like to meet the woman who could have topped her in the swimsuit competition.

"The same," said Johnny. "She's now a real estate broker. She put the whole dinner together. She's bringing her boss. I told her she could have some sort of inside track to get some business from us."

"What the hell are you thinking? Who is this broad?"

"It's Miss Texas! Now here's the thing —

I don't want them to pay. You pick up the tab. Okay?"

"Really?" I asked. I wasn't objecting to the request, just reacting to the oddness of his interest.

"Listen, I've also invited her to fly with us on the helicopter tour tomorrow. That'll give you and the boys a chance to talk to her and see what you can do for her."

"Just one more thing," I asked. "How long has this been going on?"

Johnny responded with a wink and a grin, which told me that it really didn't matter and I really didn't need to know.

"So, you don't really give a shit about the project, do you?"

"Certainly!" he responded with the look of mock innocence with which he had been amusing audiences for decades. "Looks as if I'll have to be visiting Houston a lot over the next few years."

That night we had an excellent dinner at a Houston steak house. Phyllis McGuire and Mike Davis were invited to join us, and Mike insisted on picking up the tab. The bill amounted to more than $2,000, on top of which Mike left $5,000, which was his normal percentage. Miss Texas was stunning. Johnny was happy.

But Johnny wasn't happy for long. Acrimony developed between him and the main local investor, a very shrewd fellow named Hugh Pike. Hugh felt, as most normal people would, that Johnny's presence would be invaluable when prospective tenants and subdevelopers were coming in to discuss deals. For a while Johnny agreed and complied. Then there came a point when he didn't. The relationship with Miss Texas had ended, and so did his interest in going to Houston. Eventually Johnny bought out all the partners, and years later Willowbrook became a roaring success.

I had a lot of time to think about Johnny's involvement in the Willowbrook deal while another deal we were involved in was having difficulties. Eight investors, including me, Johnny, and my law partner Arnold Kopelson, had formed a group that took over the ownership of the Garden State Bank in Hawaiian Gardens, California, a town about twenty miles south of Los Angeles. Our plan was to rename it the Commercial Bank of California, relocate it to Los Angeles, and, using all of our assets and connections, turn it into a profitable bank serving our clients. The bank needed to raise more money if it was to succeed; most of us couldn't afford to put in more money, and Johnny didn't want to. He had also pledged to promote the bank with appearances at several small gatherings, but he reneged, claiming it was too tiring for him. Eventually we had to sell the bank, and all the investors lost their money.

Arnold Kopelson was very angry with Carson for his refusal to promote the bank and put up more money, and he was furious with me for taking Johnny's side. Arnold maintained that a million dollars would have saved the bank, an amount that was chump change to Carson. Looking back, I think he was probably right. Our friendship ended in a rancorous lawsuit, with my saying and doing things I now regret in order to protect Carson and my relationship with him.

In seeing how things went down in Houston and with the bank, I began to feel that there was a problem with this relationship. Johnny was willing to make appearances and use my law firm and the investment group we assembled in order to promote his connection to Miss Texas, but he wouldn't make appearances or bolster the bank's investment group, even if it cost my friends and me money and lost me the friendship of Arnold Kopelson, a man I really liked and admired. More and more, I was beginning to think that the relationship

I had with Carson might have been suitable and even beneficial to a young man just embarking on his career, but that it didn't work so well for a more mature person who had a more prominent place in a wider world.

The last time I saw Rick Carson was at *The Tonight Show* anniversary party that took place on the *Queen Mary* in October 1987. It was marking twenty-five years of the Carson era, and NBC really tried to impress, inviting not only the people who worked on the show, but also network executives, the entertainment press, Johnny's family and friends, and others. Dinner, dancing, and entertainment were part of the festivities, as was a casino area, where people could play blackjack, roulette, and craps. Rick was playing in the casino and drinking heavily. His father went to see him in order to keep him under control, and a screaming match ensued. Johnny lost his temper and began yelling, and Rick responded in kind. Johnny pulled back his fist — he was going to slug his son — but somebody stepped in and hustled Johnny away. Not long before I would have been one of those stepping in. This time I left the boat and headed home. I realized as I left that the situation between Johnny and me

425

was going downhill fast. I hated the way he spoke to his son, and I hated that I had become his "cleaner." And I suspect that he probably had his issues with me. I was less available to play tennis with him. I became increasingly intolerant of his lack of civility toward company employees. In general, we were growing apart, and our friendship was lost.

A couple of weeks later, October 19, on so-called Black Monday, the stock market lost 22 percent of its value. Johnny and I were scheduled to play tennis at eleven a.m., but he called and asked me to come over early. By then the market was three hours into its historic freefall. "Do you realize how much money I lost today?" he asked me the moment I walked in. "Why the hell didn't you warn me to get out of the market?"

I didn't know what to say. I never had anything to do with his portfolio. Fred Kayne had always managed it, but earlier in the year, Alex had persuaded Johnny to let Michael Klein, an old friend of hers who worked at Bear Stearns, guide his investments. But all that was irrelevant. The stock market had suffered the largest one-day percentage decline in its history, and Carson was blaming me.

Now everything could be blamed on me.

FIFTEEN:
1987–1988: THE END

There were many things Frank Sinatra admired about Johnny Carson, but the thing he truly envied was Carson's wealth. Frank, to be sure, had plenty of money, but like a lot of entertainers, he had put his money into real estate. It was safe and profitable, but it wasn't particularly liquid. Johnny had real estate investments, too, as well as stocks and bonds, but unlike Sinatra or Crosby or Hope or any of the other truly wealthy entertainers, Johnny had *The Tonight Show,* a cash cow that week after week paid him hundreds of thousands of dollars in salary and fees and expenses. And it was relatively easy money. Sinatra had to travel the world giving concerts, incurring in the process all sorts of expenses for himself and those who traveled with him. Johnny had to drive to Burbank.

But even before his ownership of *The Tonight Show* relieved him of ever having to care about money, Johnny didn't much care about it as long as there was enough of it. Even when he and I first met and he was working under terrible contracts prepared by his negligent advisors, he still had plenty of cash, and he spent it like he never gave it a thought. Once he got control of *The Tonight Show,* however, he was earning so much that it was like Monopoly money. He was free to do literally whatever he wanted. He could ignore a sweet deal from Coca-Cola because he didn't want to make a lasting commitment. When he didn't like modeling for photographers for two days a year, he could afford to close down his multimillion-dollar clothing company; when he got tired of playing nightclubs, he bailed on his dates in Las Vegas; when he decided he didn't like going to see the rushes of movies in production, he closed up his company's successful movie division; and when he got tired of being the CEO of Carson Productions, he decided to rid himself of the company.

The truth is that Johnny never liked anything having to do with business. That was not only evident from the trust he placed in an entirely unworthy Sonny Werblin, but it was also clear two years later when he placed the same level of trust in me without having performed much more scrutiny, still depending only on his less-than-reliable gut. For a long time, I was able to shield him from most of the necessities of business, but that had become harder to do in recent years, and the problems that Johnny could no longer ignore were serious and painful.

Having to approve firing a friend, John McMahon. Having to condone firing his son Rick. Dealing with the stubborn Ed Weinberger. Hearing his name embroiled in the DeLorean.

More than one hundred investors, including Johnny Carson and Sammy Davis Jr., put more than $12 million into a partnership for research and development while the British government produced $156 million in grants and loans in return for DeLorean locating the factory in Northern Ireland.

Johnny's biggest regret about the investment was driving the car. It broke down on his first test drive, and to make matters worse, he was driving the DeLorean when he was arrested for a DUI in 1982. The monetary loss of the investment was of no real consequence to him. However, the arrest for drunk driving in that car caused Johnny to never drive it again.

One final difficulty involved a writer for

The Tonight Show who wanted a raise. He was making $4,000 a week, and the producers thought that was a just and appropriate amount. When I declined his request, the writer marched into Johnny's office and repeated his request. Instead, he got fired, but Johnny, who had carefully insulated himself from ever having to talk money with those who worked for him, was disturbed by the whole outrageous intrusion.

By the late '80s, Johnny's heart and breathing problems were worsening, and he was taking cortisone, which affected his mood and left him with less patience for managing problems. Moreover, Alex was having an effect on his business decisions, as new wives in any marriage are wont to do. She talked Johnny into replacing his longtime art dealer, Tom Paul, and hiring her father instead. When Fred Kayne (his longtime stockbroker) left Bear Stearns, Alex had campaigned for him to be replaced by her old friend Michael Klein. I honestly don't know if these changes happened by coincidence or if she had a plan. I certainly don't know if she ever considered replacing me with someone she thought could do a better job as her husband's lawyer.

Even as Johnny's mood soured and his

interest flagged, Carson Productions had turned the corner. *Amen* showed Weinberger in full possession of his creative magic, and in a sign of tremendous confidence in Carson Productions, Paramount, the company for whom Weinberger had helped create *Taxi,* offered $50 million to us in production financing. That meant being able to hire more writers, commission more scripts, and produce more pilots.

That tremendous news, however, did nothing to alter the fundamental trajectory of Carson's feelings: he announced that he had decided to sell the company. Relying on Michael Klein of Bear Stearns to act as the company's investment advisor, Johnny set the sale price of the company at $90 million, which I thought was unrealistic.

"Look at the record," I told Johnny. "We've had five series on NBC, not one of which ever made it past twenty-two episodes. We had a modest hit with *Mr. President,* but we structured the production costs so poorly we had to beg Fox to put us out of our misery. So there isn't anything in the library to sell. We currently have a hit in *Amen,* but we need three more years of production before we can get into syndication and make some money. After that, we've got a couple of miniseries and TV movies. The only thing we have of real value to sell is *The Tonight Show,* and while I have no idea who might contemplate paying $90 million for this collection of odds and ends, I have no doubt that whoever it might be, he or she is going to do exactly what Coca-Cola did and require you to commit to do the show for a few more years."

"Well, that's ridiculous," replied Carson. "I won't agree to that bullshit demand. I'm going to go year by year, and they can go fuck themselves."

And that's where we left it. I wasn't dissatisfied with his stubbornness. If he held his ground on $90 million, we would probably end up not selling and instead use the Paramount money to create new shows.

But once word got out that Johnny was interested in selling, Weinberger called. "I wasn't going to mention this," he hesitantly began, "but I've been approached by the Tribune Company. They told me that if I wasn't happy with the terms of the sale of Carson Productions, then they would like to talk to me about running their television operations." But that wasn't what he had really called to tell me. "Here's the thing. It would be much better if they bought Carson Productions," he argued. "*Amen* could continue to remain in production and build value, and you and I could remain in our positions." Implied but unspoken was the additional benefit — we wouldn't be working with Johnny anymore.

I liked the picture Ed had painted, and so unbeknownst to Carson, I met with the Tribune people. After long consideration, they advised me they would offer $60 million for the business, with Weinberger and me remaining as senior management.

I was disappointed at the price. I didn't think we would be offered the $90 million Bear Stearns was seeking, but neither did I believe that the company would go for as little as $60 million. I thought that $65 million would be right. In the past I would have known how and when to share this kind of news with Carson, but with his new heightened level of anger, I was unsure of myself. I called Fred Kayne for advice.

"Don't tell Bear Stearns about this," he warned me. "It really wasn't up to you to talk to other people about selling the company. Let them get the best offer they can, and you keep the Tribune offer under your hat for now. We'll see if maybe you should mention it later."

Fred also gave me some good personal advice. "Face facts," he said. "He's involving new people. It's because so far he likes what he's hearing from them, so give them some space to show what they can do. But don't make the mistake of underestimating Alex or Michael Klein. Don't think they'll play nice. Michael Klein cannot help himself — he will find a way to screw you."

That was sound advice, but for some reason, I chose not to follow it. For whatever reason, I felt compelled to advise Michael Klein of the offer. "Keep it confidential," I told him. "Consider it a backup. If everything else fails, that deal is out there."

"Of course, Henry," Klein agreed. "This is *entre nous.*"

Whereupon he directly went to Carson and told him that Ed Weinberger and I were trying to steal his company.

Carson summoned me to the Malibu house. It had been a long time since we had last played tennis together; it was just no fun anymore. I'd heard that he'd been expanding the place; now it was enormous. I'm told that when Bob Newhart came to visit, he asked Johnny, "Where's the gift shop?"

Johnny didn't say why he wanted to see me, although I knew that if Michael Klein had broken his promise to keep a secret — and if twenty years in law practice had taught me anything, it's that nobody keeps a secret — Johnny would be angry with me. I just wasn't prepared for how angry.

He didn't even bother to ask me to sit down. "I hear you're trying to steal my god-damn company," he said when I walked into his living room. "Sixty million, huh? Where the fuck did that number come from? You and Weinberger got a sweet deal for yourselves?"

The implication that Ed and I had finagled some other way of getting paid in order to keep the price down was insulting, but I never got the chance to address it. "I've talked to Ed Hookstratten," Johnny continued, referring to one of Beverly Hills's most prominent lawyers. "He'll take over. Let's talk about you. What's fair between us?"

At that moment I realized the guillotine had fallen. No need to offer an explanation, no point in engaging in a discussion, and certainly no call for sentiment or nostalgia. "One year's compensation paid over the next twelve months," I said plainly, "and my share of the proceeds when the company is sold."

"It's a deal," he said. We shook hands, and I left. And just that fast, my eighteen-year association with Johnny Carson came to an end.

■ ■ ■ ■

Years before, when I was officially hired as Carson's full-time lawyer, he told me what he wanted. "I don't expect to be somebody's only client," he said, "but I need to know that I'm number one." Over the years, a lot of people failed to satisfy that stipulation: Bruno and Shields, the William Morris Agency, Sonny Werblin, Arnold Grant, three executive producers of *The Tonight Show,* three wives, and Joan Rivers. Now add to that list the name of Henry Bushkin.

Had I been disloyal? Hardly. I did nothing that harmed his interests. But it is true that at some point his goals and my goals, which had always been united, diverged. I negotiated a contract that got him ownership of *The Tonight Show,* which enabled the popular, successful, well-paid Carson to become an astronomically well-compensated entertainer. The contract also could have allowed him to be a rich, powerful, and influential producer of films and television programs, the likes of which Hollywood had yet to see, if only that was what he wanted. I helped him walk through that door, but after seeing what life was like on the other side, he decided that it wasn't for him. He didn't want the aggravation, and he certainly didn't need the dough.

But having walked through that door with him, I discovered that I didn't want to help him throw it all away, and I didn't want to just be his adjunct, his enforcer, his "quicker picker-upper." I had discovered that I liked running the company, doing deals, working with creative people. Running Carson Productions suited me. I couldn't and wouldn't do anything to hurt Carson's interests, but I hoped he wouldn't act in a way that would hurt mine. He had done so too often already.

So our interests were in conflict.

As I thought about it, talking to the Tribune people didn't seem like that big a crime. I told Klein about it; it wasn't like I had tried to keep it a secret, which would have been a worse offense. Perhaps he had been looking for an excuse for some time. Maybe I should have kept playing tennis with him; maybe I should have been warmer to Alex, who had moved Fred Kayne, Bob Trapenberg, and Michael Hattem out of Johnny's life like so much old furniture, and who perhaps had come to see me as a worn and soiled settee. Maybe there were so many maybes that when Carson caught a whiff of a betrayal, he dropped the hammer first and felt badly about it later.

Once I was gone, Johnny had Ed Hookstratten, his new attorney, fire Ed Weinberger and shut down production. One hundred people lost their livelihoods. Weinberger later sued the company for the money due him under his contract and lost profits. He won.

Over the next year, I spent considerable time working with Hookstratten, bringing him up to date on two decades' worth of Carson's affairs. Despite a fraught atmosphere, Ed and I worked well together, and we remained friends. The issue that promised the greatest potential for anger and bitterness, the amount due to me for my percentage of Carson Productions, was handled with professionalism. I got more money than I would have under the proposed terms of the company's sale to the Coca-Cola Company, but I lost the friendship of the most interesting man I had ever known. I was not a winner in the deal.

In 1988 Ed Weinberger and I made one more attempt to salvage Carson Productions. We targeted Taft and Westinghouse, the big station groups, but never got a deal off the ground. As my distance from Carson grew, I began to see that I didn't have an interest in staying in show business per se. What I enjoyed was the law and business. I liked setting up deals, negotiating terms, and knowing the law to create advantages and benefits for my clients and myself. When eventually I took a job again, it was "of counsel" in a law firm, where I found that working for savings and loans and banks to be as rewarding and fruitful as working for Carson. It's true that I did take a flyer at becoming a movie producer with 1990's *Spontaneous Combustion,* written and directed by Tobe Hooper of *The Texas Chain Saw Massacre.* Alas, *Spontaneous Combustion* did not catch fire, and that ended my movie career.

Johnny terminated our relationship in a mere three-minute conversation. A swift unceremonious end to a long and profitable run. There was no final act; it felt as if someone unplugged the projector in the middle of the movie.

But there was a twisted epilogue, much of which played out in court. My ouster rumbled through Hollywood like a storm amid accusations of backstabbing and other forms of character assassination. I was angry. I lost the one client I had devoted my life to for nearly two decades. And Johnny had insisted that I work for him alone — any time spent on others was considered an insult. My partners at the firm handled other clients that I brought in, like Neil Simon. If Neil invited me to New York to view a rehearsal, I knew I'd better fit in a reason for the trip that would benefit Johnny. I would tell him that I was going to visit with NBC, and that usually was enough to satisfy him. But by 1988 our ties were frayed to the point of dysfunction, and our friendship was shredded by others with their own agendas in mind.

Johnny and I never had a written contract, so at the end he agreed to one year's salary as my severance plan. But the unpleasantness didn't end with an awkward handshake . . .

About six weeks after my final meeting with Johnny, I got a call from Norman Marcus, my accountant as well as Johnny's. Johnny had decided to sell his apartment in Trump Tower and was livid that he was losing money on the sale. Johnny claimed I should cover his loss, since I had suggested that he buy a place there. I was more shocked at Norman's gall than at Johnny's grievance. Norman also informed me I would no longer be a client of Ernst & Young.

"Obviously we can't continue to represent

you" were his parting words to me. They wanted me to be a guarantor on Johnny's investment — that is, they wanted me to make him whole should he sell the condo at a loss.

"Obviously you can go fuck yourself," I said. A week later he called to let me know that the severance pay Johnny and I agreed upon would be stopped. He would keep it in order to recoup his loss on the apartment sale.

Meanwhile, Ed Hookstratten demanded that two decades' worth of files be handed over immediately. My firm foolishly agreed to send them our original files and Ed agreed to have a copy service duplicate them. But six months later we were missing a page, a crucial page. It was a one-page letter allowing my firm to represent Johnny Carson in the Willowbrook investment partnership. The project had twenty investors. Each investor signed such a letter. Of the twenty signed letters, nineteen were found. Only Johnny's was missing.

We were fucked. Carson's side brought in hired guns — a Los Angeles law firm that accused us of malpractice. They claimed because we could not produce that letter, it left our firm on the hook for Johnny's entire investment.

My frustration and anxiety were mounting. That somber, numbing meeting with Johnny in his Malibu home seemed like it had happened decades ago. What I thought was a simple, albeit sad, end took a nightmarish turn. When that letter went "missing," it signaled the beginning of a lengthy legal battle that would gnaw at me continually for four years.

The story of the end of the Carson–Bushkin relationship proved irresistible for the media because I was accused of everything except sodomy with a duck (an expression Johnny often used when facing accusations from one wife or another).

The journalists reporting on the split printed whatever the Carson lawyers' publicity machine meted out. Those reporters showed no skepticism whatsoever; none of them ever called me to comment on anything Carson's people had told them. His story was the one they wanted to believe. According to the reportage, he was the good guy and I was the one who betrayed him.

We notified our insurance carrier of the claim made by Johnny's camp. They hired Irell & Manella to investigate the claim. Eventually, Irell agreed that without the letter, there was a technical but real act of malpractice. We were technically negligent for not being able to produce that letter. It was obvious to my partners and me that someone on the other side, we didn't know who, had trashed the letter during the six months our files were in their possession. Ed (and his firm) denied that anyone had trashed the letter, but since we had sent them the original, there was no proof that the letter had ever existed.

Our insurance carrier then claimed that the missing letter indicated collusion between Johnny and me — that we were setting them up to cover the Willowbrook investment. That ninety-three-acre parcel of land in Houston was suffering from a recent downturn in the economy — as were all such investments at the time. My firm and Irell & Manella urged the carrier to pay the $15 million claim from the Carson camp. They refused, and once Hookstratten got wind of the refusal, he filed a "massive malpractice" lawsuit against the partners in my firm.

In the lawsuit they alleged that I was negligent to advise Carson to buy a place in Trump Tower. They also claimed that I used company funds to pay for the vacations that Johnny and I took at Hôtel du Cap for the past eleven years. I couldn't believe what I was hearing. Those unbelievable summers on the French coastline that had produced such fond memories for me — now soured by these ridiculous accusations. In fact, NBC had paid the costs for those trips, specific terms that I'd negotiated with Dave Tebet.

My stomach churned as I listened to these claims. I rubbed my hand around my neck, feeling for bolts. Surely I was some kind of monster to have the townspeople turn on me like this.

I phoned Bob Shapiro, a friend — and one of the best lawyers I know. He was also a good friend to Hookstratten and I thought he could mediate a successful conclusion and put an end to this ugly affair.

"They want your stock in the Carson companies," he told me. "If they get that, the insurer will know there's no collusion and they believe Johnny will get paid," he said.

I flatly refused. Judy had gotten everything else in our divorce a few years earlier, and I wasn't about to hand over my last asset. But, anxious about the effects this suit could have on the firm, my partners put the pressure on me.

"Give them that and this will all go away." I was stuck. Hold on to my last piece of financial security and dig my heels in for a lengthy battle with the Carson camp. Or acquiesce and leave my financial future to the fates. I held out just long enough that the Carson side agreed to assign to me their "bad faith" claim against the insurance company. (Once the claim was assigned to me, who now bore the brunt of the insurer's refusal to pay up, I could go after them in court.) I gave Carson's camp my stock, and they dropped their lawsuit.

After the settlement, my good pals at Ernst & Young informed me I was receiving a 1099 with more than $2 million in phantom income. Which means I now had a tax liability in excess of $1 million courtesy of Carson. I had escaped the lawsuit, but now I had no clients, no real income, and I owed more than $1 million in taxes.

I then filed a bad faith action against the insurance company. The case came to trial in 1992. Their defense against my claim was simple: Henry Bushkin is a bad guy. They went through the complaint Carson's camp had filed against my firm. They subpoenaed a primary lawyer from his camp to testify about all the allegations that the earlier lawsuit had made against me.

The lawyer said the complaint was filed because they had suspected wrongdoing.

But they could not prove I'd done anything wrong because I hadn't done anything wrong. And after nine weeks of deliberation, the twelve-person jury came to the same conclusion. The debate among the jurors focused on how much I was entitled to for my stock and the emotional distress I had been put through. They awarded me $11 million. Plus, they said that the insurer was also subject to punitive damages. They wished to settle immediately and offered an additional $6 million. I agreed because the total sum would offset the amount I'd lost when I turned over my stock to Carson.

Whatever justice I ultimately got in court, I was still considered guilty in the court of public opinion because I could not tell the full story of that case. My nondisclosure agreement with the insurer prevented me from saying anything on the subject when I made the deal with them. Even if I had been able to reveal the truth, the media wasn't really interested by this time. There's been a lot of research recently on how hard it is to dislodge an impression once it's been implanted in someone's mind. (This is why political attack ads don't have to be true to be effective. The other side can point out their inaccuracies, but the voter's mind privileges the memory of the original accusation, which was juicier than any counterargument ever could be.) Perhaps no amount of good press after the trial could have unseated the impression of me that had by this point become ingrained in the public's mind.

In the ensuing years, I have had many adventures. I practiced law; built 150 single-family homes; moved to London; took on a business in Kyrgyzstan; then came back to California, where I ran a large computer distribution business; practiced more law; and got involved with an international trading company based in Hong Kong. So much has happened to me since Johnny and I split, so far am I removed from that world, that as I've been working on this book, I have at times felt as if I were an interloper in my own past. But I do know for sure that in the years since I left Carson I have been happier than I was during the years I spent with him. There are fewer things I regret, and there are no feelings from that time that compare with the sadness I feel over the pain I caused some of my friends and loved ones during the Carson years, especially Judy Bushkin and Arnold Kopelson.

I never saw Johnny after we broke up, but

one day in 1988, while he was in the midst of selling his apartment in Trump Tower, he called me to complain because the buyers were taking too much time to finalize the sale. For a moment, it was as if nothing had changed. He called me to bitch, yet he was not going to call the lawyer actually working on the matter. I was surprised by the call and was mostly amused by his predicament, but I was glad that I had no responsibility in the matter. He was funny and charming, and for a while I hoped that this call might signal a reopening in our relationship, a period when he might call from time to time and we could talk as the real friends we almost but never quite were. However, he did not call back, and in time I concluded that he had dialed my number by reflex that day, not by choice. It was simply a mistake. And I was disappointed. The truth is that I was excited he had called. The truth is that I had missed him and I hoped he was missing me too.

All the time I worked for him I knew that nobody in Johnny's life was really necessary to him. There were a lot of guys who had worked for him who had great relationships with him and who one day found themselves gone. We had a relationship that lasted a long time, but I always knew it could and would end. But until it happens, you don't really believe it will, and even after it happens, part of you keeps thinking he'll change his mind. Once I realized that there was no going back, I became angry — angry that I'd been fired, angry that he didn't miss me, angry at myself for having sacrificed so much for a man who had so little appreciation for what I'd given up.

After I left, Johnny's world continued to shrink. Rick Carson died in 1991. I never watched *The Tonight Show* after Johnny fired me, except for the night that Johnny returned from his hiatus and offered his tribute to Rick. I thought Johnny did a good job. I sent him a note of condolence, but he never acknowledged it. I was told that at some point following Rick's death, Johnny apologized to Chris and Cory, his surviving sons, for not being there when they needed him.

The following year, Johnny retired from *The Tonight Show* with a spectacular send-off, full of tributes and emotion. It was entirely deserved. That program drew more than twenty million viewers, but I was not among them.

At some point, Johnny and Alex separated, although they never divorced. Their eighteen years of marriage put her in first place among the Carson wives. He spent a great deal of time in his last years on his boat, alone with his crew, who took care of him.

On January 24, 2005, at Cedars-Sinai Medical Center, Johnny died of respiratory failure due to emphysema. He was alone. According to published reports, he left an estate worth in excess of $450 million, money that came primarily from his owner-ship of *The Tonight Show.* He never did sell Carson Productions, and perhaps that was the best choice after all. In 2012, his still-considerable estate was able to transfer $156 million to the Carson Foundation for distribution to the Children's Hospital of Los Angeles, the Los Angeles Free Clinic, Planned Parenthood, and other charities.

When Carson died, just like the character Diana in *A Chorus Line,* I thought I ought to be feeling something, but nothing emerged. The news media deluged me with calls, no doubt thinking that I would be a Vesuvius of memories, insights, and emo-tions, but I refused them all. I couldn't work up any noble sentiments about the man, and I did not want to look like I was taking a cheap shot.

My feelings began to emerge sometime after his death, and mostly what I felt was sadness. I thought it was terrible that he died alone, without the company of anyone who really cared — separated from his wife; his two surviving sons incapable of providing any sort of comfort; so many of his friends dismissed, alienated, or turned away. Long before emphysema took Johnny's life, the disease he caught from his mother killed his spirit. In the end, it's true, we each must die alone, but the love and friendship we share with one another show that we do not live alone. And of all men, Johnny did not live alone. He lived with millions, among whom were a small, very fortunate group who really did care about him. I began to think that had he and I remained as we once were, there would have been a celebration of his life, and he would have left this world far happier than he did.

But perhaps not. He had too keen an appreciation for how much work and talent and discipline went into success to be flattered by praise and adulation; nobody knew better than he when he was good and when he wasn't. Perhaps that's why in the end he mostly gave up trying to create and sustain friendships and relationships; perhaps he concluded that he wasn't any good at it and stopped trying. Which is too bad, because of all the things I valued about working with him, the thing I cherished most was the sense that I was helping him. He made you feel so good that you were happy to be helping him. I think the same was true of Joanna and many others as well. Had he allowed it, had he offered any encouragement, many of us would have continued to try.

I do not think he would have wanted a celebration; but I do like to think that he would have been happy with this book. I've tried to show him in all his complexity, in his huge talent and great vivacity, and with his tremendous appeal and charisma and sense of fun, and also with his failures and shortcomings and even cruelties. A man so suspicious of flattery and sentimentality might have appreciated my attempt to paint an accurate portrait of the most thrilling, fun, frustrating, and mysterious relationship of my life — a portrait of a man I loved.

ACKNOWLEDGMENTS

I would like to express my gratitude to the many people who saw me through this book; to all those who provided support, talked things over, read, wrote, offered comments, allowed me to pick their brains, and helped me complete the manuscript.

Above all I want to thank Jacquelin Jordan and the rest of my family, who supported and encouraged me when I was little more than a reclusive houseguest.

My friends Fred Kayne, Michael Hattem, Bruce Singer, and Mel Markman provided great advice and friendship during the time in which I struggled to finish the work. Their insights and observations helped set the tone and pace of the book.

The initial spark to write this book was ignited by my friend Ed Hookstratten. "Hook" said to me one day in early 2008, "Why not write the book about you and Johnny? No one knew him like you did."

Hook reminded me that he worked for Johnny for more than nine years and knew very little about him personally. With any unpleasantness years behind me, I decided he was right. It was Ed who got me here.

Last and not least: I beg forgiveness of all those who have been with me over the course of the years and whose names I have failed to mention.

ABOUT THE AUTHOR

Henry Bushkin is a lawyer living in Los Angeles. For eighteen years, he was Johnny Carson's personal legal adviser, fixer, confidant, and close friend.

The employees of Thorndike Press hope you have enjoyed this Large Print book. All our Thorndike, Wheeler, and Kennebec Large Print titles are designed for easy reading, and all our books are made to last. Other Thorndike Press Large Print books are available at your library, through selected bookstores, or directly from us.

For information about titles, please call:
(800) 223-1244

or visit our Web site at:
http://gale.cengage.com/thorndike

To share your comments, please write:
Publisher
Thorndike Press
10 Water St., Suite 310
Waterville, ME 04901